THREE YEARS IN THE SADDLE

AROUND THE WORLD ON A BICYCLE

By
Dave Cobley

Bloomington, IN Milton Keynes, UK

AuthorHouse™
1663 Liberty Drive, Suite 200
Bloomington, IN 47403
www.authorhouse.com
Phone: 1-800-839-8640

AuthorHouse™ UK Ltd.
500 Avebury Boulevard
Central Milton Keynes, MK9 2BE
www.authorhouse.co.uk
Phone: 08001974150

This book is a work of non-fiction. Unless otherwise noted, the author and the publisher make no explicit guarantees as to the accuracy of the information contained in this book and in some cases, names of people and places have been altered to protect their privacy.

First published by AuthorHouse 6/5/2006

ISBN: 1-4259-3990-2 (sc)

Printed in the United States of America
Bloomington, Indiana

This book is printed on acid-free paper.

My journey brought me into contact with communities where, despite the most basic living conditions, people lead their lives in a dignified manner – upholding ancient traditions, caring for each other and showing kindness to strangers. 'Three Years in the Saddle' is dedicated to those people and published in aid of Practical Action. This charity seeks to protect the livelihoods of people living in similar communities, by using small-scale, intermediate forms of technology to promote sustainable, community-led development

ACKNOWLEDGEMENTS

My thanks are extended to my brother John, who spent endless hours proof reading and also produced the excellent maps, which appear at the beginning of each chapter. The journey itself would probably never have happened without the support and advice of my friend Mathew Ives, who introduced me to cycle touring, built the wheels and gave me a crash course in cycle maintenance prior to my departure. My parents supported me throughout the journey – taking care of my affairs at home, faithfully sending letters to me via 'poste-restante' in nearly every major city en-route and nearly contacting 'Interpol' at one point when they had not heard from me for a while! Finally, my thanks and appreciation go to the countless people around the world who opened their homes to me and helped me along the way.

INTRODUCTION

There had to be a better way of getting to work. Sitting or standing in a crowded carriage on the London Underground for three hours each day, for a journey that was no more than ten miles each way by road, seemed like such a waste of time. Attempting the journey by car would have been even more of a nightmare - even if I could have afforded to buy one! My friend, Matthew, who was a mechanic at the local bike shop, came up with the solution. Having talked me round to the idea of cycling to work, he promptly fixed me up with a brand new mountain bike – a 'Ridgeback 603'.

To my surprise, I actually enjoyed riding across London every day, especially overtaking all the motorists that were stuck in traffic jams! My journey time was cut in half and my fitness grew rapidly. Matthew's next suggestion was a cycling holiday in the French Alps and, though it sounded more like hard labour than a holiday, he eventually managed to talk me into this as well.

Growing up near Dover, I had often wondered what life was like across the English Channel - in France and beyond. As school friends returned from summer holidays in America, Australia, Thailand and Spain, my determination to visit such places one day grew. In particular, one country that fascinated me was India, having read stories about Mother Theresa and her work with the 'poorest of the poor'.

My first taste of foreign travel was an 'inter-railing' trip around Europe, after finishing University. This had satisfied my curiosity to some extent, although my main memory of the trip is the feeling of sheer mental exhaustion that comes from spending countless hours on long train journeys and trying to visit as many countries as possible in three and a half weeks. Towards the end, all the cities started to look the same and I just wanted to get home.

As Matthew and I cycled from the Calais ferry port down towards the Alps, that travelling dream came alive once more. I loved the sense of freedom, and of not knowing what lay around the corner or where we would end up each night. The cycling added a whole new dimension to the experience, giving us much more independence and ensuring that we spent time in the ordinary places as well as the cities and tourist centres. The holiday ended a little prematurely, however, when Matthew crashed on the descent into Grenoble. His shoulder was injured and we had to take the train back to London. By then, however, my mind was made up. This was the way to travel.

It took the best part of two years for me to save up enough money and gather equipment together for a long cycle tour. During this time, however, there was never any doubt in my mind that my dream to travel around the world was at last going to come true. People can be sceptical about those who deviate from 'conventional' patterns of living but, as friends warned me about the dangers lurking in countries that they knew very little about, or the stupidity of giving up a secure job, my determination only grew. The practical support came mainly from Matthew, who helped me to strip down the Ridgeback and completely rebuild it with 'top of the range' Shimano components. He also built me a sturdy pair of wheels, which he promised would be free from spoke breakages. (His promise was almost kept – the first spoke breakage occurring in the last few days of my journey!)

My official plan was to cycle to India, and then decide from there what to do next. Secretly though, I had hopes to travel far beyond India – perhaps even as far as Australia. There were some fears in my mind about problems that may occur on the road, such as loneliness or mechanical failures, but I never allowed these fears to become an excuse not to at least give it a try.

The three-year journey that followed was the most rewarding experience of my life so far. Problems did arise, but my confidence grew as they were overcome, either with the help of strangers or by using my own inner resources – which had far greater depths that I had ever imagined! Despite the political and economic chaos in so many countries, the world is a beautiful place and there were kind, hospitable people, in every country, who help me to appreciate it.

For me, cycling was a great way to travel. The exercise helped to keep me fit and I learnt to really appreciate the daily basics of food and shelter, which are so often taken for granted as we lead our busy lives in the West. My mode of transport also opened up doors to remote places, off the beaten track, where some of the greatest discoveries were to be made.

TABLE OF CONTENTS

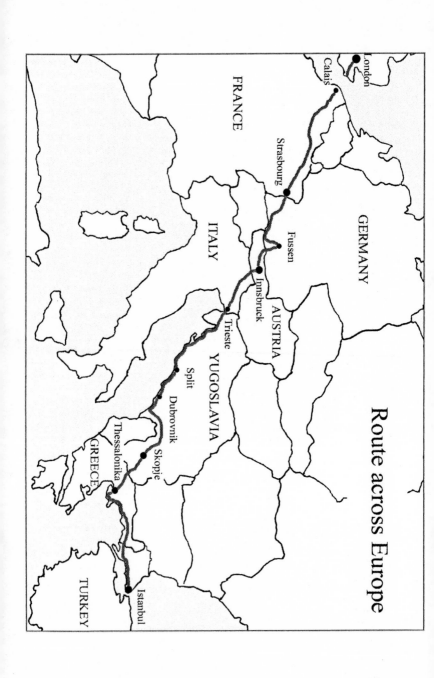

Route across Europe

CHAPTER ONE

THE JOURNEY BEGINS

London to Istanbul

ON A COOL SEPTEMBER MORNING IN 1990, my journey began. Over the past year, I had been making careful plans, accumulating touring equipment and considering how best to deal with the various problems that may arise on the road. In the last few days, this careful planning had turned into a mad rush of visiting friends, and repeated trips to the local bike shop to check that I had every vital piece of equipment that might be necessary. Now these concerns were behind me and my mind was at ease. Ahead of me lay the open road and, hopefully, a wonderful adventure.

My starting point was Kilburn, in north London. The heavily loaded bike felt rather unstable at first, and my journey nearly came to a premature end when one of the large rear panniers came loose as I was crossing the Thames on London Bridge. This caused me to wobble to an emergency stop, as the early morning traffic somehow snaked past me. Having made the necessary adjustments, and responded appropriately to the various insults that came flying at me from irate drivers, I carried on down the Old Kent Road, through the outer suburbs, and on towards Dover on the A2. With my head full of thoughts about what might lie ahead, and the life that I was leaving behind, the miles passed quickly.

While eating my lunch outside a supermarket in Sittingbourne, an old man glanced down at me. He looked at the bike, then back at me:

"You look like you're going a long way, Chief", he said, slowly.

"I'm heading for India", I replied

"Really. When did you start?"

"This morning", I answered, fairly casually.

The old fellow stared for a few moments in disbelief and then shuffled away, muttering to himself. This was the first of countless roadside encounters. As with most of them, it was my mode of travel – the bicycle – that provided the catalyst for conversation.

I rode seventy-three miles on that first day to reach a small campsite on a hillside overlooking Dover. An hour or so was spent setting up my 'Jetpacker' tent – which seemed ever so much smaller now than it had done in the shop – and preparing the first meal on my brand new 'Whisperlite' petrol stove. As it turned dark,

I wandered down to the local pub for a quiet drink to mark the end of my first day on the road.

The white cliffs of Dover bid me a final farewell from England, as the ferry headed out across channel to Calais. Only my second day on the road and already in a foreign country! Full of enthusiasm, I rode south from Calais across rich farmland, interspersed with huge processing plants, to reach a small family-run campsite near Bethune.

My spirits were dampened a little the next day, as grey clouds and persistent drizzle turned the industrial plains of Northern France into a rather bleak landscape. After a late start, it turned into quite a struggle to reach the next campsite marked on the map before nightfall. My bike lights had been left behind in London as part of a ruthless last minute luggage-reduction exercise, so there was nothing for it but to set up camp for the night in a roadside field. In the weeks to come, I was to increasingly enjoy these 'wild camps', as I called them, but that first time it was a little scary! My fears were eased considerably, however, when the silence was broken by the arrival of two English girls, who cycled into the field and set up camp close by. They were riding together from Amsterdam to Bologna and I was glad of their unexpected company.

3

In the morning, the girls were able to make use of my extensive toolkit to tune up their bikes, before we went our separate ways. The weather was miserable once again and I rode all day in pouring rain to the town of Charleyville. Camping loses its appeal when you are soaked to the skin, so I was pleased to find a Youth Hostel here. There were no other guests, but the warden was happy to prepare a fine meal just for me, and he even produced a bottle of wine for us to share together afterwards.

The Vosgue Mountains provided my first real test of stamina. The climbs were steep but, with low gearing, I was able to settle into an easy rhythm and enjoy the rugged scenery. It took a couple of days' to ride through the range and into Strasbourg.

It was very satisfying to have reached such an important city as Strasbourg after just one week, and the large International Youth Hostel made an excellent base. It was just a short walk into the city centre, which was dominated by the soaring spire of the old Gothic Cathedral, and I joined a crowd of tourists to witness the daily procession of mechanical apostles around its astronomical clock. My favourite area, though, was an old part of the city known as 'La Petite France', where canals were lined with narrow cobbled streets and beautifully restored Tudor houses, decorated with flowers.

Feeling refreshed after my city break, I crossed the Rhine into Germany. From the border it was a short ride into the Black Forest, where the landscape is a stunning array of dense spruce forest, deeply cut valleys, mountain lakes, vineyards and orchards. Dotted among the hills were beautiful villages and old thatched farmhouses. The scenery was so distracting that I took several wrong turnings! However, each unplanned detour was well rewarded with breath-taking views.

By now I was quite comfortable with the idea of 'wild camping'. This practice was certainly not encouraged by the authorities in most countries of Western Europe, so I settled into a routine of finding well-hidden sites, setting up my camp just before nightfall and leaving soon after sun-rise. I also tried to ensure that no traces of my camp were left, so as not to disfigure the landscape in even the slightest way.

On reaching the larger towns, I usually stayed in hostels, where the luxury of a comfortable bed, clean linen and a shower was greatly appreciated. At Villengen, in the south of the Black Forest, my hostel dormitory was shared with three other touring cyclists – all heading in different directions. Covering the floor with maps, we swapped stories and compared our planned routes.

Having crossed the mountainous Black Forest, it was good to ride across flat terrain again, along the northern shore of Lake Constance – a giant lake at the meeting point of Germany, Switzerland and Austria. I followed the shoreline for two days to reach the town of Lindau, before heading north again through the Allgauer Alps. This was a spontaneous diversion from my planned route, on the advice of an old man who had taken my photograph by the lakeside, and then warned me that it would be a crime not to visit King Ludwig's 'fairy-tale castles' at Fussen.

As the road snaked its way up through the mountains towards Fussen, it soon became clear that this detour was going to take a little longer than expected. It was a tough ride, but the rugged mountain scenery was quite inspirational. On a clear, starry night, I camped by the roadside on the edge of a deep ravine, before descending into the ancient town of Fussen. It was a Bank Holiday weekend and the large Youth Hostel here was full for the night, but the management allowed me to sleep on my own mat on the floor of one of the dormitories.

Early the following morning I rode to Schwangau, a few miles from Fussen, to visit the famous castles, which are former residences of the Bavarian royal household. There were hordes of tourists around the coach park and souvenir shops, but the mountaintop castles were all but obscured by clouds. Nevertheless, I joined the crowds of tourist swarming like insects up the steep, narrow road leading to the entrance of 'Sommerweg' – the most famous of King Ludwig's extravagant creations. As I got closer, the towers and turrets of Sommerweg gradually emerged from the clouds, almost like a romantic vision. It was a magical moment and I silently thanked the old man for his advice.

From Schwangau, I rode directly south into Austria. Riding through the beautiful Tirol region of Western Austria was surprisingly easy, with the smooth highway following the flat valley floors between huge snow-capped mountains. Each evening, as sunset approached, I was able to find idyllic camping spots by following trails leading into the forest, which would eventually lead to a clearing. On one morning it was raining heavily, so I stayed dry and warm in my tent until mid-afternoon!

The Youth Hostel at Innsbruck provided a few days relief from the rigours of roadside camping. Surrounded by towering mountains, Austria's capital city has a wonderful setting. The central area was quite compact and it was relaxing to wander aimlessly around the well-preserved Baroque palaces, churches and museums.

It was a long, gradual climb from Innsbruck on the Brenner Pass road towards the Italian border. Following an old Roman route, this amazing highway has been carved through the mountains with the help of tunnels and a series of colossal bridges. It was a slow journey that morning, as I made frequent stops to gain breath and to try and comprehend the incredible amount engineering skill that must have gone into creating this concrete masterpiece.

At the border, I met Mike and Sheila – an Anglo-Canadian couple that had been cycle touring around Europe for the past three months. They were 'wild camping' all the time and managing to survive on less than a 'fiver' a day between them! We rode together for the rest of the day and it was a great experience to be able to learn from seasoned cycle-tourists. Travelling alone has many advantages but, on a long journey, there are times when it is nice have some company on the road. They were the first of many 'road partners' for me, all of whom were to enrich my journey.

That night together we reached a village called Mauls, where we received permission from locals to camp on the football field. We pooled our resources for supper and spent a moonlit evening chatting over a bottle of wine. It was a great evening, and my new friends filled me with confidence that I too could survive on the road for a long time. It also transpired that I had met Mike before, while he was working at a London bike shop called 'On Your Bike'.

We rode together again for a couple of hours in the morning, before parting company. Mike and Sheila took the road south to Lake Guarda, while I continued on an easterly route towards the Dolomites. There was a vague arrangement to meet up again in Yugoslavia, but this never materialised.

It felt a little strange to be suddenly on my own again, so I tried not to dwell on my thoughts too much and just concentrate on riding hard. The miles passed quickly and by mid afternoon I found myself at a small town called Dobbiaco, on the edge of the Dolomites. Foolishly ignoring the huge black clouds looming overhead, I peddled on into the mountains. Sure enough, the thunderstorm arrived within half an hour, so I came to my senses and hurriedly retreated to Dobbiaco! Here it had not even rained and I was able to dry out my wet clothes on the town campsite.

In the morning the skies again looked fairly ominous. However, there was not much to do in Dobbiaco, so I set off into the mountains again. This time the rains held off and, despite the grey skies, the Dolomite scenery was dramatic and captivating. The towers of craggy limestone rock rising abruptly from the roadside were reminiscent of Cheddar Gorge, though on a much grander scale.

Arriving at one mountain pass, I stumbled upon the beautiful Lake Misurina. Having known nothing about this famous tourist destination, it came as a lovely surprise at the end of a tough climb. A few minutes were spent chatting at the lakeside with a group of English tourists that were on a twelve-day European coach tour. I slightly envied them for the comfort of their luxury coach, while they seemed to envy me for my freedom in being able to travel with so few constraints.

An exhilarating ten-mile descent brought me down into the town of Auronzo, where I sampled one of Italy's specialities – pizza! The sun came out at last, as I embarked on another steep climb, and the glistening mountains began to look a little less angry!

That night, I reached a village called Lorenzago, high in the mountains. Having chosen a camping spot about half a mile from the edge of the settlement, I decided to spend the evening in the village plaza. After cooking my evening meal, I washed the utensils in the fountain and then had a wash myself. There was nobody else in the square at that time, but I was conscious of the stares of several pairs of eyes from the surrounding houses as I carried out my evening routines. Strangely, I felt no sense of embarrassment. It was as if my bicycle was the licence of an authentic traveller and I had every right to treat the plaza as my home for a few hours, before heading off into the forest to sleep.

Continuing eastwards into the province of Udine, I came to a junction where a narrow side road led towards a small settlement up in the hills. A signpost, indicating 'Raveo 3kms', immediately brought me to a stop. Some months earlier, a friend had given me the address of a lady named Aura, who lived in Raveo, Udine. My friend had assured me of a warm welcome if I visited her on my way through Italy. Having presumed that Raveo was a suburb of Udine City, I had planned to phone Aura that evening in order to let her know that I would be arriving in Udine the following day. However, it dawned on me now that Raveo was in fact a tiny village, just a couple of miles off my route. Though reluctant to turn up without warning, it seemed such a coincidence to be passing so close that I had to call in.

On reaching the village, I was soon able to find Aura's address. As I stood at the door, waiting for a reply to my knock, a small crowd of villagers gathered round – anxious to help. They all knew Aura well, and told me that she had moved to another house in the village. This weekend, however, they remembered that she was visiting her elderly sister, Dirce, in another village called Pesaris, ten miles further up the valley. I was quite ready to thank them and forget the whole thing, but one lady insisted that I should ride on to Pesaris, and that she would phone ahead to say that I was on my way.

It was a tough climb up the valley to Pesaris and I felt quite exhausted on arrival. Riding hard and camping wild for the past few days was beginning to take its toll. Not having an address to look for this time, and with no specific instructions, I just rolled into the cobbled square at the centre of the village. On seeing me, a young boy jumped up and indicated that I should follow him.

The boy led me to a ramshackle old stone cottage on the edge of the village, where an elderly lady was standing at the doorway. She spoke no English, but I gathered that she was Aura's sister Dirce. Her welcome was warm and, once inside, I was directed upstairs to the bathroom, where a hot bath was waiting for me. The bathtub was rather small, but I wasted no time in jumping in to soak my aching limbs. Later on, Dirce served up a delicious meal of pasta and soup, over which we made a good stab at communicating with each other via my phrasebook. She managed to explain to me that Aura was away in Austria, but was due to return in the morning, and insisted that I must rest with them for a few days.

The following morning, Aura duly arrived. She spoke perfect English, having lived in Hampshire for twenty years, and seemed delighted at my surprise visit. We lunched with Dirce, before returning back down the valley to Aura's home in Raveo. Over the next couple of days, I was introduced to almost every inhabitant of the village and made to feel part of a very close community. Aura had returned to Raveo, her native village, after the death of her husband some years previously. She told me that the only thing she missed about her life in England was privacy. Here in Raveo everyone knew everything about each other's lives!

I set off from Raveo feeling rested and uplifted by the warm wishes of an entire village community. Many of its inhabitants had lived there all their lives and I wondered what they really thought of my transitory lifestyle. Aura had been a wonderful hostess and I felt especially indebted to Dirce, who had responded to my needs at such short notice, despite not being able to speak my language. Aura told me that Dirce liked to collect postcards, so I resolved to send her one as often as possible for the remainder of my journey.

Riding on towards Udine City, the skies blackened and streaks of lightening were closely followed by loud thunderclaps. There was nowhere obvious to shelter so I struggled on, and soon found myself riding under the full force of a ferocious storm. The crosswinds were so strong that I had to lean into them in order to keep my balance. A smile appeared on my face, however, as I thought of my friends back in Raveo, whose thoughts would surely be with me as the storm reached their village.

My strength was draining fast as I battled against the winds, so it was some relief when a roadside motel came into view. Nightfall was approaching and the storm showed no signs of abating, so I gave in to the elements and checked in for the night. Twenty pounds seemed like money well spent on this occasion, although it turned out to be the most that I would ever pay for a night's accommodation!

The storm died out overnight and I set off under clear skies. It was not long before Udine City came into view, neatly encircled by hills and dominated by its castle, which stood on a wooded hill right in the centre. I rode down from the hills towards this focal point, through the smart outer suburbs and then cobbled streets and romantic archways of the 'Old Town'. After a late breakfast at one of the trendy street cafes here, I recklessly entrusted all my belongings to the waiter and walked up to the castle. From the castle walls, the Adriatic Sea was just about visible, far away to the south.

The day was still young, so I rode on to Gradisco, where an enormous war memorial provided me with another opportunity to stretch my legs. Endless lines of memorial plaques decorated a series of huge steps, leading up the hillside to a small chapel and eternal flame. It was an impressive tribute to the men of this town that had sacrificed their lives in the two World Wars.

Back on the bike, I peddled on into the evening to reach the city of Trieste, not far from the Yugoslav border. Trieste is tucked into a deep bay, surrounded by steep hills. At the harbour, I made enquiries after accommodation and was told that all the campsites were situated well out of the city. There did not appear to be any cheap hostels either, so I decided to compensate for the previous night's motel expenses by passing the night at the main railway station. With the bike safely secured to waiting room seats, I settled down for the evening with a newspaper and my first letters from home, collected from the main post office.

It was raining heavily again in the morning and I had not slept too well, due to a noisy demonstration that was taking place late into the night in the streets around the station. I had not managed to find out the purpose of the demonstration, other than to make as much noise as possible! The day started slowly with a few lazy hours at the station café drinking Cappuccinos and watching the world go by – an activity that seems to be something of a national pastime in Italy. Eventually the rain eased off, and I climbed slowly out of Trieste to reach the Yugoslav border by late afternoon. A thoroughly bored looking border guard waved me across with a cursory glance at my passport, and I set up camp for the night behind a restaurant in the border town of Kozina.

The road across the Istrian Peninsula was bumpy and pot-holed – the first really rough road that I had encountered, but a luxury road compared to some that I would meet later on in Asia! After riding for most of the day under grey skies, across the bleak Slovenian peninsula, the seaside resort town of Rijeka was a welcome sight. I sat down to rest for a while on a promenade bench and was immediately engulfed by smiling locals, who gathered around to inspect the bike and ask questions about my journey. One of them made what he considered to be a generous offer for the bike, and seemed quite offended at my refusal to sell! It dawned on me then that I had reached Eastern Europe and my high-tech bike would arouse quite a bit of curiosity from now on.

I rode south a little from Rijeka on the Adriatic Highway, which follows the Dalmation Coast all the way down to the Albanian border. That night I reached a campsite at the small village of Bakerac, which is set in a beautiful bay. Sharing the campsite with me were Stephen and Lily - a 'Geordie' couple that had been cycle touring around Eastern Europe for several months now. They were heading south, like me, but planning to use local ferries to hop between the islands just off the coast. We shared a meal together and spent the evening solving most of the world's problems, around a small campfire on a chilly late September evening.

In the morning, Stephen and Lily headed off on the morning ferry, while I continued south on the Adriatic Highway. It was tough going, up and over numerous capes, but the spectacular coastal vistas provided ample reward. The road was quite perilous, with long stretches where there were no barriers to protect me from a sheer drop into the ocean! I saw several cars embedded into the cliffs, which served as a vivid reminder that the utmost caution was necessary. Fortunately, there was not too much traffic, but I could understand why the road was apparently closed to cyclists in the busy months of July and August.

Over the next few days, I made good progress and enjoyed glorious weather for a change. There were plenty of idyllic roadside camping spots along the coast, although one night I got a nasty shock on pitching the tent in the corner of a seemingly empty field. I was awoken in the early hours by the sound of bells and snorting, an animal of some description circled my tent, obviously giving it a close inspection. Praying that it was not a bull, I tentatively stuck my head out of the tent, at which the animal fled. I had not been able to identify it in the darkness but, reassured by its fear of me, nodded off to sleep again to the sound of distant bells. When daylight came I emerged from the tent again to see my overnight companions for the first time. Standing on the other side of the field were two young ponies, who did not seem to mind posing for a photograph!

Having parted company with the ponies, I decided to make a detour inland. There was no particular reason for this, other than to take a break from the coastal highway, which, though breathtaking at times, was something of a 'tourist trail'. I followed a minor road inland which, according to my map, would meet up with the Adriatic Highway about fifty miles further south. Stopping at a roadside café for some water, I was taken aback by the reaction of the local farmers gathered there. There was an eerie silence for a few moments as I walked in, but soon these rugged looking men were gathering round and trying to persuade me to join them for a beer. This was politely refused as it was only 8.30 a.m. and a long road was lying ahead! Instead I was plied with coffee. My unexpected appearance was clearly a source of amusement to these people, but they seemed to be genuinely appreciative of my efforts to see the 'real' Yugoslavia.

One aspect that disappointed me as I ventured inland was the huge amount of rubbish lying all around, marring a wild and rugged landscape. It seemed that little thought was given to the environment in these areas that tourists were unlikely to see. However, the detour was well worthwhile as I barely encountered another vehicle all day and thoroughly enjoyed the ride.

Back on the Adriatic Highway, I sampled a Yugoslav Youth Hostel at the busy port of Sibenik. It was a luxurious hostel and, with the tourist season drawing to a close, I had the whole place all to myself! The town itself was equally impressive - built on steep hillsides overlooking an island-studded inlet. The focal point was a huge Gothic Cathedral called the Castle of St. Anne.

A further day's riding over numerous capes brought me to the even more impressive city of Split. There were no cheap lodgings to be found here, so I decided to sleep rough. It was a warm, moonlit night and, in any case, I wanted to visit Split's famous 'Old Town' at first light – well before the daily tourist invasion. After a refreshing swim in the sea I settled down on the promenade with a picnic supper and a newspaper. As the evening drew to a close, and the promenade strollers began to drift away, I found myself a sheltered bench next to the ferry port, where I could bed down for the night.

Awaking at first light, I re-loaded the bike and went to explore the 'Old Town'. This was one of four renowned ancient settlements on the Adriatic coast – all of which are World Heritage sites. As expected, the narrow cobbled streets and courtyards were almost deserted at this hour and I was able to cycle slowly around, soaking up the atmosphere. A market was setting up for the day in one of the larger courtyards, and a stall-holder offered me a giant tomato to eat with my bread and cheese for breakfast.

It was still early in the morning when I rode out of Split, and this was one of those rare days when the riding seemed almost effortless. Following the Adriatic Highway, the rugged coastal landscape became increasingly rocky and barren as I rode on and on. As evening approached, I started to think about somewhere to camp, but was unable to find a patch of land, between the rocky hills that lined both sides of the highway, that would be large enough to pitch the tent. There was nothing for it but to keep riding, until I eventually arrived at the village of Neum. Here there was a small, deserted campsite, where I could finally make camp in semi-darkness. My cycle computer proudly indicated that the magic figure of one hundred miles had been covered that day!

Another long day's riding brought me to Yugoslavia's top tourist destination – Dubrovnik. Although it was now mid-October, the large campsite here was fairly crowded with holidaymakers, and among them were Stephen and Lily. They had been there for a couple of days already and were planning to take the morning ferry to Southern Greece, so we celebrated their last night in Yugoslavia with a meal together at a local restaurant. Their trip was due to end in a couple of weeks' time, so I did not think that our paths were likely to cross again. However, the travelling life is full of unlikely encounters, and I would bump into Stephen again six months later at Changi Airport in Singapore!

A whole day was spent exploring Dubrovnik's famous old walled city, which lies like a jewel in the ocean, separated from the modern part of the city by a causeway. The old city was beautifully preserved, despite having survived numerous earthquakes, and still largely inhabited. It was very relaxing to lose myself in the maze of alleys and stairways, which thread their way around the Dalmation stone churches, houses and museums. Particularly interesting was the Historical Museum, housed in the Rector's Palace, which tells of the life and times of the Ragusa Republic, as Dubrovnik was once known. From here the Rector ruled, a month at a time, and during this period he was not allowed to leave the confines of the Palace, for fear that he would be distracted from his duties.

Back on the Adriatic Highway, there was yet more dramatic coastal scenery, with sweeping views back to Dubrovnik necessitating several photo stops! A day's riding brought me to the Bay of Kotor, where tiny fishing communities, scattered along the shores, nestled beneath towering mountains. These mountains separate the Dalmation coast from the inland regions of Montenegro and Kosovo. At the town of Kotor itself, I was able to camp free on a motor-camp that was now officially closed for the winter.

The next day began with some more sightseeing in the 'Old Town' of Kotor, which is another impressive living museum of ancient architecture. Though much smaller than the old towns of Split and Dubrovnik, the fantastic setting of this settlement, squeezed between huge mountains and the sea, and complete lack of tourists, made this easily my favourite of place on the Dalmation Coastline. It was also to mark the end of my long ride on the Adriatic Highway, as my journey from here would take me inland, in order to avoid the closed land frontiers of Albania. I would now have to find a way through those towering mountains!

It was the toughest climb of my journey so far. I crawled uphill on a steep, zigzag road rising 1200 metres up the sides of Mount Lovcen to Cetinje – the former Capital of Montenegro. Much encouragement came from a coach-load of German tourists that passed me three times. Each time that the coach pulled in for a photo stop, I was able to regain the lead during the time that it took the fifty or so passengers to file in and out for their photos. The coach would then overtake me again, with the passengers cheering me on with greater enthusiasm each time. This really spurred me on and helped to take my mind off the aching legs!

With one final look back at the Dalmation coast, now almost obscured by clouds, I continued downhill from Cetinje into the mountainous region of Montenegro. That night I camped at another 'closed' campsite on the edge of Titograd – the State capital.

It was raining steadily as I set off early in the morning, while Titograd was still sleeping. Once clear of the city, the road passed through rocky canyons, following fast flowing rivers. The grey skies above, and many long dark tunnels, gave the landscape a rather hostile look.

As if to emphasise this, the sound of a sudden, deafening, gunshot awoke me from my thoughts and almost knocked me from the bike! The bullet had been fired above my head from a passing truck. The driver was leaning out of the cab and gave a loud laugh as the truck hurtled on. Regaining my composure, I recalled the numerous warnings that I had been given, while riding down the tourist-friendly coastal highway, about the dangers of travelling inland. I had taken these warnings fairly lightly, but now began to review them in a more serious light. I cycled on with some trepidation!

Still in a state of mild shock, I was befriended by a family of day-tripping Yugoslavs, who kindly shared their lunch with me in the gardens of an old monastery at Moracca. After lunch, the resident monk gave us a short guided tour of the ancient buildings, which dated back to 1256. It was a pleasant diversion, which helped to calm my nerves a little.

It was still raining steadily as I set off from Moracca, planning to ride just another fifteen miles up the valley to the larger town of Kolassin. After just a couple of miles, however, the day's second unsavoury incident occurred. A couple of farmers were herding a group of ponies, sheep and bulls along the road towards me. As I slowly rode past, one of the bulls suddenly leapt across the road into my path. I swerved to narrowly avoid a collision, but the car following was unable to stop and skidded into the bull. The bull seemed to be unhurt, though slightly ruffled, but there was a huge dent in the side of the car. A heated argument ensued, with the driver and one of the farmers apparently arguing as to who was at fault, while I waited anxiously in the pouring rain for the verdict. The debate lasted for a few minutes, before ending as suddenly as it had begun. Both parties seemed to have accepted the situation philosophically and there were handshakes all round. Attention then turned to me, and I was sent on my way with an encouraging pat on the back from one of the farmers!

Drenched and exhausted, having been riding mostly uphill and in pouring rain all day, I finally reached the sleepy mountain town of Kolassin. Heading slowly into the centre of the town, I was approached by two young boys, who offered me lodgings for the night. This seemed to be a godsend, so I followed them without question. The boys lived at an old farmhouse with their parents, grandfather and several older brothers and sisters. None of them spoke any English, but I was warmly welcomed. It was not long before my wet clothes were hanging up to dry and I was warming myself by the fire with a glass of brandy. Dinner was a delicious vegetable stew with freshly baked bread, and the evening was spent communicating via my phrasebook. The tiny book was a source of great interest and amusement! Climbing into a comfortable, warm bed, I was able to reflect on the most eventful day of my trip so far.

The rain continued through the night. Over breakfast, my hosts informed me that it was not uncommon for it to rain continuously for over a week in these parts. They insisted that I should stay with them until the weather improved, which was fine by me as my legs were still aching from the previous day. The family members came and went throughout the day, while I sat with granddad working on my language skills and reading. Everyone gathered at meal times, and virtually everything that we ate had been produced on the farm. I admired their simple, hard-working and self-sufficient way of life.

By the following morning the rain had eased off at last, and I walked into town to buy some small presents for my hosts. These were presented at lunch and then my departure was made, as the sun finally broke through the clouds. I was completely refreshed and ready for whatever lay in store!

I rode for several more days through the mountainous countryside, camping by the roadside but eating at café's more frequently as it became colder. The usual dish – and often the only choice – was a 'mixed grill', which, though not particularly interesting, at least filled me up. From Yugoslavia's highest settlement – a village named Louce, at 1350 metres – I finally left Montenego behind and descended onto the plains of Kosovo.

Riding was easier now and less lonely as well, with farmers invariably waving and calling out greetings from the fields as I rode past. Young children often rushed to the side of the road to greet me as they saw me coming, and this helped to take my mind off the monotony of the Kosovan plains.

Early one afternoon I cycled into the city of Pristina. With its massive grey apartment blocks, and dusty streets full of chaotic activity, this city was quite a shock to the senses! While searching for lodgings, I was besieged by moneychangers that wanted to buy my dollars, and children dressed in rags that tried to hang onto the bike as I rode along. There was no sign of a campsite or cheap lodgings, and sleeping rough here was clearly out of the question, so I decided to head on towards the larger city of Skopje, some fifty miles further south.

I had planned to camp somewhere by the roadside en-route to Skopje but, helped by a strong tailwind, I flew across the plains to reach a large motor-camp on the edge of the city, just before nightfall. The site had an impressive range of facilities, including a live band live in the on-site café!

Skopje proved an interesting city to explore. It was almost completely destroyed by an earthquake in 1963, and a massive effort had clearly gone into its reconstruction. In the heart this modern, sprawling city, remnants of the 'Old Town' have been carefully restored to provide a reminder of the city's ancient past. Crossing an old stone footbridge brought me into a maze of narrow alleyways threading through a bazaar to the Skopje Town Museum, at the heart of 'Old Skopje'. The museum's clock was stopped at 5.17am – the time of day when the first earthquake tremors rumbled beneath the city.

Riding south from Skopje, I inadvertently found myself on what appeared to be a motorway. Being a little uncertain as to whether cycling was permitted on Yugoslav motorways, I turned off onto an old cobbled road, which seemed to follow the same route. Riding over the cobbles proved to be thoroughly uncomfortable, however, so I rejoined the motorway at the first opportunity. There was plenty of horn tooting from passing cars and trucks, as I cruised along the hard shoulder, but I think that the drivers were just being friendly!

Having traversed all six independent states of Yugoslavia – most of which are now independent countries, of course - I reflected on the marked differences in terrain and climate between each one. Here in Macedonia – the southern-most state - it was a mixture of agricultural plains and gentle rolling green hills, and it was becoming very warm as I approached the Greek border.

Just north of the border, a couple of Western cycle tourists had stopped at the roadside to mend a puncture. This was a welcome sight, as I had not seen another cycle tourist since leaving the Dalmation coast, and they seemed quite pleased to see me as well.

'Mike the Bike' – as he introduced himself to me – was from Vancouver, Canada. He seemed to be immensely proud of this fact – insisting that there was no better place to live! He worked at home each winter to make enough money for cycle-touring in North America or Europe in summer – a routine that he had followed for the past seven years. He was very talkative and a mine of touring information, so I was to learn much from him as we cycled together over the next few weeks.

Mike's older and quieter companion was Bob – a 47 year-old divorcee from Ohio, U.S.A. At his own admission, he seemed to have reached something of a mid-life crisis – prompting him to leave behind a secure job and comfortable lifestyle, in order to experience life on the road. He had spent three months on an organised group cycle tour in Russia, before catching a train from there to Belgrade in order to continue on his own in Europe. He had met Mike in Belgrade and, since they were both heading to Istanbul, they had teamed up.

We rode together across the border into Northern Greece. The pace was a little slow, but it was great to have company on the road again and the miles seemed to go by quickly.

With the trained eye of a seasoned traveller, Mike spotted an empty barn in the corner of a roadside field, which would provide us with shelter for the night. We were soon settled in, and spent the evening drinking cheap local wine and playing cards by candlelight. Bob told us that, despite having to do without so many of the luxuries that he was used to, he felt as happy now as at any stage of his life. His only regret was that he badly missed his two young children. I admired his courage at leaving so much behind in order to make his dream come true.

In the morning we rode into Thessalonika – Greece's second largest city. Here we checked into the Youth Hostel, where there were some interesting characters in residence. These included a quiet Japanese guy, of stocky build, who had spent the past eight months walking from Portugal to Greece. He planned to walk as far as Istanbul, before flying home from there to Hiroshima. This man's incredible journey made my own efforts seem quite insignificant!

Apart from Bob and Mike and I, there were another five cycle tourists staying at the hostel – including Peter from Australia. I struck up an instant friendship with Peter, and a year later we would be living for a while as close neighbours in Alice Springs. Most uplifting for me at this time though was to meet an English backpacker who had recently travelled through Iran. He had obtained his visa in Pakistan and had experienced no difficulties while travelling through the country, despite the fact that the First Gulf War was well underway in neighbouring Iraq and Kuwait. This was the first really positive information that I had received on my intended route through the Middle East.

Thessalonika – the birthplace of Aristotle – seemed a surprisingly modern city, although there were still some remains from Roman times, including much of the old city walls. Strolling around the shops, offices and apartment blocks, I stumbled upon several old Byzantine churches, containing beautiful mosaics, some of which were over a thousand years old. After a couple of restful days taking in these sights, and enjoying some very tasty food in the local restaurants, we were ready to head on. Peter was invited to join us for the ride to Istanbul.

*

On the morning of our planned departure, I was laid low with a tummy bug. After some debate, we decided that Peter and Bob would set off together, while Mike and I would follow the next day, assuming that I was well enough by then. Our cycling pace would be faster than theirs, so we expected to catch up them up in a day. We would meet up on the campsite at Asprovalta, and then continue on to Istanbul together.

The next day I was feeling much better, although my energy levels were a little low, having not eaten anything for a couple of days. It would probably have been sensible to spend another day in Thessalonika building my strength up. However, not wanting to upset the arrangements, I agreed to travel.

The road signs were quite confusing as we headed out of Thessalonika and, having covered over twenty miles, we found ourselves to be on entirely the wrong road. Instead of riding due east towards the Turkish border, we were heading in a southerly direction towards the Mediterranean coast. Each of us had put too much faith in the other's road sense, and hence we had not bothered to stop and consult the map earlier. We laughed about this, but it was a depressing blow as we would not now be able to reach the appointed meeting place with Bob and Peter that evening. After some discussion, we decided that we might as well continue on this road to the coast and then cut back inland the following day. Hopefully we would be able to catch up with our friends somewhere en-route to Istanbul.

The riding was a real struggle for me, due to lack of energy, but Mike was patient and encouraged me to rest frequently. We eventually reached the coastal town of Gerikini, where our troubles really began! Spotting a seemingly idyllic camping spot by the sea, we pushed our bikes through a gap in some fencing. There was plenty of shade, and a nice flat grassy area to pitch the tents. However, while walking barefoot after a swim in the sea, it became apparent that the ground was covered in tiny sharp thorns. On inspecting the bikes we then saw that all four tyres were rapidly deflating!

Quickly abandoning our campsite, we retreated to the concrete balcony of a locked-up holiday home nearby. A long evening was spent picking the numerous thorns out of the tyres by candlelight. It became quite therapeutic after a while, and we were able to laugh about a difficult day. Somehow these kinds of difficulties are much easier to cope with when they are shared.

The next day I was feeling much stronger, and really enjoyed riding with Mike. He kept me entertained by reciting Monty Python sketches and telling me stories from his years of cycle touring. It was late October now and, with the tourist season over, many of the towns that we passed through were like ghost towns. They were full of unfinished buildings and deserted holiday homes, with cafes and shops that had long been closed for the winter. It was a good day for riding, with clear skies and a cool breeze, as we headed back inland. When we did, occasionally, encounter strong headwinds, we were able to reduce the workload by riding in each other's slipstreams.

On reaching Asprovalta, we checked the campsite for news of Bob and Peter. They had stayed the previous evening, as arranged, but had not left any messages for us. We were both feeling good, so we rode on for a

32

couple of hours and camped by the roadside in a half-built apartment block, which was strangely situated in the middle of nowhere. There seemed to be no shortage of free shelter for passing travellers in Greece at this time of year! As usual we set off again at first light, so as to avoid being discovered.

We were riding due east now, towards the Turkish border. By early afternoon, we had made it to Kavala – an attractive Mediterranean town, which sits on a peninsula jutting out into the ocean. We went straight to the town campsite, to check for news of Bob and Peter. Again their names were in the guest book, but they had left that morning without leaving a message. However, we were both long overdue for a shower, so we checked in anyway and spent the afternoon washing clothes and relaxing by the pool.

I shall never forget one character that we met the next day, on the road to Komotini. His name was Tony - a well-weathered, middle-aged man, who had cycled from his home in Manchester to Turkey, and was now on his way back. He had no expensive touring equipment, and was riding on a very old, single-speed, bicycle that seemed to be held together by bits of string and slightly suspect welding jobs. He was travelling very light indeed and sleeping rough at nights without even a tent. His diet was based strictly on his motto - 'No Cook, No Kill'. This meant that he only ate raw vegetables soaked in olive oil, fruit and oats. As if to prove this, he was carrying a large jar of olive oil! An hour or so passed very quickly, as we chatted with this rather eccentric and unique cycle-tourist. As we were parting company, he gave my smart mountain bike a brief inspection.

"That bike will take you round the world five times over!" he said casually, without a hint of envy.

We set up camp in the woods, just a few miles before the Turkish border. It had not rained for several weeks in these parts, so I was not able to push the tent pegs very far into the rock hard ground. This did not worry me too much as it was a fine evening and the skies were clear. However, I learned that night that you can never take fine weather for granted – at least not in Europe!

The thunderstorm that struck during the night was ferocious and, despite plenty of shelter afforded by the trees, my poorly set up tent soon collapsed. I should have got up to rebuild the tent straight away, but instead tried to hold it up from the inside, hoping that the torrential rain would ease off a little first. This did not happen, and before long I was shivering in a pool of freezing water! I had no choice but to desert my flooded home and go in search of Mike. His tent had stood firm, so I was able to borrow some dry clothes and shelter there until dawn. It had been a camping nightmare – but some valuable experience gained!

It was still raining steadily as we packed up our gear in the morning and cycled to the border. Here we spent a couple of hours in the café, warming up and recovering from a traumatic night! Later on, with the rain still pelting down and temperatures barely above freezing, we crossed the border into Turkey. We were both in need of rest, and I needed to dry all my clothes out, so we checked into a cheap hotel for the night in the border town of Ipsala.

The next morning we were in no hurry to start cycling again, so we went for a walk in the streets around the hotel. As we strolled around, there were friendly shouts and smiles from all directions and, before long, we were invited into a worker's café for tea. We sat there for several hours, communicating in sign language and drinking endless cups of delicious Turkish tea – for which all offers of payment were refused. It was quite a welcome to Turkey and it seemed as though we had entered another world, simply by crossing the border.

From Ipsala we rode for three days on a busy highway that followed the shores of the Sea of Marmara. The weather was fairly miserable and it was quite hard to resist the temptation to accept one of the frequent offers, from passing truck drivers, of a ride into Istanbul. Our polite refusals seemed to cause much bewilderment, but we were both determined to reach the famous city under our own steam.

Even harder to resist was the temptation to stop too often at roadside cafes, from which the locals would often be waving at us and inviting us in. We always received a friendly welcome in these places, and usually the opportunity to warm up for a while by a roaring fire, while drinking delicious fresh tea. There was often a game of backgammon going on as well, and it was amazing to watch the game being played so fast that you could hardly see the pieces move! In the evenings, these cafes became meeting places where Turkish men would gather to socialise and watch football on television.

We arrived in Istanbul on the morning of October 25th 1990. This city is known as the 'Gateway to the East', and all the hardships of the past seven and a half weeks paled into insignificance as I caught my first glimpse of Asia across the Sea of Bosphorus. The geographical significance of this city meant more to me than its historical importance. My desire to travel further was as strong as ever, but now it was time to rest. I had cycled across Europe.

Riding into the city through the busy suburbs was a hair-raising experience! Old cars moved bumper to bumper through narrow streets at a frantic pace, while we competed with donkey-drawn carts and criss-crossing pedestrians for the remaining road space! To add to the confusion, most motorists seemed to find it necessary to constantly blast their horns, as they were driving along. With some relief, we finally reached the Sultanahmed district, in the heart of 'Old Istanbul'. This area contains most of the city's tourist attractions, including giant mosques, palaces and the biggest bazaar in Asia. It was also something of a 'Traveller's Village', with numerous guest houses and hostels. We checked into one called the Topkapi Hostel, which was cheap and cheerful.

Peter arrived in Istanbul the following day and we bumped into each other (almost literally!) outside the General Post Office. He had somehow managed to lose Bob along the way, and was concerned for his safety. However, Bob turned up himself a few days later, and the four of us shared a dormitory at the Topkapi Hostel. Bob seemed very pleased at having cycled alone for the first time - and survived! It seems that Mike and I overtook them somewhere around the border, and that they had become separated shortly afterwards, when Bob took a wrong turning.

One of Istanbul's highlights, for me, was a visit to the Topkapi Palace. This was the main residence for Ottoman rulers from the 1450s to the 1850s, and once housed over five thousand residents – many of them concubines and eunuchs. It is now maintained as a museum and every room contained eye-catching exhibits. The hill-top Palace gardens were a blaze of colour and a tranquil oasis in the heart of the city. The gardens overlooked the Golden Horn – a four-mile inlet, which flows off the Bosphorus Sea, separating the European side of the city into two parts.

Not far from the Topkapi Palace stands a spectacular red-domed mosque called Ayasofya. Built around AD532 - using ivory from Asia, marble from Egypt and columns from the ruins of Ephusus – it took ten thousand men and six years to complete, and is now considered one of the world's greatest examples of Byzantine architecture. Just a few yards away stands the colossal Blue Mosque, with its shimmering blue tiles and six minarets. Built more recently, in 1609, the Blue Mosque was apparently intended to outshine the Ayasofya. I would certainly not have wanted to have to judge between the two!

A few miles form the grand old buildings of Sultanahmed, I discovered the slum area of Fener. Here washing hung across narrow cobbled streets from the windows of grubby apartment blocks and children were playing football in the streets. Strolling around this area, I felt entirely at ease and was greeted by friendly smiles from almost everyone that I saw. It was interesting and refreshing to sample some ordinary city life, away from the influences of tourism. I resolved to make similar efforts to discover the more ordinary districts in other cities that I would be visiting along the way.

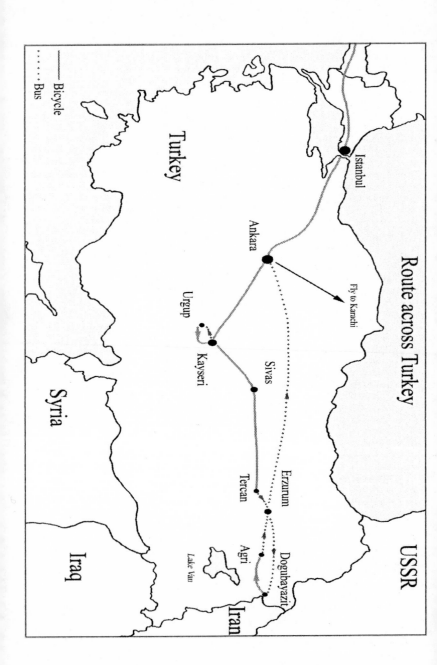

Route across Turkey

Turkey

USSR

Istanbul

Ankara

Fly to Karachi

Urgup

Kayseri

Sivas

Erzurum

Tercan

Agri

Doğubayazit

Lake Van

Syria

Iraq

Iran

——— Bicycle
········· Bus

CHAPTER TWO

COLD TURKEY

Istanbul to the Iranian Frontier

A WEEK DID NOT SEEM LONG ENOUGH in Istanbul but, with winter fast approaching, I was anxious to head eastwards across Turkey as soon as possible, before the high mountain passes in the centre of the country became in-passable due to snow. My recent travelling companions – Mike, Bob and Peter – had all decided to head back to the warmer climes of Greece, so it would be a solo journey again. I was armed with Indian and Pakistani visas, easily obtained in the city, but no Iranian visa. The Iranian Consulate had been extremely negative about the idea of me trying to cycle across Iran, so I resolved to try again in Ankara.

Another hair-raising ride through the bustling suburbs brought me to the Bosphorus Suspension Bridge, which spans over one mile to link Europe and Asia across the Bosphorus Straits. Police Officers stationed at the bridge were adamant that the morning traffic was far too heavy for me to ride across. One of them was quite sympathetic to my cause, however, and ordered the driver of a passing truck to give me a lift over! The driver was happy to oblige, and even offered me a lift all the way to Ankara – some three hundred miles further east. He seemed puzzled at my insistence that I wanted to travel there under my own steam, but wished me well as he dropped me off on the other side of the bridge.

Surprisingly, the Asian side of Istanbul seemed somewhat calmer and quieter, with the streets and plazas wider and less cluttered. Within an hour I was clear of the suburbs and making good progress along the Marmara coast. Several drivers hooted and waved as they drove past, and there were frequent shouts of encouragement from the roadside. Istanbul seemed far behind already and it was good to be on the move again.

That night I checked into a backstreet hotel in the large coastal city of Izmit. The reception staff here kept me chatting most of the evening. One of them was able to act as an interpreter, having apparently studied English at Cambridge University, and the bicycle was, as usual, the main focus of attention.

The busy highway between Istanbul and Ankara forms part of the main overland truck route between Europe and the East. With no network of back-roads to use as an alternative, I had to battle against a stream of heavy trucks, which tended to create an almost permanent dust storm. Cycling goggles were helpful, but could not keep the dust out of my eyes when the wind was blowing, and sometimes I had to stop for a while to recover my vision.

Eighty miles east of Izmit, I reached a small isolated town called Kaynasli, where there was a small hotel. The Manager was fast asleep behind the reception desk when I walked in, which was understandable when he explained that I was his first guest for several days. Together we hauled my loaded bike upstairs to what he assured me was the best room.

While dining at the café next door to the hotel, I was engaged in conversation by a group of young local lads. The main topic was football – a sport that is followed passionately in Turkey. After dinner, my new friends invited me to what I gathered was some sort of a dance, or disco, in the next village. We walked a couple of miles along a dirt track to reach the village, which was alive with the sound of celebrations. A few hundred people, of all ages and mostly in traditional dress, were gathered in the village plaza. A band was playing lively folk music and there seemed to be a general state of excitement. On our arrival, my friends proudly introduced me as a visitor from England. I was immediately surrounded by a sea of smiling faces and served with a glass of wine and sweetmeats.

I was just wondering whether this was normal village entertainment for a Saturday night when, suddenly, all became clear. A battered, brightly painted, old car drew up, and out stepped the bride and groom! At this point many candles were lit and a human tunnel was formed, through which the happy couple made their way to the centre of the festivities. The dancing began now but, with so many people crowded into the square, there was only room for a few people to dance at a time. We watched, and occasionally joined in, the celebrations for a couple of hours, before walking back to Kaynasli by the light of the moon for a 'night-cap' and game of cards in the café.

After a typical Turkish breakfast of soup with freshly baked bread, I made an early start the next morning. The bleak terrain was becoming increasingly hilly, but I sometimes managed to give my legs a rest by hanging onto the back of slow moving trucks while going uphill. The drivers always seemed to find this highly amusing and gave frequent 'thumbs up' signs to show their approval. One truck towed me uphill for five miles!

By late afternoon I had reached the village of Aykarma, which lies at 1500 metres above sea level – the highest point on the highway between Istanbul and Ankara. There was no hotel here, so I set my tent up behind a very smart restaurant, which was owned by a friendly, English speaking, couple. They allowed me to take a shower in their private quarters, before sitting down to an excellent meal in the restaurant. Glad to be inside on a bitterly cold evening, I ate my dinner as slowly as possible! I need not have worried, however, because there were no other diners that night, and my hosts invited me to join them for a drink afterwards anyway. They told me that it normally snows in Aykarma at this time of year, so I was lucky to have arrived in such good weather. Nevertheless, the temperature dropped to well below freezing that night and I was glad of my four-season sleeping bag!

From the heights of sleepy Aykarma, it was a fairly gentle descent into the huge basin in which Ankara lies. This was just as well, because I was feeling some discomfort from an old knee injury and in need of rest. The problem would often recur in the future – usually after some tough riding in mountainous areas – and the solution was always a few days' rest.

The huge metropolis of Ankara is encircled by a ring of hills. These natural barriers tend to trap the air pollution, and the city is known to have the highest levels in Turkey. Though the sun was shining from a clear sky, the air over the city did seem very dark as I approached.

Budget accommodation was much harder to find than in Istanbul, but I eventually tracked down some cheap lodgings in the Ulus district of 'Old Ankara'. The family that run my hotel were very welcoming and I was soon introduced to many of their friends that lived in the neighbouring houses. Within a couple of days I found that I virtually had the 'freedom of the street'! Next to the hotel was a tea-shop, then a kebab takeaway, and I was unable to walk past either without being invited in to sample their products at no charge! In the evenings the street would turn into a football pitch and a delegation would knock on my door to invite me to join the game. It seemed strange to have been accepted so readily into a backstreet community in such a large, modern city as this.

Perched on a hilltop close to Ulus is 'The Citadel'. Within these imposing fortress walls lies a tranquil old Turkish village – unchanged and utterly remote from the city of skyscrapers below. This is where Ankara began, and a stroll through the narrow, car-free, cobbled streets was like stepping back in time. People quietly went about their daily business here, seemingly oblivious to the gazes of occasional tourists. It was captivating enough for me to return several times during my stay.

Modern Ankara is a planned city, whose prime concern appears to be Government – perhaps due to its strategic position in the heart of the country. I made several visits to the diplomatic districts, in search of the elusive Iranian visa. The British Consulate kindly gave me a letter of recommendation, explaining my desire to cross Iran as part of my overland journey to the East, but this cut no ice with the Iranian Embassy! My only hope now was to try again in the eastern city of Erzurum, where there was a small Consulate with a reputation for being more relaxed over the issue of visas.

On the morning of my departure from Ankara, a sizeable crowd gathered to see me off. This show of affection was very touching, and it seemed that I had known them for much longer than the five days that had passed since my arrival as a stranger in their city. Within minutes of my grand departure, the chain snapped, as I tried to force the pedals round on a steep little incline. Another crowd quickly gathered round to watch as I carried out the repair in a shop doorway. Having rejoined the chain, a bowl of soapy water was produced for me to wash my hands, and I was on my way again to the sound of cheering and shouts of encouragement!

It was midday by the time that I had cleared the sprawling city suburbs. Days were shorter now, with the onset of winter, so I decided to skip lunch in order to cover as much ground as possible before nightfall. The Central Anatolian region is an area of great historical importance, with many civilisations having risen and fallen here - including the earliest human communities, dating from 7500 BC. It was hard to appreciate this, however, on a grey, rainy day, as I moved slowly across the bleak and empty landscape.

With nightfall approaching fast, a truck driver pulled over just in front of me as I struggled uphill, just outside the town of Keskin. He was carrying milk churns to the city of Kayseri – a hundred miles further on – and offered me a lift there. With snow expected any day now, I had been warned that some of the mountain passes in Central Turkey could soon be blocked for the winter. For this reason, I had decided earlier in the day to start accepting lifts. Otherwise I would have to make an enormous detour in order to avoid the mountain ranges. Nevertheless, this first lift was hard to accept, with my cycle ride being unbroken up to this point. There was some hesitation, but something made me nod to the driver. I was soon seated comfortably in the driver's cab, with the bike firmly secured on top of the milk churns behind.

On arriving in Kayseri (known in biblical times as Ceasarea), we went straight to the city bus station. My driver was known to all the bus drivers, and it was arranged that I would stay with them that night. Several of them were gathered round a stove in a small common room, relaxing at the end of their day's work. The conversation was animated and I was able to join in occasionally, having picked up quite a few phrases by now. Late in the evening, most of the drivers drifted off to their homes and I settled down to sleep on the couch.

The night was short, as I was awoken early with a breakfast of bread, cheese, chocolate and tea. One of the drivers had promised to take me to the nearby town of Urgup, in the heart of the Cappadocia region. This was not on my route, but I had heard that Cappadocia was an area not to be missed. Breakfast was hurriedly consumed and we were soon on our way.

It was not far to Urgup, but the lift was a blessing because it was now snowing heavily! At around 9am, we approached the town and I caught my first glimpses of Cappadocia. The area was engulfed by volcanic lava thousands of years ago, and the soft volcanic rock has been eroded by wind and rain into enormous, strangely shaped, pillars and cones. The resulting landscape is fantastic and quite surreal.

Situated in the heart of the Cappadocian wonderland, Urgup is a strange town whose life is divided between farming and tourism. Deserted cave dwellings are a feature of the region, but in Urgup many people still live or work in houses built into the rock. The large hotel that I checked into was quite conventional, however, and luxurious by the standards that I was used to (there were even 'sit-down' toilets with paper!). With the tourist season long over now there were very few other guests, so I was able to negotiate a room at about half the usual rate.

The day was hardly begun so, after a second breakfast at one of Urgup's many restaurants, I set off on the bike to visit one of Cappadocia's highlights - the underground city of Kaymakli. This is one of three underground cities in the region that have been excavated and lit for visitors. There are eight levels below the ground and a maze of tunnels and stairways connecting tiny rooms, including churches, common dining rooms and even tombs. There is room to accommodate thousands of inhabitants, supplied with water by underground springs, and air through elaborate ventilation systems. It is likely that Kaymakli was never continuously occupied, but served as a fortress for refugees in times of trouble and persecution. At all entrances, and at many points within, there are great round blocking stones that were used to seal off passages as required. As I crawled through the tunnels, my guide pointed out storage jars for oil, wine and water, communal kitchens blackened by smoke and incredibly deep wells. I was gradually able to imagine a whole community living happily beneath the ground.

Using Urgup as my base, the next few days were spent exploring the region by bike and on foot. Clambering over pillars and rock faces, the unique landscape changes continuously and I became quite entranced. Particularly fascinating was the famous

Goreme Valley, which is an amazing complex of two dozen churches and monasteries, built into the cliffs. Some were decorated with the scratched remains of beautifully painted frescos, mostly depicting Saints and biblical scenes.

A group of eight English cycle tourists were also staying in Urgup, and it was not long before we met up. They were the first English-speaking people that I had encountered for some time, so it was a nice change to spend a couple of evenings relaxing and chatting in my own language!

Urgup was covered in a thick blanket of snow as the English cycling group set off on their journey back to Istanbul. A blizzard was blowing and it was bitterly cold but, with the high passes of Central Turkey still to come, I knew that I could not afford to delay my own journey any longer. Wrapped up in five layers of clothing, I rode back towards Kayseri. On the long climb out of Urgup, I looked back on Cappadocia for the last time. The rich mixture of colours was now obscured by snow, but the weird rock formations were still very much in evidence.

On reaching Kayseri I thought about searching out my bus driver friends again. However, I decided that a good night's sleep in a hotel would be more beneficial, so that I would be able to cover good ground the next day. Cheap lodgings were very easy to find at this time of year, so the effect on my budget was fairly negligible. That evening, I strolled around the ancient streets that surround Kayseri's fortress. As I was admiring the wealth of medieval buildings, a young, well-dressed man sidled up to me. Speaking fluent English, he expressed heartfelt interest in my wellbeing. After exchanging pleasantries for a couple of minutes, the conversation took a sudden turn:

"You know, many Englishmen that come to Kayseri are interested in the fine carpets that are made here". Having been lured into several carpet shops during my time in Istanbul, I had no wish to spend half an hour in one now and stated plainly that I did not want to buy carpets. The commission agent to accept this but still insisted on shadowing me back to my hotel, presumably hoping that I would change my mind!

It was well below freezing when I set off from Kayseri the next morning, so I rode as fast as possible in order to keep warm. Heading into the mountains now, I climbed slowly to a high pass, and then nearly froze on the descent! Settlements were few and far between, and it was well into the afternoon before I reached a small café for lunch. The café was full of truck drivers and, as usual, I attracted plenty of attention. The owner even insisted that I write him a list of each country that I had been through, and each country that I was planning to visit in the future! It was hard to escape, but I did so by explaining that I only had two hours left to reach the high mountain town of Sarkisla before nightfall.

It was just enough time, and I checked into a small hotel in Sarkisla that had been recommended by the café owner. With no energy left to explore the town, I spent the evening consuming tea and delicious cakes in the cake shop across the road.

In the morning, I was straight back to the cake shop at first light, for a breakfast of warm bread, straight from the oven, with honey and hot milk. Then, armed with a good supply of pastries, I set off for the city of Sivas, some fifty miles east. There were no settlements marked on my map before Sivas, and the road would not drop below 1,000 metres, so I was determined to avoid a cold mountain camp by making it to Sivas before nightfall.

The highway was a thin straight line across a snow-covered mountain plateau, which was set alight by the early morning sun. It was a pretty scene, but before long I was riding into freezing winds that swept across the plateau. Every turn of the pedals required great effort and I soon started to doubt whether I would make it to Sivas in daylight. There was no question of turning back, so I tried not to think about the prospect of camping, as I concentrated on keeping the pedals slowly turning.

By mid-afternoon, the blustery headwinds had developed into a full-scale blizzard, and I had managed only twenty-eight miles – just over half way. At this point, I was put out of my misery as a truck pulled over for me. This time I had no difficulty at all in accepting the lift. However, the journey to Sivas was not over yet! The truck had already punctured twice that day, leaving them a wheel short after using the spare. To compensate for this, they had somehow managed to secure the rear axle to the chassis by chains. Unfortunately, the chains gave way within a few miles and we almost overturned. A lengthy delay ensued while further chains were used to re-secure the axle, and I wondered whether I would be better off chancing it against the elements. My good-humoured companions seemed completely unfazed by the situation, however, so I kept faith in them. Before too long, we were lumbering into Sivas.

It was no problem finding lodgings in Sivas, which was a large and surprisingly modern looking city, lying at an altitude of 1300 metres. It was wonderful to relax and rest the aching limbs in the warm, friendly atmosphere of a smoky teahouse, at the end of a day that had turned out to be a real endurance test!

My morning explorations of Sivas revealed a smattering of old Seljuk buildings, many now in ruins, giving evidence of the city's place in Turkish history as a Seljuk capital, through which dozens of invading armies have passed. It would have been nice to have stayed longer to rest and discover the city further. However, winter seemed to be deepening by the day now and I knew it was essential to cross this huge mountainous region, which makes up the bulk of Turkey, as soon as possible. By mid-morning I was on the road again

My journey was mainly uphill from Sivas, so it was slow going again. The weather was a little kinder than the previous day, but I was now troubled again by my recurring knee problem. I had managed about sixty miles, before giving in to the pain, and deciding that it was time to make camp for the night. There was no more than an hour's daylight left, and there was no sign of any settlements where I might at least find somewhere warm to shelter for the evening. The options were limited, so I just pulled off the road a little and started to clear some of the deep snow by the roadside, in order to make a pitch for the tent. However, just like the previous evening, help was at hand at just the right time! Before I had even started to unpack the tent a minibus pulled up. The driver had only stopped to relieve himself, but, realising with horror that I was planning to camp out in these Arctic conditions, ushered me hurriedly into his bus. The bus was empty, so there was plenty of room for the bike in the aisle. We were soon heading for the next big city of Erzincan – some 120 miles further east.

It seemed that I was somehow destined to get across these mountains safely and without having to test out my survival camping skills! From the warmth of the bus, I was able to fully appreciate the beauty of this rugged terrain. The steep mountains, covered with snow-clad fir trees, were no longer threatening but there to be admired. The highway turned to cobbles for one ten-mile stretch, which, though not particularly comfortable in the bus, would have been horrendous on the bike. It was a lovely journey, not least due to my cheerful driver who seemed pleased at the opportunity to learn a few English words, in exchange for the lift!

Erzincan was once renowned as one of the most beautiful cities in Anatolia. However, a series of earthquakes – the worst killing forty thousand people in 1939 – have left most of the Seljuk mosques and palaces in ruins. Despite rebuilding programmes, the city is still known mainly for its earthquakes today. Nevertheless, my overnight stay turned out to be quite a memorable one – and not because of an earthquake!

Having been kindly deposited in the city centre, I stopped the first person that walked by to ask for directions to a cheap hotel. This person was an English teacher named Erdal and he insisted that I should stay at his home. He lived with his wife and baby in a small flat, below his parents' flat, and we all spent the evening together in the parents' flat. After a lavish dinner, I assisted Erdal with an English lesson that he was giving to one of his students that had come round for some extra tuition. Later on we settled down to watch a soccer game on television, involving Manchester City and Leeds. It was strange to watch my hosts getting so involved in a game that seemed quite irrelevant to them in this remote Turkish city.

After an early breakfast with Erdal, before he went to work, I spent an hour drinking tea in his father's wool shop before setting off myself. Feeling refreshed after receiving such excellent hospitality, I covered twenty miles quite effortlessly before entering a steep-sided river valley. My progress slowed dramatically as I encountered strong headwinds which, channelled by the high valley walls, did their best to force me backwards. It was so cold now that my water bottles froze solid and I could not feel my feet at all!

There were no settlements at all along the valley and there were no places to shelter, so I just kept battling along into the wind at a snail's pace. This time I was not rescued by a passing truck – probably because it was too dangerous for a truck to pull over on the narrow, winding road through the valley.

In a state of near-exhaustion, I finally reached the mouth of the valley by late afternoon. Feeling quite dazed, I rode a further ten miles across a snowy plateau to the town of Tercan. I had no energy left to go through my usual routine of shopping around for the cheapest lodgings in town, so I just checked into the first hotel that I saw. It turned out to be quite a luxurious one, and I had my first hot shower since leaving Istanbul! The Manager was a chirpy character, with a reasonable grasp of the English language, and we spent an evening chatting together over beer and crisps. It was a nice way to unwind at the end of the toughest day's riding of my trip so far.

Fifty miles east of Tercan lies Erzurum. This is the largest city of Eastern Turkey and, at an altitude of 2000 metres, generally the coldest. The hotel manager had warned me that most of the journey from Tercan was uphill. After my frightening experience of the previous day, when I had nearly collapsed from exhaustion, and taking into account the lingering pain from my knee injury, I decided to resort to public transport. This was another landmark decision – a bit like when I took my first lift a few weeks before. It felt like a bit of a 'cop out', but I think that I was starting to realise that travelling does not have to be about pushing yourself to the limits of endurance each day. The bicycle was my preferred means of transport, but there would be times when other options would be more suitable. After all, I was not in a competition! Turkey has a very efficient inter-city bus service, and the journey to Erzurum cost me just over one pound, including a small surcharge for the bike!

Erzurum is an exotic city full of ancient streets and buildings but, with daytime temperatures at around minus twenty degrees, I was not too interested in sightseeing. Instead, I headed straight for the Iranian consulate, in search of the elusive visa.

My hopes rose as I stood in a queue behind two German backpackers, who were granted visas on the spot. When my turn came, however, I was told that I would have to wait for at least six weeks, while my passport was sent to Tehran, and that even then my application would probably be refused. On hearing my protests, the official simply turned away slightly and told me to blame Margaret Thatcher, who was apparently making it hard for Iranians to come to Britain at the time!

The news was demoralising, as it seemed that the overland route to Asia was now closed to me. With the Iraqi invasion of Kuwait having recently taken place, and a full-scale war raging in the Gulf, my planned route through Iran was the only feasible one at this time. After a good deal of thought, I decided to travel on by bus to the border town of Dogubayazit and make one last attempt to obtain a visa there. If unsuccessful, I would have to return to Ankara to get a flight over the Middle East. Dogubayazit lies on the plains, much lower than Erzurum, so at least it would be warmer there.

I took an immediate liking to Dogubayazit – a rural town just twenty miles from the Iranian border. To the south of this isolated settlement was a range of bare, jagged hills, while to the north was a vast, flat expanse of golden wheat fields and grazing land. Out of this flatness arises snow-capped Mount Ararat – an enormous, conical volcano which has figured in legends since time began – most notably as the resting place of Noah's Ark. Mount Ararat looms large over the town and dominates the landscape.

I had barely climbed off the bus when I was greeted by a couple of Australian girls, Diedrie and Gillian, that had been in town for a couple of months now. Gillian was dating a local guy, and Diedrie had injured her arm, so it had suited them both to stay put here for a while. The summer tourist season was long gone now, so they were quite surprised at my unexpected arrival. That evening, they invited me to an engagement party, at which I was introduced to many of the locals. The newly engaged couple had come from a nearby village for the party, which was held in a room above the cake shop.

Hidden in the hills to the south of Dogubayazit, lies the ruined palace of Ishak Pasa. Together with the Australian girls, as well as several children that followed us from the town, I set off the following morning to hike to these ruins. It was a lovely, sunny day, and we hiked for a couple of hours before the pointed domes and stripy minarets of Ishak Pasa came into view. Constructed in 1784 by a Kurdish chieftain named Ishak, using an unusual mixture of architectural styles, this remote palace must have once been an incredibly impressive sight. We had a picnic there, while the children played in the ruins, before heading back into town as the sun was setting over the hills.

That evening, as I walked around the town, I sensed hostile glances directed at me from several directions. A friendly guy called Mehmet, who owned a small cigarette shop next to my hotel, helpfully explained to me that many of the young men were jealous with me for having spent the day with Diedrie! Apparently, she had spent the last few weeks resisting the advances of several local suitors. With my arrival on the scene, it was naturally assumed that I was her partner, and hence the reason for her resistance. The situation became even more volatile the following day, when I received a verbal death threat from a fiery young lad called Mamo, who claimed to be Diedrie's rightful lover! I was not sure whether to find this amusing or threatening, but decided to take no notice, and not even bother to explain to him that I was not remotely interested in any romantic involvement with the object of his desires.

It was a relief to escape from this madness by cycling the twenty or so miles across the plains to the Iranian border. Here I made a final attempt at obtaining a visa, but to no avail. I knew now that the game was up and I would have to find my way back to Ankara. By way of consolation, the Turkish border guards allowed me to ride across into the 'no man's land' between the two frontier posts, so that I was able to get to within a few yards of Iranian territory. However, noticing that the

Turkish soldiers posted in the hills around the border post were keeping a close eye on me, I did not linger here for too long!

On my way back to the town, I visited a giant crater that was apparently formed when a giant meteor fell on the area in the 1920s. Some soldiers were stationed in a hut nearby, and we chatted for a while. Like most of the Turkish soldiers that I had met on this journey, they were thoroughly bored and hated their compulsory military service.

Arriving back in Dogubayazit, I was surprised to discover that the Australian girls had left town and that I was suddenly back in favour. Mehmet, the cigarette seller, explained to me that the girls had left to prevent me from coming to any harm. Mamo approached me again, this time to apologise for his behaviour and offer to buy me a drink. I politely refused and returned to the hotel to prepare for my own departure.

Early the next morning I had a farewell breakfast with Mehmet, before setting off on my journey back to Ankara. Ararat was completely obscured by the morning mist, and Dogubayazit was slowly waking up as I waved to my friend and cycled out of the town. I had decided to ride across the plains to Agri and then take a bus all the way back to Ankara, nearly a thousand miles back towards the west. From there I would jump on the first plane to Pakistan.

The riding was fairly easy, although there was still some pain from my knee injury, which had given me so much trouble in the mountains. Of greater concern today though were the throngs of wild-looking children that rushed from the surrounding fields as I approached. Armed with stones, they would shout the word 'para' – meaning money – and then shower me with stones as I passed by. This happened twice, leaving me quite sore from bruises, so I devised a cunning plan! The next time I spotted a crowd of these little urchins waiting at the roadside ahead of me, I slowed right down on my approach. Expecting me to stop and hand out money, they dropped their weapons and held out their hands. Just as I was arriving, I suddenly stood on the pedals and sped off. By the time they were able to react I was just about out of range, and laughing at the angry cries behind me. I used this ploy three or four times that day, and it always worked.

Reaching Agri, I checked into a small hotel, which seemed to be occupied mainly by teachers from a local college. Walking around the local bazaar, in search of somewhere to eat, I was approached by a young man who invited me to his home for dinner. We walked to his house, where a family of twelve were quickly lined up to welcome me. I sat with the men of the house on cushions on one side of the simply furnished living room, while the women waited on us. A tablecloth was laid on the floor and we were served a traditional Kurdish meal of fresh nan bread with rice, meat and fried onions. One of the daughters had clearly been given the task of constantly watching my glass, and filling it as soon as it became empty, which made me feel a little self-conscious!

The family were lined up again for my departure after dinner, and two of the sons walked me back to my hotel. On the way, they explained to me that Mohammed, The Prophet, had taught that it was very important to show hospitality to strangers, and that they were pleased to have had the opportunity to do this! Back at the hotel, we found the teachers in the middle of a chess tournament. My friends bid farewell and disappeared into the night, and I was soon engaged in a game of chess.

A luxury coach carried me back to Ankara, where I was reunited with my friends in Ulus, who had made me so welcome a fortnight earlier. News of my return spread quickly and several local people came to see me at the hotel. I spent the next couple of days drinking tea and playing street football with them while waiting for my flight to Pakistan. They seemed delighted at my unexpected return, and it was with great sadness that I departed from them once more on the day of my flight. However, a new adventure was waiting for me. I had never before been on an aeroplane!

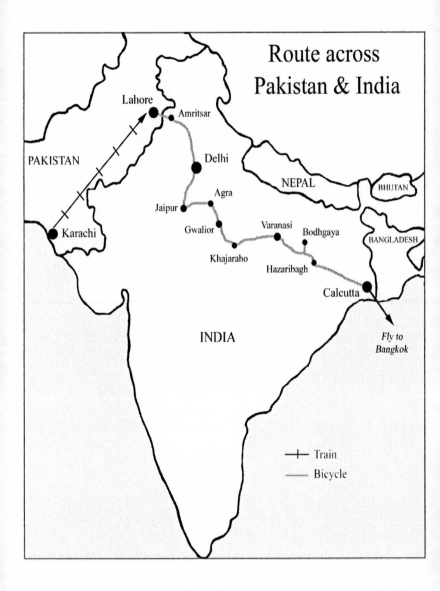

Route across
Pakistan & India

PAKISTAN

Lahore
Amritsar

Delhi

Jaipur
Agra

Gwalior

Khajaraho

Karachi

NEPAL

BHUTAN

Varanasi
Bodhgaya

BANGLADESH

Hazaribagh

Calcutta

INDIA

Fly to
Bangkok

—⊢— Train
~~~~~~ Bicycle

CHAPTER THREE

BACK-ROADS AND BEYOND
Karachi to Calcutta

A MASS OF BRIGHT LIGHTS FILLED THE night sky, signalling that we were about to land in Karachi. Up to this point, I had enjoyed my first experience of flying, but it was about to turn into a nightmare! To start with, only three of my five bags arrived on the luggage carousel. On reporting this to the luggage department, they eventually managed to locate one of the missing bags, but not the other. Still missing was a large rear pannier, containing most of my camping gear.

Enlisting the help of one of the porters, who had followed me around for a while in hope of earning some money from my predicament, I had my first encounter with Asian bureaucracy and corruption. The porter escorted me around numerous offices, where I filled out various forms and had my passport inspected countless times. I also handed out five-dollar notes fairly liberally, having been assured by my guide that this was essential practice if any progress was to be made. In the end, I received a firm promise that every effort would be made to locate the bag, and was told to come back in the morning.

It was nearly midnight by now and I had yet to obtain local currency, so we visited the airport bank, which was supposed to be open all night. Despite the '24 Hour Bank' sign, and the abundance of staff that clearly had little to do, we were told that the bank was actually closed! The porter whispered apologetically that I would have to hand over another five dollars in order to entice them to change a travellers' cheque for me.

Having collected his own tip, the porter then pointed me to a government hostel next to the airport where I would at least be able to get a few hours sleep before returning in the morning. It had cost me nearly fifty dollars to get the airport officials to do the jobs that they were supposedly there to do, and there was no guarantee that I would get the pannier back. It was not the best of introductions to Pakistan!

Early the next morning, after a fitful sleep, I went straight back to the airport baggage department. The pannier had still not been found, but an important looking official cheerfully told me that he had faxed Turkish Airlines in Istanbul, and that I should return in a couple of days time.

Riding into Karachi, my senses were bombarded by noise, rich aromas and bright colours. The bustling, chaotic suburbs were just how I had imagined an Asian city to be. I was soon absorbed by my surroundings, and began to feel positive about my journey again for the first time since my arrival the previous evening. It seemed as though I had been transported into a different world and there was so much to discover.

I checked into a simple hotel next to the railway station. Beneath my balcony was a busy little open-air restaurant, so I went down for my first proper meal in Pakistan. The restaurant Proprietor was a jovial character called Mohammed. He showed me to what he insisted was the best table and brought me several little tasters to help me decide what to order. He knew a few words of English and introduced me to everyone that came in as his 'good friend from England'!

Over the next three weeks I could often be seen up on my balcony, surveying the frenzied activity in the streets below. The continuous flow of everyday life was frequently punctuated by collisions between overloaded buses, petty squabbles and practical jokes. Sometimes the locals would call me down for a cup of tea, and Mohammed would always insist on sitting me at his special table, despite my protests when he had to move another customer!

There were two reasons for my prolonged stay in Karachi. Firstly, I was waiting for the missing pannier, and each morning I took the bus to the airport in the vain hope of a miracle. The officials there got used to my visits and were happy to just let me search through the lost luggage rooms by myself. Eventually I had to accept that the bag was gone forever. It was probably stolen from the luggage carousel before I had even got there.

The second reason for my inertia was that I had been laid low with a severe stomach bug, which may have been a reaction to the new spicy diet. I avoided taking any medication, in the hope that I would adjust naturally and build up some resistance to such stomach complaints.

Due to my poor health, I rarely ventured beyond the little community around the railway station. However I did make one journey by bus to the famous Clifton Beach. I was lucky to be able to squeeze into the crowded bus, as many of the passengers were either sitting on the roof, or hanging onto the sides. The conductor bravely clambered all around the outsides of the bus collecting fares as we hurtled along! Despite the crush inside the bus everyone seemed good-humoured, and the old man next to me insisted on paying my fare as we arrived at our destination. Clifton Beach provided welcome relief from the city, and I even treated myself to a brief camel ride along the shores.

After three weeks I was more than ready for a change of scene. However, I was still not fully recovered from my stomach complaint, and felt far too weak to attempt to cycle any distance. I decided, therefore, to take the train up to Lahore – a city renowned for its beauty – and continue my recovery there. Hopefully I would be able to start riding again from there, and travel across India during December and January - the coolest months of the year.

The railway platform was complete chaos, with people and animals running in all directions. Enlisting the help of a porter, I somehow managed to get the bicycle registered and onto the train. This involved filling in several forms and presenting my travel documents to various minor officials. This country seemed to love bureaucracy, and I was fairly resigned to this by now. Eventually, the porter led me to my carriage and collected his tip.

The train departed at 11.30pm – an hour late. This was unusually early, apparently, and everyone seemed delighted that we were leaving so promptly! I had booked a sleeper for the twenty-hour journey, but soon discovered that my 'helpful' porter had led me to the wrong carriage. The train was far too packed for me to try and find my carriage, so I just stood in the corridor, surrounded by my luggage. Fortunately, some of the passengers got off at the first stop in Hyderabad, at 2am, and the guard was finally able to lead me to my carriage. It was not easy though, as my bags had to be passed from person to person along the corridors!

My fellow passengers in the six-berth carriage took a great interest in me – asking numerous questions about England, and insisting on sharing their food with me. At one point the train stopped by a field, and some of them jumped off to collect sticks of sugar cane, which were then shared around. We reached Lahore some five hours late but, surprisingly, the journey had seemed to pass very quickly.

One man in the carriage had invited me to stay at his home in Lahore, not far from the railway station, and we arrived there soon after midnight. The house was simply furnished and rather cramped, with three generations living under the same roof. A tasty meal was quickly prepared for us and a rope bed was placed in the kitchen for me.

The family could not have been more hospitable, but there was obviously a shortage of space, and many mouths to feed besides mine, so I decided to move on the next day. After breakfast my host accompanied me back to the railway station to retrieve the bike, which had been stored there overnight. We parted company there and I rode across the city to the Salvation Army hostel, which would be my haven for the next fortnight.

The hostel was run by a plain-speaking Yorkshireman, who had been living in Pakistan for seven years. It was full of long-distance travellers that were resting up from the rigours of the road and the atmosphere was wonderfully relaxed. I knew straight away that this was the place to stay until I was well enough to start riding again.

Lahore is rich in culture, with exquisite palaces, tombs, mosques and theatres. Most Pakistanis that I had met were rightly proud of this city and I had frequently heard the favourite saying; 'You have not lived until you have seen Lahore'. The centrepiece of the city is the Lahore Fort and Badshahi Mosque, and I came here on several occasions with my new friends from the hostel. We were usually engaged in conversation by students that had gathered there in the hope of improving their English by speaking with tourists. They were always polite and it was interesting to learn about their lives, as well as trying to correct some of their misconceptions about life in the West.

For a change from sightseeing I spent a few days watching test cricket at the Gadaffi Stadium, where Pakistan were taking on West Indies. For a ticket costing forty rupees (less than one pound) I was able to watch the match from the comfort of a shaded armchair in the first class enclosure! The Pakistanis are passionate about their cricket, and there was a football match atmosphere in the stadium, despite the fact that the West Indies had already won the series.

I was eating normally again at last and, as my strength returned, my enthusiasm for the road ahead grew. I knew that I would be more dependent on the locals than before, having been unable to replace the lost camping gear, but felt ready for the challenge.

With some difficulty, I managed to achieve a reasonably equal weight distribution on the bike with my three remaining panniers and an old sleeping bag, which had been given to me at the hostel. The sleeping bag was tied to the front rack in place of one of the small front panniers, which was, in turn, used at the back to replace the missing rear pannier. The small pannier at the back was then loaded with heavier items, such as my tool kit. It looked a bit odd, but at least the bike was fairly stable.

On December 17th 1990, over a month since landing in Pakistan, I loaded up and rode to the Indian border, thirty miles east.

It took three hours to complete the border formalities, as the contents of my bags were carefully scrutinised. The guards were courteous and apologetic – explaining that they were under strict orders to search all luggage thoroughly, because some Nigerians had been caught smuggling heroine the previous day. I felt a buzz of excitement as I was finally waved across into

India. This was a country that had fascinated me since childhood, and had been one of the main inspirations for my journey.

I rode a further twenty miles on a shady highway to the famous Punjabi city of Amritsar. Here I spent some time searching for a tiny backstreet hotel, where I had arranged to meet a group of backpackers that had also left the hostel in Lahore that morning. On arrival, however, there was a message to say that they had taken a quick look at Amritsar and decided to take the train straight on to Delhi!

At first light I was strolling into the city centre to visit one of India's most famous sights – the Golden Temple. The streets were already alive with the hustle and bustle of street traders, bicycle rickshaws and street dwellers preparing for the day ahead. The bicycle rickshaws seemed to be the main form of city transport, and one painfully thin rider was barely able to keep up with my brisk walking pace, as he struggled under the weight of his three hefty passengers.

After washing my feet and donning a headscarf, I was allowed to enter the Golden Temple complex. The atmosphere inside the complex was one of calm and tranquillity, in stark contrast to the chaotic streets outside. Positioned in the centre of a large pool of holy waters, and surrounded by grand white temple buildings, the Golden Temple itself is quite small and entirely coated in gold. Perfectly restored, since it was damaged by Hindus in retaliation for the assassination of Indira Ghandi in 1984, the splendour of the place surpassed my highest expectations.

Later in the day I visited a small park which was the scene of the Amritsar massacre in 1919. Here the Imperial Order was ended by the brutal act of an English Officer who ordered his troops to fire without warning on a prohibited meeting, killing 379 people. A small gallery in the park houses an enormous painting depicting the scene of the massacre in gory detail. It was a moving and uncomfortable experience to visit this place.

My first taste of 'Indian directions' came when I stopped on the way out of Amritsar to check that I was on the right road for Delhi. I was actually heading north on entirely the wrong road, but the two young men, presumably eager not to disappoint me by admitting that they did not know the correct answer, directed me straight ahead with confidence. The mistake became obvious a little later when I passed a sign warning me that the road ahead into the northern State of Kashmir was blocked by snow! I rode back into Amritsar to start again, resolving that in future I would conduct a survey of at least five people when I needed directions.

Riding south at last on the Grand Trunk Road across the Punjab plains, I felt a great sense of expectancy and adventure. The highway was well surfaced and lined with tall trees, which offered plenty of shade from the warm winter sun. The Punjab is India's richest State, and the lush landscape of green fields and pastures seemed to confirm this.

At my regular 'tea stops', a large crowd of onlookers always gathered. Most wanted to examine the bicycle and some made quite determined efforts to try and figure out how the gear systems worked. Indian bikes did not have this sort of technology, and it seemed to fascinate them.

With my strength and fitness building up rapidly now, I followed the Grand Trunk Road through the Punjabi cities of Jallunder and Ludhiana, spending a night in each. The journey was uncomfortable at times, due to the uneven road surface and heavy traffic. The main rule of the road appeared to be that 'size matters', and I was frequently forced off the road by trucks and buses that seemed to have no regard at all for smaller vehicles, let alone bicycles. Another irritation was the great clouds of dust that these heavy trucks always left in their wake, and I sometimes had to stop for a while until I was able to see properly again.

I noticed in the towns that women were not afraid to smile at me and make eye contact, suggesting a greater sense of freedom and confidence than in Muslim Pakistan and Turkey. This was quite refreshing to see and, over the next few weeks, I got the impression that attitudes were generally a little more liberal here.

In Ludhiana I was drawn into a tiresome conversation with a well-spoken Indian Stock Exchange worker, whose hotel room was next to mine. He could not understand why anyone would wish to travel so far, and concluded that I must have been sent away following a family quarrel. He seemed even more convinced of this when I mentioned that I had not lived with my family for six years, and was totally unable to accept my alternative reasons for travel. He also gave me the usual warnings about India being far too dangerous for bicycle travel.

Soon after crossing the State border into Haryana, I caught up with a Dutch cycle tourist called Ramon. He was riding a bicycle made by the Taiwanese firm 'Giant'. He had bought the bike in Amsterdam and set out to ride it from there to the Giant factory in Taiwan, where it had been built. Apparently, the people at 'Giant' were so impressed with this idea that they had supplied the bike and touring equipment free of charge. We rode together into the ancient Sikh capital of Ambala.

We found shelter that night at a Sikh temple on the outskirts of Ambala. The Sikhs have a great tradition of providing hospitality for travellers and we were made to feel most welcome. After a simple, but satisfying, meal of 'dal and chappattis', we were shown to a small dusty room within the temple, containing two rope beds. The only requests made of us were that we obeyed the simple Temple rules of removing our shoes and covering our heads. On our departure we made a small contribution towards rebuilding work that was taking place, and we were invited to keep the headscarves that we had been given, in case we visited other Temples along the way.

Ramon was an entertaining road partner as we cycled on towards Karnal, although I found him to be rather eccentric. He was riding in jeans and a heavy jacket, which seemed ridiculous to me, and carrying an incredible amount of luggage. All of it, he claimed, was absolutely necessary. He was also full of amusing anecdotes – most of them based on various love affairs that he had had on his journey. At Karnal we called at another Sikh Temple, but were told that there was no sleeping accommodation here. Instead we were directed to a larger temple on the other side of Karnal, and sent on our way with a large bag of sweetmeats.

As promised, we were warmly received at the larger Temple. It was in a state of half-completion, but luckily the sleeping quarters were ready. After dinner, we were invited to the resident Guru's quarters to meet him and his disciples that were gathered there. It was explained to us there that the Sikhs regard the whole of humanity as 'One Body'. Hence their desire to provide hospitality to strangers – no matter what they believe, or where they come from.

In the morning we went for breakfast at the home of one of the Sikh families that lived nearby. Ramon had been taken ill overnight, so a doctor was sent for. He clearly needed to rest for a few days, so it was decided that he would stay here with the Sikhs until he was fully recovered, while I carried on to Delhi on my own. We were planning to take different routes after Delhi in any case, so there was little point in me waiting for him.

Delhi was ninety miles south which, on the flat highway, was just about manageable for me in a day. The Indian capital city seemed like a magnet, drawing me in, and I peddled hard along the Grand Trunk Road, after leaving Ramon at the Temple. By late afternoon, I found myself rolling into the city centre. I carried on a few miles further south to the wealthy southern suburb of Chanakapuri, where there was a huge international hostel, which had been recommended to me. The hostel resembled a school building and was full of noisy young Indian students, but it was very cheap and the facilities were excellent. The only other foreign guests were a New Zealand missionary family that I had previously met in Lahore. They had been living in Northern Pakistan for two years and were taking a short holiday in India.

It was Christmas Eve and I recalled with some satisfaction that, on the morning of my departure from

London, I had predicted to friends that I would be in Delhi for Christmas. Things were going according to plan!

On Christmas morning I shared a cake with the New Zealand family, but it was a rushed celebration as they were catching a train south that morning. The hostel had completely emptied out and I suddenly found myself feeling rather alone on Christmas Day. To keep my mind occupied, I took a bus into the city, and strolled around the Old Delhi district. The narrow streets here were lined with crippled and sick people, for whom Christmas Day was just another day to try and survive. This was the first example of mass poverty and hardship that I had come across in Asia, and I have recalled the scene to my mind every Christmas since.

Overlooking the crowded streets and bazaars of Old Delhi was the Red Fort, which is a huge symbol of Delhi's past greatness as the centre of the Mogul Empire. The vast, imposing red sandstone walls appeared to go on for miles, on either side of the grand entrance passage, which crosses a dry moat to the main gate. Resisting the advances of several young turbaned Sikhs, who sprang up from all sides to offer their services as guides, I walked through the gate onto a grassy courtyard leading to various halls, which were built mainly in marble and filled with priceless treasures.

This contrast between the harsh reality of life on the streets of Old Delhi and the incredible wealth and grandeur of the Red Fort was hard to understand and accept, but also quite fascinating. As I was to discover, this dichotomy was fairly typical of city life in India.

Back in Chanakapuri, the hostel was still eerily empty when I returned that evening. The canteen was open though, and I awoke the chef from his slumbers so that he could prepare my Christmas dinner!

Boxing Day was spent visiting some of the numerous tombs, ruined fortresses and mosques that are scattered throughout the southern part of the city. Many of these were lying side by side with huge modern structures, which seemed quite ugly by comparison. Perhaps the most memorable sight was Qutab Minar. Built in the twelfth century from red sandstone, and soaring to a height of 72 metres, this ancient tower was the first great monument of Muslim rule in India and a symbol of Muslim dominance at the time.

My general plan now was to follow the Great Trunk Road across Northern India to the north-eastern city of Calcutta. However, I decided to travel first in a south-westerly direction, in order to take in Jaipur and some of the desert State of Rajastan.

The Jaipur road was bumpy and dusty, which made riding difficult, but I was feeling quite refreshed, after my Christmas sightseeing break, and managed to cover eighty miles in a day to reach the village of Behror, midway between Delhi and Jaipur.

Asking around for accommodation, I was offered the use of a garage for the night! As I was wheeling the bike in, a large English-speaking man called Mehabir emerged from the crowd of onlookers and said that I should leave my things in the garage, but come and sleep at his house. First though he insisted that we should celebrate my arrival with a drink. A bottle of whisky was produced from somewhere and a small crowd gathered together for my welcome party!

Eventually, Mehabir signalled that it was time to make our way to his home for dinner. As we staggered across a field on a dirt track, slightly the worse for wear, we were suddenly set upon by a ferocious dog. The animal belonged to Mehabir and he quickly called it to order, but not before I had been bitten on the arm and leg.

Mehabir was full of apologies as we reached the house, and he immediately sent one of his sons into the village to fetch the Doctor. Meanwhile, my wounds were dressed and we sat down to a feast that had been prepared by Mehabir's wife, who had been sent word of my arrival. The boy returned with news that the Doctor was away for a few days, producing another burst of apologies from Mehabir! I assured him that I was fine, however, and would be able to get the wounds checked out at the hospital in Jaipur the next day.

Despite the unfortunate incident with the dog, it had been a most enjoyable evening in Behror. Mehabir and his wife were the perfect hosts and even insisted on giving up their bed for me, despite my protests. For breakfast, Mehabir's wife had prepared some 'lado', which is a delicious and filling sweet substance made from butter, sugar, milk and nuts. Then my slight wounds were dressed again, and the family gathered together to wave me off.

The riding was a pleasure that morning, as it was much cooler than of late. The Rajastan landscape was mostly scrub desert, with a few trees lining the road. The villages that I passed through were quite picturesque and the country folk, in their bright clothes, seemed to stand out from the desert surroundings. Camels seemed to do much of the work in this part of India, and I frequently overtook lines of them pulling heavy loads.

Reaching the back of a long traffic jam, I made my way between the stationary buses and trucks for a couple of miles to the cause of the hold-up. A truck had overturned, spilling a huge load of rubble across the road to create a complete blockage. I managed to carry my bike over the rubble, providing some light relief to the police and truck drivers that were trying to clear the road.

Riding into Jaipur, I stopped to ask for directions to the Jaipur Inn, which had been recommended to me by Mehabir. The directions that I received were quite straightforward, but this did not stop another cyclist from following me - insisting that he would help me to find the place. The man was very drunk and meandering all over the road, so it was certainly not a welcome development. Despite my insistence that I did not need any help, however, it was impossible to shake him off.

On reaching the Jaipur Inn, my companion followed me in and immediately started to demand commission from the receptionist. The Chinese receptionist refused, at which the drunken Indian became quite threatening. Punches began to fly between the two, and within seconds three burly hotel employees arrived on the scene. The hapless commission agent was given a thorough beating and then thrown out. Attention then turned towards me, and I thought for a moment that they were going to give me the same treatment. However, they quickly accepted my assurances that I had not encouraged the man in any way, and left me to carry on with the business of checking in.

In the morning I went straight to the Jaipur Hospital for treatment on my dog bites. I joined a long queue in the waiting area, but was immediately ushered straight into the Doctor's room. This was quite embarrassing, but no one seemed to mind at all. Fortunately I had been vaccinated against rabies before my trip, so a tetanus booster was all that was required. The charge for this was just two rupees, and the young Doctor insisted that we exchange addresses so that we could write to each other in the future!

There was plenty to see in and around Jaipur and, despite the scary events of my first night there, my stay at the Jaipur Inn was most enjoyable. One great excursion was a hike to the ruined Tiger Fort, which stands on a hilltop overlooking the city. From here I hitched a ride on the back of a hay truck, over the hills to the nearby Amber Palace. Before long, the Palace came into view below us, rising from the slopes of a steep hill beside a small lake. It was a majestic sight, and no less impressive on closer inspection. The ancient walls were covered in decorative art both inside and out, and the views of the surrounding hills from the top ramparts were an added bonus.

I had not planned to travel any further into Rajastan, but could not resist the temptation to join some of the backpackers at the Jaipur Inn who were heading down to the famous desert town of Pushgar, about a hundred miles south, in order to celebrate New Year. The Chinese receptionist agreed to look after the bike for me, while I travelled by bus with my new friends.

Pushgar is built around a clear lake in which the white lakeside buildings are perfectly reflected. It was also something of a backpackers' haunt, and the New Year parties were in full swing when we arrived.

Pushgar is considered to be a very holy place, and I took a break from the partying to visit one of the hilltop

Hindu temples, a little out of town in the desert. On reaching the temple, I was greeted by an Australian lady that had been living here with a Hindu family for ten years. She told me that she returns to Australia for two months each year in order to earn money to pay for her keep in India for the rest of the year. She claimed to have found peace and fulfilment in the Hindu faith, and hoped to spend the rest of her life at this remote desert temple.

With the New Year celebrations still continuing, I returned alone to Jaipur. It was a relief to find that my bicycle and belongings had been well looked after by the Chinese receptionist.

My next target was Agra - the third corner of India's 'Golden Triangle', which is formed by Delhi, Jaipur and Agra. The landscape became greener and camels were replaced by horses, as I rode eastwards and left the Rajastan desert behind. As usual there were plenty of local cyclists of all ages on the highway, riding between their villages. At one point I was trailed for several miles by a pack of about ten of them, each taking turns at overtaking me. Each time the rider that had overtaken would quickly tire from his exertions, and I would have to move back to the front again. This was all very good-humoured and created a welcome diversion.

Stopping at the village of Dousa for lunch, I was invited into the kitchen of a roadside café to choose from the various pots of steaming curries. Unfortunately, my random selection turned out to be the hottest dish that I had, or have since, ever attempted to eat! My sense of moral responsibility to finish my plate was reinforced by the fact that, as usual, I had a large audience of curious villages silently observing me throughout the meal. I am sure that they had never seen a plate of curry eaten as slowly as that before!

It was a relief to get back on the bike again after my marathon lunch! However, progress was fairly slow on the hot, dusty highway. My chunky mountain bike tyres were starting to wear thin now, and I punctured twice while swerving off the road to avoid the trucks that thundered past without deviating on my account in the slightest. To make matters worse, I encountered occasional hordes of stone-throwing children, who were disturbingly accurate at times. With Calcutta still over a thousand miles away, I began to harbour serious doubts about the wisdom of trying to cycle across India!

I stopped that night at a guesthouse by the entrance to the Baratpur Bird Sanctuary. This is the largest bird sanctuary in Asia, containing birds of every colour and species imaginable. It was a relief to escape from the noise and fumes of the highway as I spent the whole of the next day relaxing and strolling around the tranquil grounds of the sanctuary. Much of the park is marshland or lake, and there were plenty of herons and other waterfowl. The highlight of the day, though, was the sighting of a large python, which slithered down a hole as I was trying to get close enough for a good photo.

A short ride the following morning brought me to the famous 'ghost city' of Fatepur Sikri, which was built on a rocky ridge in the sixteenth century by the great Emporer Akbar. It functioned briefly as the capital of the Mogul Empire, only to be abandoned after just fourteen years – most probably because its water supply failed. Fatepur Sikri has been deserted ever since and, as a result, has changed very little since its glory days. I was escorted around the well-preserved ruins by a couple of young students of English, who both seemed delighted at the opportunity to practice with a native speaker of the language. A new town of Fatepur Sikri has grown up below the ridge on which the ruins lie and I lunched here at the home of one of the students, before setting off for Agra, which lies just twenty miles or so to the East.

Riding through the sprawling city of Agra, I caught my first glimpse of the Taj Mahal. The huge white dome, rising above the city, was a majestic sight. The streets around the Taj were surprisingly downmarket, and I was able to obtain a room for just twenty rupees (about 40 pence) at a hotel with a wonderful rooftop view of the great monument.

At dawn I paid the first of several visits to the Taj Mahal. Some people have been disappointed on visiting the Taj, perhaps as the highlight of a 'once-in-a-lifetime' trip to India, but for me it was a breathtaking experience. The scale was beyond anything that I could have imagined, and the first pale rays of sunlight produced a surreal shimmering effect.

The history of the Taj only enhances its magic. It was built in1648 by the Mogul Emporer, Shah Jehan, as a token of love for his deceased wife. He brought in skilled craftsmen from the furthest reaches of the known world, in order to realise his dream of building her a memorial that would surpass anything the world had ever seen, in terms of beauty and extravagance.

While I was peacefully admiring the 'Masterpiece in Marble', there was drama in the streets nearby. Apparently a man had been shot in the leg, sparking off a riot between local Hindus and Muslims. As a result of this outbreak of violence, the area came under an immediate curfew. This meant that all shops and businesses were closed, and any Indian people seen on the streets were liable to be arrested. The curfew did not apply to foreign tourists but, by the time I had made it back to my hotel, everyone had checked out, save for a Swiss cycle tourist named Beat.

The curfew continued for a couple of days and, as I walked the streets with Beat, the atmosphere was tense and the silence quite eerie. We visited the Taj frequently and, with Agra now a 'no-go' area for tourists, there were rarely more than ten people wandering around. We considered ourselves very fortunate to have the Taj Mahal – perhaps the world's most famous building – virtually to ourselves!

We were also fortunate that a local café owner sneaked us into his café at mealtimes. Trading was officially banned during the curfew, but he managed to obtain supplies form his neighbour's grocery shop, in order to produce meals for us. We were charged at no more than regular prices, despite the obvious risk that he was taking.

Beat was a fascinating character and we got on very well. He had been roaming around the world for six years now – the last three by bicycle – since growing disillusioned with his life as a Zurich banker. He was finally ready to go home now, and was riding back to Switzerland. He had cycled from Calcutta, and warned me that the highway ahead of me was in such an appalling state that it was almost 'unrideable'. Beat had avoided the highway by cycling through the countryside on back-roads, and had been surprised to find that many of these were sealed and in good condition. Apparently, one legacy of colonial times was an excellent network of roads. While the highways have suffered over the years through lack of maintenance, most of the back-roads see little motorised traffic and, hence, are still in good condition. With this knowledge in hand, I resolved to follow Beat's example and stick to the rural roads as much as possible.

After an early morning breakfast with Beat, we wished each other well and parted company. The curfew had been lifted and there were signs that things were getting back to normal as I headed south out of the city towards Gwalior.

The highway that day led me out of Uttah Pradesh, through a corner of Rajastan and into Madya Pradesh. Northern India is incredibly flat, on the whole, and it was a nice surprise to actually encounter a few gentle hills! As usual, I was feeling quite energetic after a few days rest and was able to make good progress. I stopped just once – to accept an invitation for tea and cookies with a group of men that were in charge of a highway toll barrier. By mid-afternoon, I had covered eighty miles to reach Gwalior.

My first port of call was a Government Circuit House, where I hoped to find a bed for the night. These colonial mansions are found at most towns and villages around India, and their purpose is to accommodate Government Officials as they travel around the country. In practice, however, they tend to be underused, and passing foreigners are allowed to stay in them at the discretion of the local authorities. However, on this occasion, the official in charge completely ignored me for ten minutes, before looking up from his desk to tell me that there was no room. It was the same story at the local Sikh Temple, although they were somewhat more polite there! Finally, after a long search, I found some cheap lodgings in quiet little side street.

On a hill rising sheer from the plains sits the giant Gwalior Fortress, overlooking and completely dominating the city. It is one of the oldest forts in India, dating back to at least AD525. According to legends, it was built by a local leader who, having been cured of leprosy by the Hindu Saint, Gwalipa, was directed by the Saint to build a fort on the spot. I had enough energy left that day to climb the steep path to its gates and explore the complex of temples and monuments within, before descending again for my evening bowl of curry.

From Gwalior I rode east on minor roads, following a route that had been recommended by Beat. It was a pleasant and tranquil ride through hilly countryside, without the deafening noise of traffic that I had been used to on the Grand Trunk Road. I sampled local speciality dishes for breakfast and lunch, as the locals looked on with delight, politely allowing me to finish my food before bombarding me with questions about my journey. By the time the sun had dropped I had covered over ninety miles, to reach the town of Mauranipaur. Before beginning my quest for lodgings, I sat down at a tea-stall and was persuaded to try some 'pan'. This is a collection of herbs, mixed in a red paste and wrapped in a leaf. It seemed to be very popular in India, and presumably explains why so many of the people that I met had red teeth. I bit off a small piece, but found the taste of it so disgusting that I had to spit it out immediately – much to everyones' amusement!

That night I did manage to stay at a Government Circuit House. The caretaker put me through to the local magistrate by telephone, and permission was granted straight away. The whole building was put at my disposal for the nominal fee of five rupees! I was brought a complimentary meal by one of the servants, and slept that night in a magnificent four poster bed with mosquito net.

Another long day's riding on country roads brought me to the village of Khajaraho, which is the site of some world famous Jain temples. The temples are decorated inside and out with intricate nude sculptures, depicting various aspects of the life cycle. On close inspection, the detail of these carvings is quite amazing. It remains a mystery as to why such a large group of extraordinary temples were built at such a remote location.

A rest day was spent wandering among the temples and talking with village children – most of whom had picked up plenty of English words from the constant stream of tourists that make their way here. All of them begged me incessantly for coins, pens or anything else that they might keep as souvenirs or, more likely, try to resell to other tourists. It was quite sad to see this negative influence of tourism on these children.

That evening was spent relaxing on the balcony of my small hotel, and chatting with some of the backpackers from various countries that were gathered there. There was some impromptu entertainment when a noisy dispute kicked off on the street below. It ended with one of the antagonists firing a gun in the air, which immediately brought the local police running. The protagonists were quickly dispersed, and an armed guard was considerately positioned on the roof of the hotel for our safety.

Heading east, I rode along country lanes that were sometimes smoothly paved, while at other times deteriorated into bumpy gravel tracks. My locally bought maps were proving pretty inaccurate, so I had to stop frequently for directions. As I had already found out, this can be a precarious business. Eager to appear helpful, the country folk would often send me down the wrong road, rather than admitting that they did not know the way. Eventually, though, I reached the town of Banda and again managed to find accommodation at the local Government Circuit House. The caretaker made several phone calls on my behalf, before announcing with great satisfaction that I was to be looked after at no charge. He then showed me to my quarters, and invited me to join him and his family for dinner at their house nearby.

Like most of the homes that I had been lucky enough to visit in India, the caretaker's home was simply furnished and immaculately clean. We sat on the floor to a meal of vegetable curry, boiled eggs and chapattis, which seemed to be in never-ending supply. When I finally insisted that I could eat no more there was a brief interlude before tea, biscuits and sweetmeats were served. Even my cyclist's appetite was more than satisfied!

After dinner, the caretaker took me on a tour of the neighbourhood, which included a visit to the home of an elderly relative who spoke English well and was totally blind. More food was served here and we chatted for over an hour. He told me that he hoped to be cured one day if he could save up enough money to go to Madras for an operation. On parting, he requested a photograph together. I did not have my camera with me, but promised to return in the morning.

The caretaker also introduced me to an elderly couple from Norway, who had set up a Mission in the town some forty years previously, and had lived here ever since. On hearing my intended route, they insisted that I should stay with some missionary friends of theirs in the village of Karwi, which was about a day's ride away. They promised to ring ahead and make the arrangements.

The next morning I returned to the caretaker's house for breakfast. Knowing that I had a long ride ahead of me, my hosts served me with a stack of eight thick potato pancakes. Anxious not to offend, I determinedly ate my way to the bottom of the pile. This was a big mistake, because another four pancakes were brought out just as I took the last bite! I was struggling now, but managed to eat another two for the sake of politeness. I then walked round to the blind man's house for the promised photo, which was followed, inevitably, by more refreshments, before returning to the Circuit House to prepare for my departure.

The caretaker was waiting for me and, to my surprise, had gathered together various local government officials to see me off! There was tea all round and lots of handshakes before I finally set off for Karwi.

Beat's suggestion to travel across India on the back-roads was turning out to be excellent advice. The journey was slower, but much more enjoyable, and I was starting to feel completely immersed in the country. The warm send off from Banda gave me quite a lift, and the riding was most enjoyable that day.

Despite the late start, I was on course to reach Karwi quite early in the afternoon, so I made a slight detour to visit the riverside town of Chitracut Dham. There happened to be a festival taking place in this picturesque little settlement, so I was greeted by colourful and noisy celebrations. I spent a couple of hours enjoying the carnival atmosphere and chatting with some of the revellers, before heading on to Karwi as the sun was starting to set over the river.

At Karwi, the Norwegian missionaries gave me a warm reception. The two elderly sisters had arrived in this tiny settlement shortly after the Banda Mission was set up. As well as running a church, their work in the village had included the setting up of a school and a hospital.

The next morning, the sisters invited me to spend the day with them, so that I could enjoy some home cooking and find out more about their work in Karwi. We started with a visit to the Mission Hospital, where I was given a grand tour by the Nurse-in-Charge. She told me that people came from as far away as Allahabad – some ninety miles away – for treatment, and that there could be as many as 800 patients present at one time. There was a team of five Indian doctors, supported by nurses and auxiliaries, and they were dealing mainly with dysentery and tuberculosis cases as that time. The hospital was completely funded by the Norwegian missionary society, which the sisters represented, and most of their equipment was sent direct from Sweden. I was impressed with the general level of cleanliness - which would have put many hospitals in England to shame - and the friendly atmosphere throughout the place.

After my brief tour of the hospital, the Nurse deposited me on the school bus for a visit to the school. The bus was crowded, but a seat was vacated for me at once. We arrived just in time for morning assembly, which consisted mainly of prayers and songs, before the children dispersed. They seemed very well behaved, but could not help staring at me as they marched off to their classrooms! Next I was given a tour of the school by one of the teachers. As we entered each classroom the children rose as one and said 'Good Morning' in unison. It made me feel like royalty! There were over a thousand children in attendance, from Karwi and the surrounding villages, with at least fifty to each class. My tour concluded with a visit to the Headmaster's office, where I was proudly given a demonstration of the school's 'pride and joy' – a loud speaker machine by which the Head could speak directly to each classroom from his office.

The school bus then appeared again to take me back to the sisters' house for lunch. The spread included European luxuries such as cheese, home-made bread and jam, which was a real treat for me. The sisters were most entertaining, and seemed to take great pleasure from spoiling me. I could not help admiring their dedication to the work that had begun in this remote village so many years before, and which they hoped to continue until the end of their lives.

My panniers were loaded to bursting point with supplies that the sisters had prepared for the road ahead. They also gave me excellent directions to follow as I crossed the plains to Allahabad. Without these I could have ended up anywhere, because the intricate network of country lanes was quite confusing at times, and many of the junctions were not sign-posted at all.

It was late afternoon when I crossed the Ganges on a great iron bridge, which leads into the city of Allahabad. The sisters had told me that an important Hindu festival was taking place in the city – presumably the same festival that was being celebrated in Chitracut Dham, a few days before. However, this did not prepare me for the amazing scene, which met my eyes when I looked down from that bridge. The sun was beating down on an endless vista of temporary dwellings along the shores of the Ganges. Amongst these were thousands of pilgrims swarming to and from the holy waters. The river itself was dotted with pilgrims performing their bathing rituals, and small rowing boats taking them to and from the shore. The most intense activity was centred close to the point at which the River Yamuna joined the Ganges. Apparently, this confluence of the two great rivers is a particularly sacred site, and the actual point of the confluence was completely hidden by a great mass of humanity. I stopped on the bridge for at least an hour, just trying to take in the enormity of this gathering. It was later explained to me that this festival of cleansing is called the Magh Mela, and takes place each year at the beginning of Spring.

Needless to say, the city hotels were all crammed full, but I was allocated some roof space and a rope bed at a small hotel near the centre of the city. Once settled in, I made my way back to the Ganges to experience the festivities at ground level. Despite the impression of complete chaos from the bridge, I was surprised at how well organised everything seemed to be on closer inspection. The tents and makeshift huts were divided into groups, according to the localities and castes that they represented. There were rows of barbers attending to pilgrims that were waiting to have their heads shaved and stalls selling all manner of snacks and souvenirs. The waters of the Ganges were sprinkled with rose petals and marigolds, thrown by Hindu women as offerings to the Gods. Despite the frenzied level of activity, the overall atmosphere was calm and sombre.

From Allahabad, I rode on the Grand Trunk Road again towards another ancient and holy city – Varanasi. It was uncomfortable to be battling against the traffic again, after several days of meandering along country lanes, but the journey was enlivened by some of the colourful characters making their way up and down the highway between the two great cities. There were pilgrims with long beards, some on foot and some riding buffalo carts, all sorts of animals - including elephants and a dancing bear - and even a wedding procession. The trucks and buses were slowed down considerably by the great number of other road users and there were frequent traffic jams. One of these hold-ups was due to a sacred cow deciding to lie in the middle of the highway for a few minutes!

On reaching Varanasi, I headed for the old part of the city, where there were numerous hostels and guesthouses. Amidst a maze of narrow alleyways I found the Yogi Lodge – which had been recommended to me by several people. The hostel was full of travellers from Europe and Australia, whose tastes were catered for with western food and music. There was even hot water and, despite a definite lack of space, a wonderfully relaxed atmosphere. It was a real 'home from home' and a great place to unwind for the next few days.

From a small rowing boat on the Ganges, I was able appreciate Varanasi's unique shoreline, consisting of several 'ghats' (stone bathing terraces leading down to the water's edge) interspersed with palaces, temples and shrines. Varanasi is thought to be the oldest continually inhabited city in the world, and one of the temples on the shoreline is said to be over three thousand years old.

Varanasi has been at the centre of the Hindu faith throughout its long history. For Hindus, this is the preferred place to die, and many are cremated on open fires that burn day and night on the shores of the Ganges. The boat set me down at one of the famous 'Burning Ghats', where a cremation ceremony was just beginning. I watched from a discreet viewing platform, as the corpse - covered in silk cloth and flowers - was carried down the steps to be bathed one final time. After a full immersion in the holy waters, the body was then carefully placed on a pile of chopped wood. Relatives and friends of the deceased gathered around in a tight circle as the priest slowly walked around the corpse five times while reciting prayers. The wood was then set alight and the fire was soon raging. The silk cloth quickly burnt away, so that at times you could actually see parts of the body through the flames. It was a gruesome, but captivating, sight, which will not easily be erased from my memory. The body would take three hours to burn completely, before another solemn ceremony would accompany the sprinkling of the ashes in the Ganges.

Varanasi is also of great significance for Buddhists. Gautama Buddha is said to have preached his first sermon at the nearby village of Sarnath, six centuries before Christ. I jumped on a cycle-rickshaw for the short journey to Sarnath, which is now one of the four major Buddhist pilgrimage sites in India. An impressive Stupa stands on the site of that first sermon, surrounded by monasteries representing various Asian countries. The tranquil atmosphere in Sarnath, where meditation is an important part of life, contrasted sharply with the frantic levels of activity in the heart of the city.

Riding east from Varanasi, on the Grand Trunk Road, I encountered the worst stretch of highway so far. Unfortunately there were no feasible alternative routes, so I had to soldier on. The road surface was littered with bumps, cracks and huge crater-like potholes. The trucks and buses seemed to be having even more trouble than me and on several occasions I was able to overtake them, as they slowly negotiated a safe course between the craters. As usual, all kinds of humanity were manifest, as well as plenty of representatives from the animal kingdom. Rudyard Kipling once described this highway as a 'River of Life' and I could not think of a more appropriate description.

A luxury tour bus pulled in at a roadside café, where I was taking a well-earned rest from the bumpy road. The bus was carrying a group of South Korean Buddhists that were making there way to Bodhgaya – another foremost Buddhist pilgrimage site. It was quite a colourful spectacle, as they sat down to lunch in their orange robes. I was just about to continue on my way, when a delegation approached me with the offer of a plate of food. They questioned me earnestly for a few minutes, and then assured me of their best wishes and admiration! It was a touching gesture, and I resolved to make a small detour north the next day in order to visit Bodhgaya myself.

That evening I reached the large town of Dehri and was again made welcome at the local Government Circuit House. The building had clearly not been in use for a while, and the water supply had to be turned on for me. There was also a power cut so candles were lit. My quarters were quite luxurious, but I had something of a fright on suddenly seeing myself in the large bedroom mirror. My face was completely black from the traffic fumes! The Circuit House was managed by Senior District Officer Singh, who was a jovial character with a booming voice and an air of authority. He invited me to join him that evening for dinner, and delivered a pile of old hardback books on Indian culture and history to browse through beforehand!

Dinner was simple, but satisfying, and presented with great style. My host was fascinated to learn of my experiences, particularly in the villages. He concluded that India – though a poor country – was rich in culture, and that the spirit of the ordinary folk was strong. He also apologised for the appalling state of the highway – which he was deeply ashamed of – and asked me to write a brief report about it, for him to show to his superiors.

The following morning I breakfasted with Mr Singh, and submitted my report as requested. One of the tyres on my bike had deflated overnight, so a young lad was despatched to get the inner tube repaired. He returned in twenty minutes with the patched tube and I was able to make my departure. It had been yet another example of tremendous Indian hospitality and I promised Mr Singh that I would not forget my overnight stay in Dehri.

Back on the treacherous highway, I soon reached the back of a five-mile tailback, caused by an overturned lorry. With the highway completely clogged by stationary vehicles, I had to ride through deep sand at the side of the road. It was a huge relief to get back on the bumpy highway, once I had cleared the jam!

Late in the afternoon, I reached the turn off for Bodhgaya. It was just fifteen miles to the north on a wonderfully smooth, quiet lane. The village was still several miles away when I caught my first sight of an enormous Buddha statue, rising above the plains and completely dominating the landscape.

Bodhgaya is the 'Mecca' of Buddhism. It was here that the wealthy prince, Gautama Buddha, was said to have vanquished all worldly desires and gained enlightenment by sitting and meditating beneath a tree for forty-nine days. The original tree was sent to Sri Lanka, but a sapling from it was returned to Bohdgaya, where it now flourishes on the same spot. Next to it was built a great Stupa, with the giant Buddha statue nearby. Around this centrepiece are scattered numerous monasteries, offering courses and retreats that draw people from around the world. Some of these monasteries offer accommodation to passing travellers, and I was allocated a dormitory bed (which was actually just a wooden plank) in the Burmese Monastery.

That night, I came down with a virus that completely knocked me sideways. For the next five days, I saw no further than the walls of the monastery dormitory. Sharing the dormitory were a group of Americans that had come especially to Bodhgaya in order to further their spiritual development. They seemed to relish the opportunity to demonstrate selflessness, and did everything that they could for me while I was recovering from my illness.

As my strength finally began to return, I started to venture out of the monastery and explore the rather strange settlement of Bodhgaya. The population seemed to be fairly evenly divided into three distinct groups – the ordinary villagers, the monks in their bright purple and orange robes, and the western pilgrims and backpackers that were passing through. The marketplace in the centre of the village was a harmonious melting pot, where the three groups mingled together quite happily.

I could not leave Bodhgaya without attending at least one of the many lectures that were given each day at the various temples. The talk was given by a Tibetan Lama, who seemed to have no concept of 'time' whatsoever. He was still going strong when I made a discreet exit after four hours, by which time my legs were completely numb from sitting cross-legged on the ground!

With Calcutta still over three hundred miles away, I decided to avoid the treacherous Grand Trunk Road and take to the rural roads again. It felt good to be riding again after being laid up for the past five days, but it would take a while to build my strength up again, so I had to ride quite slowly. Nevertheless, the miles gradually clocked up. The usual sea of friendly and curious faces surrounded me when I stopped for tea at the village of Chauparah. An English speaker was quickly summoned, and he informed me that the last white person to pass through the village was a Yugoslavian, who had travelled through on foot about six years previously!

Riding on into the state of Bihar, the terrain became quite hilly and green. It was nice to run through the gears again, after weeks of riding on the flat. I felt stronger as the day went on, and managed quite a long hard climb under the setting sun to the pretty hill station of Hazaribagh, meaning 'a thousand gardens', which is set amidst dense forest on the Hazaribagh Plateau,

Feeling much better, after a good night's sleep at one of Hazaribagh's many guesthouses, I was on the road again soon after dawn. It was a tough ride that day, because the roads that I followed across Bihar were unsurfaced for long stretches. Another problem was that the only water I could obtain that day was a particularly foul-tasting brown liquid from the local village wells. At times I even wished that I was back on the Grand Trunk Road! It was a character-building ride though, as I kept telling myself, and eventually the town of Jhalida came into view.

The first person that I encountered in this town was a local science teacher, who quickly made arrangements for me to stay at the Government Circuit House. All the Circuit Houses that I had stayed in were comfortable and stylish, but this one was the best of all. I was even served dinner in my own private dining room! Later that evening, the science teacher brought some of his students to visit me. They had each brought an exercise book with them for me to sign. Now I really felt like a celebrity!

In the morning, the science teacher reappeared with his wife and children. We shared breakfast together and they gave me a rousing send-off. The road conditions were much better that day and it was a much more comfortable ride. My mind was on Calcutta now and I could not wait to get there. I covered nearly a hundred miles that day to reach the town of Bankura - in the state of Bengal - where permission was again granted for me to stay at the Circuit House.

Approaching Calcutta now, the villages seemed to be closer to each other and I felt obliged to stop at each one, in order to satisfy the smiling, waving locals by answering a few of their questions. One student asked me how I had managed to cross the River Thames. When I explained that I had crossed over on a bridge, he seemed quite doubtful, but thanked me anyway for the information. The question brought to my mind the first day of my journey, when one of my rear panniers had come loose while crossing London Bridge – nearly bringing my journey to an abrupt end within an hour of leaving home! It seemed like a long time ago now.

That night I stayed in a Circuit House at the town of Arambagh, only this time there was a little more bureaucracy than usual to deal with. I was instructed to write a letter explaining who I was, the purpose of my journey, and promising to vacate my bed at a moment's notice if anyone more important should turn up! It was well worth the effort because, as usual, the accommodation was excellent and it was yet another free night.

Calcutta was just sixty miles away now and I set off in the morning with a great feeling of anticipation. This city had fascinated me since childhood, perhaps due to stories of Mother Theresa's work there, and it was a tremendous feeling to be so close. The bike seemed to ride itself that day and by early afternoon I was riding across the Hoogly River, on the famous Howrah Suspension Bridge, into the heart of the city.

It is hard to describe the feelings of elation and pride that I felt while riding into Calcutta, but it was probably the best moment of the entire journey. I think that the harder you have to work at something, the more you appreciate it when it arrives, and my 1700 mile ride across India had certainly been hard work. It had also been a hugely enriching experience and I felt that I had discovered the true nature of the ordinary Indian people, who are prepared to give so much, although they have so little.

I headed straight for the 'Backpackers' Village', which is centred around Sudder street, not far from the city centre. Here I checked into the large Salvation Army Hostel, which was to be my home for the next six weeks. I had been travelling for five months now, and it was time to stay in one place for a while.

No city had left such an impression on me as Calcutta, and no city has since. There are few obvious tourist attractions – besides the majestic Victoria Memorial building, which is a beautiful palace filled with relics from colonial times and surrounded by tranquil parkland, in the heart of the city. However, the fascination comes from the sights, sounds and smells that meet you every time you turn a corner. The city was hugely over-populated and there was human activity everywhere. There were the street traders, selling the most trivial items imaginable just to earn the few rupees that they need for the daily battle to survive. There is incredible poverty, of course, and people of all ages were slowly dying on the streets from illness and hunger. The obvious hardship all around was quite overwhelming at times, but there was also an atmosphere of warmth and community spirit on the streets, which was quite amazing. The Bengalis are emotional people, and the air seemed to be constantly filled with the sounds of petty squabbles, practical jokes and general hilarity. This was a city with a soul, if ever there was one, and I fell in love with it.

The best way to get to know a city is to live and work in it, so my plan was to do some voluntary work, if possible. With this in mind I visited the residence of Mother Theresa, which was a Convent known as the 'Mother House'. I had been given vague directions at the hostel, but it was easy to find as the children playing in the streets nearby guessed my mission and eagerly led me to the door of the Convent. I was ushered in by one of the nuns, and told that I could start work the following day at the 'Home for the Dying' in Kalighat. I had not expected to actually meet the famous lady herself, but she appeared from a side room, just as I was preparing to leave. She was a tiny, frail figure, but her smiling presence seemed to fill the room. She welcomed me to Calcutta and invited me to join the Sisters for Mass.

The Sisters were gathered in the Convent chapel, which was very simply furnished. There was a small group of Westerners seated on the floor at the side of the hall, so I took my place them. The noise rising from the street below was almost deafening, and the mosquitoes were infuriating, but all this seemed to fade away at the nuns started to sing softly in Latin. It was a truly uplifting experience. Mother Theresa herself knelt on the floor at the back of the hall, until she was called upon to take a brief part in proceedings towards the end of the ceremony.

The 'Home for the Dying' in Kalighat was the first of several projects that have been established in Calcutta by Mother Theresa's 'Missionaries of Charity'. Its purpose was to offer nursing care, comfort and dignity to those that would otherwise be left to die on the streets. Besides assisting with personal care and domestic chores, much of my time here was spent providing emotional support. Most of the patients had been surviving on the streets for years, and were now being treated with love and respect for the first time in many years. Some were in great pain and most were close to death but, despite the suffering, there was a cheerful atmosphere in the home. My work here was immensely rewarding and I built up quite an admiration for the nuns, whose dedication to the place was incredible. They were taught that they should live in the same simple manner as the poor people that they were serving, and this seemed to be the reality. In particular, I noticed that there was virtually no waste, and any leftover food was immediately distributed to the beggars in the streets outside. Sister Suma, who was in charge of the home, told me of the day that an old lady brought a gift of ten paisa (less than half a penny) to Mother Theresa. One spoonful of rice represented ten paisa, and to throw it away was to waste that gift.

The big news in Calcutta at this time was the making of the film 'City of Joy' – a Hollywood production based on the novel by Dominique Lapierre. The filming was causing much controversy, with the authorities claiming that there was too much focus on the slums and street life. The first day's filming took place on Sudder Street, and a chance encounter with one of the Assistant Directors led to an invitation onto the set as a late replacement for one of the extras, who had failed to turn up. I spent three days on the set in all, with much of the time being spent relaxing with the other extras and watching the film crew at work, while waiting to be called upon. I was particularly impressed with the director – Roland Joffe – who treated everyone from the extras to the leading actors with respect, interfered only when necessary, and stayed calm while those around were pulling their hair out. The London film crew had brought over their own caterers and we were served delicious Western dishes that I had almost forgotten existed. It was an interesting experience, but unfortunately my acting ability did not seem to be universally appreciated!

The 28th of February was 'Holi Day' – an annual Hindu festival celebrating the beginning of Spring. The events of that day were memorable, and summed up Calcutta for me. Throughout the day there was music and dancing in the streets, with people celebrating by spraying water paints at each other. On venturing out for a short walk, I was soon covered from head to foot in bright colours! I had to wear this paint for most of the day because, as on most days, the water supply at the hostel was cut off for several hours. Late in the afternoon, I was sat down at a corner tea-stall and chatting with a local man named Jed, who was similarly covered in paint. He informed me, sadly, that a nearby building had collapsed early that morning, killing fifty people and injuring many others. I could hardly believe this, but walked around the block to the spot that he had mentioned and discovered that the story was true. A massive rescue operation had been taking place all day, while people had been dancing in the streets within a few hundred yards of the disaster. The mourners were starting to gather now as the bodies were carried out of the ruins. For most people, however, this seemed to be just another of life's inevitable tragedies and things carried on as normal.

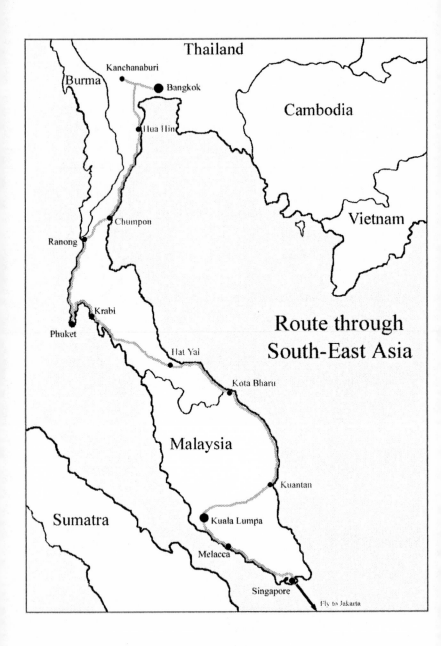

116

CHAPTER FOUR

DUAL WITH THE SUN

Bangkok to Singapore

WITH BURMA'S LAND BORDERS CLOSED AT THIS time, I decided to fly directly to Bangkok, and continue my journey from there in the direction of Australia. Money was starting to run a little short now, so I hoped to be able to obtain an Australian work visa at one of the consulates along the way.

Having slept for just a few hours in the departure lounge at Calcutta's Dum Dum Airport, I was rudely awoken by the gentle prodding of a rifle butt. A smiling Indian soldier stared down at me:

"I am like to buy your shirt", he announced

"Sorry", I murmured, still half asleep

"I am like to buy your shirt", he repeated, "How much will I pay you for it?"

My multi-coloured cycle racing shirt was well worn and tattered, but I was a little annoyed at being woken up in such a manner and in no mood to conduct a trade. The soldier seemed surprised at my blunt refusal, but just shrugged his shoulders and allowed me to turn over and go back to sleep.

It was a short flight from Calcutta to Bangkok, but it took nearly three hours to ride from the airport into the centre of the city. The six-lane highway was choked with late afternoon traffic and I had to thread my way slowly between the lines of vehicles. It felt much safer than riding in Indian cities though, because most drivers were actually following the rules of the road – for example, taking notice of traffic lights! It was almost like being back in Europe.

With darkness beginning to fall, I eventually found myself on the Khao Sahn Road, which any backpacker in this part of the world will tell you is the place to look for accommodation in Bangkok. There were numerous hostels to choose from, and I checked into a rather seedy-looking one at the back of a snooker hall. The pavements of the Khao Sahn Road were lined with food stalls selling all kinds of delicious snacks, and it was a major test of endurance to walk around that evening without buying something at each one. Eventually, I settled for a plate of Thai-fried noodles at a corner stall, and my first day in Thailand was rounded off with a lesson in the use of chopsticks!

Bangkok is a vibrant city with an amazing energy about it. Everyone around me seemed to be hurrying somewhere with a sense of purpose, as I slowly wandered around the city streets soaking up the atmosphere. Scattered among the modern apartment blocks, office complexes and shopping centres were some magnificent Buddhist Temples, providing welcome sanctuary from the hustle and bustle of the city streets. One of the most impressive was Wat Arun (Temple of Dawn), which stands serenely on the shores of the Chao Praya River. Its spire measures some 86 metres and is coated in fragments of multicoloured porcelain.

Bangkok's most dazzling monument, however, has to be the Grand Palace complex, which was only a short walk from Banglampoo. Here, perched high on a gilded alter, stands the tiny Emerald Buddha – which is arguably Thailand's most precious treasure, as it is believed that as long as the Emerald Buddha remains in Thai hands, the Kingdom will be free. In another corner of the Grand Palace stands Bangkok's oldest temple, Wat Pho, containing the giant Reclining Buddha, measuring a colossal 44 metres long and 15 metres high. The lavishly designed Grand Palace complex was quite spectacular, although a little too extravagant for my tastes. I could not help comparing it with the simple beauty of India's temples and monuments.

In Banglampoo one morning I was engaged in conversation by a very friendly man called George. Hearing that I was from England, he invited me to his home for lunch, so that he could introduce me to one of his daughters. She was planning to travel to England soon, he explained, and would be interested to learn more about the country. I had barely accepted the invitation, when a taxi pulled up and we were on our way across the city. About half an hour later, we arrived at a rather grand house in one of the wealthier suburbs. The girl, however, was strangely quiet throughout the meal, and slipped out of the room just as George was getting onto the subject of gambling and casinos. He proposed to teach me a few of his card tricks, so that we could become poker partners and make a fortune together! I was rather surprised at this turn of events but, anxious not to offend my host, tried to show an appropriate level of interest. He produced a pack of cards and invited me to join him in a game he called 'poker-jack', using counters instead of money for betting. During the game he showed me a few of his 'techniques' – which amounted to blatant cheating. It was clever and amazingly simple. I mastered the 'techniques' quickly – pleasing George no end – and hoped that would be the end of it. George, however, had only just started. He announced that some rich friends of his would be arriving soon for a real game. He would provide the betting money, so that I had nothing to lose, and we would share the winnings. By this stage I had had enough, and was about to tell him so when the doorbell rang. In came one of the expected 'players', and I was introduced as 'Mr David – a civil engineer working in the city'! George suggested that we all sit down for a quick game of 'poker-jack', before the others arrived. His friend readily agreed, and produced a wad of £100 dollar notes as he sat down! I promptly stood up and announced that there had been a misunderstanding. I was not taking part in this game, and wished to leave straight away. George looked suitably embarrassed and offended, but called one of his servants to arrange for a taxi to take me back to my hostel.

Back at the hostel, I met an English backpacker in Banglampoo, who had fallen into exactly the same trap and ended up over a thousand dollars in debt. He was anxiously waiting for his father to bail him out. I resolved not to accept any further invitations to lunch in this city!

It was good to be back on the bike again, after a two-month break from any serious cycling. I had decided to head west from Bangkok in order to visit the famous jungle region of Kanchanaburi, which is close to the Burmese border, before doubling back and then turning south towards Malaysia. The busy highway seemed incredibly smooth and cycle-friendly after the dusty, bumpy highways of India, where I was frequently forced off the road by passing trucks and buses, and it felt as though I was gliding along. When I stopped for a rest, having cleared the suburbs, two little girls came running and presented me with a slice of the juiciest watermelon I had ever tasted. Bangkok had seemed to be full of tricksters, such as George, and nearly every conversation with the locals had led to an invitation to a gem shop or a request for some sort of favour. Now the city was behind me, and the simple gift of a watermelon seemed to be a sign that I could drop my guard a little and start to discover the real Thailand.

I stopped for some lunch at a lay-by, where a group of three young men were selling iced drinks to passengers on the tour buses that seemed to pull in every few minutes. As each bus pulled up, one of the men would jump on board with a tray of drinks, followed by his friend with the collecting bowl. The third man hurried on behind with a loud speaker, through which he announced to the passengers that refreshments were coming round. In between buses the men turned their attention to me, happily supplying me with several free drinks to go with my lunch. In return, I allowed myself to be persuaded to help them out a little. When the next bus came, I dutifully jumped on behind the drinks man, carrying the collecting bowl. The passengers seemed amused at my participation and dropped their money in quite willingly. It was good fun, and I helped with a couple more buses before going on my way. It seemed sensible to leave before I became a permanent member of the team!

As it was my first day 'back in the office', I decided to stop for the night a little earlier than usual at the town of Nakhon Pathom. My clean private hotel room here was like heaven, after two weeks in a cockroach-infested dormitory in Bangkok! There was plenty of time to look around the town, which was dominated by a 120-foot high pagoda – the tallest and oldest Buddhist monument in Thailand.

In the morning I wandered down to the market in search of breakfast. Unfortunately, I inadvertently ordered a bowl of extremely spicy noodles, which had to be helped down with bread and gallons of water. This seemed to cause a great deal of hilarity among the locals! My mouth was burning for most of the morning, as I rode further west on the highway, which cut across plains of rice paddies and tapioca plantations. Eventually the plains were replaced by lush jungle as I neared Kanchanaburi.

Situated on the banks of the River Kwai, Kanchanaburi is the usual base for visiting the 'Bridge on the River Kwai', as immortalised in the film of the same name. Not surprisingly, there were numerous Backpacker Hostels to choose from. The one that I picked consisted of several small, wooden cabins, clustered around a grassy courtyard. Mine had a balcony facing onto the river.

A short evening stroll along the riverside brought me to the famous bridge, just as the sun was setting behind it. It was a beautiful scene, but rather a chilling one, as I imagined the terrible events that had taken place here. The bridge was built in 1943 by Allied prisoners-of-war, as part of the 'Death Railway' which was to connect Japanese-controlled Singapore with the Burmese capital, Rangoon. More than sixteen thousand prisoners lost their lives while building the railway - some from malaria, but others from beatings, starvation and exhaustion. This is almost equivalent to one life for every sleeper laid. Nearby was one of the war cemeteries, where there were endless rows of small rectangular memorial stones, each remembering a young soldier that had died in the camps. Many of the stones bore the inscription 'Known to God', which is used for unknown soldiers.

In the town itself, I visited the JEATH (Japan, England, Australia, Thailand and Holland) War Museum, which is laid out as an exact replica of the prisoner-of-war camp, where Allied prisoners were subjected to terrible cruelty. It houses a collection of prisoners' diaries and drawings, giving some idea of the extent of the suffering that took place.

My weekend in Kanchanaburi was a moving and harrowing experience. On my final evening, I stood on the bridge again and reflected that anyone who still thinks that war is glamorous or exciting should pay a visit to this place.

It was a strange feeling riding back towards Bangkok, as it was one of the very few occasions on my travels when I had to ride the same road twice. However, it had been a worthwhile detour, and after a few hours I was able to turn off the highway and head south on a much quieter road, cutting across the rice fields. I received plenty of encouragement from farm labourers, who usually stopped working for a brief moment to call out, or just wave, as I rode past. By mid-afternoon I had reached the village of Damnoen Saduak, which is famous for its 'floating market'. In order to catch this spectacle, which takes place each morning, I went in search of lodgings here. The locals were eager to help, despite the language barrier, and directed me to a small family guest house on the edge of the village. Once settled in, the rest of the afternoon was spent playing football with some of the village children.

This unusual village was like a mini-Venice, with wooden houses connected by a maze of waterways and walkways. As I wandered around at the first light of dawn, the place was already turning into a watery market, with traders from all over the central plains region arriving to sell their produce from wooden boats. With the enormous variety of fruit and vegetables grown in Thailand, including ten different kinds of banana, it was a colourful scene. By 8am there were so many boats that the main canal was almost blocked. If a customer on the shore wished to buy from a boat in the middle of the canal, the trade had to be conducted via three or four other boats! It was a true glimpse of years gone by, when such markets were commonplace in Thailand.

I was captivated by this strange spectacle for an hour or so, before reluctantly pulling myself away in order to start riding while it was still cool. It was not long, however, before the sun reached its full intensity and my energy started to drain away. By the time I stopped for lunch my head was thumping, and it occurred to me that I should be careful not to ride too hard in such stifling heat. However, it was only another thirty miles to the seaside resort of Hua Hin, so, after a long rest, I slowly peddled on.

It was a relief to reach Hua Hin that evening, and feel the cool sea breeze. I headed for the old part of the town, which was a lively area full of ramshackle wooden buildings – some of which were built on stilts. Many of these functioned as hotels, and I was soon settled into a cosy little room not far from the sea front. My exertions that day had taken their toll, so I decided that it was time for a rest day.

In the morning I strolled down to the beach and sat watching the fishing boats come and go. Fishermen were hard at work mending their nets and drying squid under the sun. I had decided to sunbathe for half an hour, but within a few minutes I was overcome by tiredness and fell asleep. When I woke up, a couple of hours later, one side of my body was bright red from sunburn, and even the slightest movement was painful.

I spent the rest of the day in great discomfort and did not venture from my room!

It required a great effort to climb onto the bike the next morning, after a sleepless night due to the sunburn. However, once in motion I felt a lot more comfortable and was able to put it out of my mind. The scenery became increasingly dramatic as I rolled south on the coastal highway, into Sam Roi Yod National Park. This huge Park covers over a hundred square kilometres and was famously used as a setting for the film 'The Killing Fields'. The Park is also well known for its great variety of bird-life, but the most interesting feature for me were the numerous oddly shaped limestone hills, rising dramatically above the flat coastal plains. There were some beautiful secluded sandy beaches as well, and on one of these I was able to rent a tent and set up camp for the night. This was my first camp since losing all my camping gear in Karachi, and I had the whole beach to myself that night, so it was wonderfully peaceful.

My idyllic camp was only spoilt by the sunburn, which again kept me awake for most of the night. Sunbathing was definitely off the agenda for the foreseeable future! The uncomfortable night was soon forgotten though as I started the new day to a beautiful sunrise and a refreshing swim in the ocean. It was a nice easy morning ride through the southern section of the Park to the pretty little seaside resort of Prachuap Khiri Khan.

Prachuap seemed a relaxing sort of place, so I decided on another rest day. It had been quite a lonely journey from Bangkok so far, so it was nice to meet a couple of backpackers from New Zealand, with whom to sample some of the delicious seafood that was on offer at the numerous seafront restaurants. We also climbed to the 'Monkey Temple' on a nearby hill top overlooking the bay. The resident monkeys here were quite tame, but we had to be on guard as they made frequent attempts to dive into our bags in search of food!

From Prachuap, it was another gentle morning's ride through the narrowest part of Thailand, where there are only about ten kilometres between the Pacific Ocean to the east and the Burmese border to the west. The first settlement that I reached was a town called Thap Sakae, where I discovered a tropical paradise called Thaley's Inn. The Inn consisted of a cluster of bamboo huts around a small lake, just yards from the seashore. The huts were beautifully decorated within, and surrounded by all kinds of colourful tropical flowers. It was the most tranquil place imaginable. The Thai owner, Mr Thaley, was a jovial character who spoke excellent English, having spent some years nursing in England. He gave me a warm welcome and invited me to join some of the other guests on an afternoon excursion. Within half an hour of my arrival I was clambering into the back of his truck, together with a group of six Germans and four South Africans. We were driven to an area of lush rainforest, through which we walked for an hour to reach a secluded bathing pool, fed by a gushing waterfall.

Thaley's Inn was one of those places where you quickly lose track of time, and I ended up staying there for several days. Mr Thaley arranged excursions every day to local places of interest, for which no charge was ever made. He insisted that seeing his guests happy, and being able to show them something of his country, was payment enough. In between the excursions I was able to catch up on sleep, at last, and build up my strength again for the road ahead.

Mr Thaley prepared a special breakfast of banana fritters on the morning of my departure. After several of these, I loaded up the bike and said my farewells. Reaching the first bend in the road, I stopped to look back on Thaley's Inn for one last time, and was touched to see that Mr Thaley was still standing at the gate waving me off.

While filling my water bottles at a petrol station, later that morning, I encountered a Japanese cycle tourist called Takiguchi, who had stopped for the same reason. He had been riding for two years now – mainly in Australia and New Zealand – and planned to be on the road for a further four years. He had a single-mindedness and slight arrogance about him, which I had come to recognise in most of the long distance cyclists that I met on the road. We spent half an hour or so exchanging stories and information before going our separate ways. Our paths were not to cross again, but I would think of him often, making his solitary way north while I made mine south. It was like meeting a distant relative that you know you will probably never see again, but who stays in your mind because there is a connection between you.

That evening, I reached the town of Chumpon, which is known as the 'Gateway to the South'. It was the hottest part of the year in Thailand now, so I made a very early start the next morning in order to get as far as possible while it was still cool. As the road turned inland, across the Thai peninsula, the traffic petered out and there were few settlements of any size. With so few distractions, my mind started to wander in all directions and the mile-markers drifted by almost unnoticed. I was brought back to my senses by the sight of two cycle tourists, riding towards me. They were a Swiss couple, and we sat out the hottest part of the day together, exchanging stories and advice on the road ahead, before continuing our respective journeys.

Late that evening, I arrived in the West Coast town of Ranong. Once settled into a small hotel on the main street, I wandered down to the nearby street market for some dinner. This turned out to be a traumatic experience, however, as I accidentally swallowed a whole chilli that was hidden in my fried rice. The locals seemed duly concerned, as I jumped out of my seat gasping for water, but then fell about laughing when they realised what had happened!

The coastal highway was smooth, flat and surprisingly quiet, considering the close proximity of some of Thailand's world famous holiday resorts. A gentle sea breeze provided welcome relief from the scorching heat, and the riding was much more comfortable.

An overnight stay in the seemingly mundane settlement of Khuri Buri proved quite entertaining, as the small town really came alive in the evening. A giant screen had been erected in the town plaza for an open-air film show. Apparently, this event was being staged to mark the beginning of Thailand's New Year holiday, and there was an atmosphere of great excitement as people gathered. The film itself was a typical Thai action movie, with several bursts of kick-boxing, which seemed to be going down extremely well with the crowd. My curiosity was soon satisfied, however, so I headed back to the hotel, where a raucous cabaret show was just beginning in the lounge bar. My room was directly above the lounge bar so, with sleep was clearly out of the question, I bought myself a drink and discreetly sat down in a quiet corner. It soon became clear that audience participation was compulsory, however, and I ended up singing and dancing with the locals until the early hours.

The next day, as I rode south towards Thai Muang, the New Year celebrations were in full swing. The main activity seemed to be the spraying of water and talcum powder at each other, which seemed rather infantile. Buckets of water were frequently directed at me by children at the roadside, and from cheering passengers on passing pick-up trucks. It was all very good-natured, but I did start to get a little annoyed after the umpteenth drenching!

The numerous palm-fringed beaches that I passed that day were packed with Thais, making the most of the public holiday. Just outside the town of Thai Muang, I stopped for a rest at one of these beaches and was invited to join a large group of talcum-covered teenagers for lunch. There were no English-speakers in the group, but this did not seem to matter too much as most of them were too drunk to hold a conversation anyway. When the group finally dispersed, I was called over to join another group for some more food and drink! Having given up any thoughts of riding much further by now, I accepted that invitation as well. Late in the afternoon, as the beach was gradually beginning to clear, I made my way into Thai Muang to look for lodgings.

Thai Muang lies on the northern edge of one of Thailand's most beautiful regions, which is known for its superb beaches and spectacular tropical scenery. It was just a short ride south to the famous Phuket Island, which is linked to the mainland by a causeway. Known as the 'Pearl of the South', Phuket Island boasts more than twenty-five miles of white sandy beaches, and even a National Park. The beach resorts here are highly commercialised and relatively expensive, so I headed for Phuket Town itself, which lies a few miles inland, in the southern part of the island. Here it was easy to find cheap lodgings, and the markets were full of delicious local produce – heaven for a hungry cyclist!

Phuket Town was an ideal base from which to explore the island thoroughly over the next few days. Free of luggage, the bike felt incredibly light as it propelled me over numerous capes, from which spectacular panoramic vistas opened up, as I followed the shoreline. With so much stunning scenery concentrated in such a small area, it was easy to understand why this lush, tropical island has developed into such a popular holiday resort. To satisfy my curiosity, I called in briefly at the island's most famous resort of Patong. As expected, it was over-developed, over-priced and tourist-saturated. It seemed like a huge, ugly, artificial blot on such a beautiful landscape, and it was some relief to get back to the relative normality of Phuket Town.

Back on Thailand's mainland, I followed the coastal highway round to Phang Nga Bay, where weird and wonderful limestone formations rise up from the sea. The only way to explore the Bay is by boat, so I checked into a hotel for two nights and booked onto a boat tour for the next day.

A Swiss couple joined me on the boat trip and it turned out to be a fascinating adventure, full of surprises. These included Ko Tapu (Nail Island), with its impossibly sheer rock face rising out of the water, and the instantly recognisable 'James Bond Island', which featured in the film 'The Man With The Golden Gun'. The highlight of the trip though was a stop at the old Muslim fishing village of Ko Panyi, built on stilts, where a seafood lunch of prawns and lobster was a real treat. When we arrived back at Phang Nga, the Swiss couple jumped straight on the night bus for Bangkok, and I did not see any other foreigners in the town that night. I could not help wandering why more of the beach-loving tourists on Phuket Island, that had probably travelled half way round the world to reach Thailand, did not make the short journey up to Phang Nga Bay, to take in the incredible geographical wonders that were hidden here.

Another day's riding along the increasingly hilly coastal highway brought me to the seaside town of Krabi, which was to be my next base. The highlight of my stay here was a boat trip to Pranang Beach, which lies at the end of a rocky peninsula. Not being one for lying on beaches, especially after my sunbathing mishap in Hua Hin, I straight away set about climbing one of the rocky cliffs at one end of the beach. It was a steep climb, and I regretted my decision to wear sandals that day! From the summit, however, was the most incredible view of two idyllic golden beaches lying back to back on either side of the peninsula, with a strip of palm trees in between.

Further south on the West Coast, there were several more secluded golden beaches - increasingly unspoilt and deserted - as I travelled away from the tourist magnet of Phuket and its surrounds. The ocean was never far away and the riding could not have been more enjoyable. However, it was time for a change of scenery, and I decided to ride back across the peninsula towards the less developed East Coast.

After an uncomfortable night at the town of Trang, where a small army of ants and cockroaches kept me company, I turned inland and rode hard across gentle rolling hills. It was ideal cycling terrain, as you build up enough momentum from the downhill bits to take you over the humps without too much peddling. Some heavy bursts of rain signalled the arrival of the monsoon season, which I had been expecting for a few days now. The thunderous downpours tended to last for about twenty minutes, so it was a case of finding shelter somewhere until the skies cleared again. These enforced breaks were usually enlivened through conversation with local villagers, who would run through their list of known English phrases, such as 'What is your name?' This became a little tiresome and I resorted to giving a different name each time, for the sake of variety. One of the great advantages of the travelling life is that you can be whoever you want to be!

The tranquil, rural landscape gave way to the crowded suburbs of Hat Yai, which is one of Thailand's fastest growing cities. Reaching the downtown area, I found a surprisingly clean and comfortable hostel, which seemed an ideal place to rest up and explore the city. The hostel was fairly empty, and the only person sharing my dormitory was a middle-aged Australian man named Leonard, whose sole reason for visiting Thailand was to take advantage of the cheap dental treatment available here. That night I was kept awake by his loud snoring - punctuated by frequent bursts of aggressive swearing and cursing. In the morning he had no recollection of these outbursts, and could not have been more amiable! On my second night we were joined by an abrasive American 'truckie', who had come to Thailand for cheap sex, and seemed quite proud of the fact. I took an instant dislike to this man, but could not help feeling that the three of us made an unlikely and comical trio – each of us in Thailand for entirely different reasons, but thrown together by coincidence.

The streets around the hostel were a blaze of neon signs, drawing attention to numerous restaurants, shopping precincts, glitzy bars and palatial-style massage parlours. It was like being back in Bangkok, and I could see that the American was not going to be disappointed. My own thoughts were turning to Malaysia now, however, and I spent several hours in the bookstores planning my route and reading up on the country.

The skies were clear and the temperatures were already soaring when I set off from Hat Yai early in the morning. It had been another night of frequently interrupted sleep, thanks to my eccentric roommates – Leonard with his unconscious noisy outbursts and the American arriving back in a drunken stupor at four-o-clock in the morning - so it was some relief to be on the road again. It was a hilly ride at first, but the terrain gradually flattened out towards the East Coast.

The waters of the Gulf of Thailand looked a little murky compared to the crystal clear West Coast waters, but this did not stop me from 'taking the plunge' at the first opportunity. Already splashing about in the ocean were a young Thai couple, who were touring their country by motorcycle. Conversation was tricky, due to the language barrier, but they invited me to share their lunch of roast chicken and sticky rice, as we relaxed on the beach during the hottest part of the day.

That evening I reached the fishing town of Pattani, which lies on the banks of a river, close to its estuary. After checking into a rather ramshackle old Chinese hotel, I went for a sunset stroll along the riverbank. Fishermen were mending their nets and hauling in their catches, while children were playing in the dirty river waters. Everyone acknowledged me cheerfully as I walked by, usually by asking 'Pai nai?' (Where are you going?), which appears to be a form of greeting in this part of the world! There were several mosques dotted around the town - serving as a reminder that Malaysia was not far away now.

The next day I followed the coastal road south towards the larger seaside town of Narathiwat. Despite the sea breeze, it was another blisteringly hot day and I began to feel quite dizzy in the afternoon. Eventually I had to just stop for a while until my head stopped spinning. A garage attendant noticed that I was in a bad way, and invited me inside to rest inside for a while. I sat there until early evening, drinking iced tea and chatting with the attendant in between customers, before riding a further ten miles to Narathiwat.

On arrival, I checked into another old wooden Chinese hotel, similar to the one in Pattani. My appetite was gone completely, so I just had a shower and went straight to bed. It turned out to be a long night, as I broke into a shivering fever and had to make repeated visits to the toilet. The hotel was obviously doubling as a brothel, and the corridor that led to the toilet was lined with scantily dressed prostitutes. They seemed to find it increasingly amusing as I kept reappearing from my room and dashing to the toilet!

The next few days were spent slowly recovering from what was probably a dose of sunstroke. Much of that time was spent lying in bed, or sitting on the hotel balcony and chatting with another cycle tourist, named John, who had arrived the day after me. John was a fifty-seven-year-old Auckland 'docker', who had taken three months' leave in order to ride from Bangkok to Singapore. He had not done any cycle touring before, and his friends at home thought him completely mad to undertake such a venture at his age. He was clearly having the time of his life, however, and I admired his courage. His company was greatly appreciated and helped the hours to pass quickly. John was not travelling on a tight budget, and had been staying in rather expensive hotels for most of his trip. However, having found that he had little in common with the regular tourists and business people that tended to stay in these places, he had decided to try this budget hotel. The plan had paid off, he told me, as he had met me! His sentiments led me to thinking that perhaps my more limited means were no disadvantage. Once you get used to a certain level of comfort you can be quite happy with it, and it is the people around you that make the difference.

On the first day of May 1991, John and I set off together for the Malaysian border, just forty miles south.

I was feeling much better, although still quite weak, having only just started to eat properly again. John was a keen marathon runner and was clearly in good condition. He had a lighter load than me as well and set a good pace, which I struggled to match. However, my pride would not allow me to let the old man get too far ahead! By the time we reached the border town of Sungei Ko-Luk, I was feeling quite sick again, and angry at myself for having tried to keep up with John.

John could see that I was struggling, and his encouragement gave me the strength to keep going. We crossed the border and rode much more slowly towards the port city of Khota Bharu, just twenty miles further south. As is often the case, the border was like a magic line and we noticed little differences on the Malaysian side straight away. Everything seemed a little smarter and tidier. Even the roadside fruit stands were stacked more neatly!

At Khota Bharu we checked into a Backpackers' Hostel, where a dormitory bed for the night set us back less than a pound each. The town prides itself as a cultural centre and we were entertained that night by a free show of traditional music and dancing, as well as top-spinning and Malay wrestling, which was staged in the main theatre by the local tourist board. Three days passed easily in this lively town, as I continued to get back to full health before attempting any more cycling. One place that I visited frequently during this time was the central market, housed in a huge, coliseum-like building. The ground floor – reserved for fruit and vegetables – was known as the womens' market, as all the stall-holders were all women. Viewed from the balconies above, it was a blaze of colour and activity, which was quite captivating.

John made his departure a day before me, in order to keep up with his carefully planned schedule, but I hoped to catch up with him further south. The extra day helped me to regain my strength, and I rode quickly along the smooth, traffic-free, coastal highway. It was a lovely ride, with the ocean to my left and a landscape of rice-fields, rivers and green forested hills to my right. The miles seemed to slip by easily and I travelled much further than planned to reach the village of Merang, some eighty-five miles south of Khota Bharu.

Unbeknown to me, I had already caught up with John, who was staying at Merang's only hotel. We did not meet though because, on asking for directions to the hotel, I was invited to stay with a local family instead. They lived in a small, simply furnished cottage, and I had my evening wash at the garden well before joining the family for a tasty dinner of fried noodles and fresh fish. They all spoke excellent English and were very interested to hear about my journey and learn about life in England. I had not experienced hospitality like this since India, so it came as a welcome surprise.

From Merang, I rode to Marang – another small fishing village, further down the coast. There was a guest house here called Kamals, which had been recommended to me by a Swiss friend called Stefan, who was working with me in Calcutta. It did not take long to find the place and, to my great surprise, Stefan was there to greet me himself! He had travelled straight down from Calcutta to visit his Malaysian friends here, before returning home to Switzerland. It was great to see him again and we spent a couple of days together in Marang, relaxing on the beach and reminiscing about Calcutta.

A little further down the coast, I stopped for the night at Rantau Abang. The guest house here was run by an English lady who was travelling through Asia four years previously, when she fell in love and decided to settle down in this sleepy little coastal village. She had not been back to England since, and told me that the only thing she really missed was the changeable English weather! Among the guests was a Dutch unicyclist, who told me that he would like to travel around the world by unicycle one day. The only problem he had yet to resolve was how to carry enough luggage for such a trip, as panniers cannot easily be attached to a unicycle. I could only suggest a small backpack full of money!

Rantau Abang is known for its giant leatherback turtles, which come up onto the beach several times each day to lay their eggs. The turtles are best seen at night and there were plenty of local tour operators offering evening expeditions. However, I had heard that the local children can be quite cruel to them, and that they are bothered by the torchlight beams that are flashed at them by crowds of tourists each night, so I decided to forego the pleasure of visiting them.

The East Coast highway was proving to be an excellent cycle route. The terrain was mostly flat and there was virtually no traffic so, despite the tropical heat, it was quite a comfortable ride. My next overnight stop was at the tiny beach resort of Cherating, where I rented a cabin at Mac Long Teh's Guest House. Cherating is known to have several residents that are over a hundred years old, and Mac Long Teh herself was well into her eighties. She had been running the guest house for over thirty years now, but there was no sign of her enthusiasm diminishing. Every meal was a feast and there was a terrific atmosphere about the place. Not surprisingly, there were quite a few travellers in temporary residence, and they all seemed to agree that Mac Long Teh's was probably the best value accommodation in South-East Asia. It was here that I bumped into John again. He was staying at a guest house nearby and, on hearing that there was another cyclist in the village, had come round in search of me.

Reunited with John again, we rode south together to the city of Kuantan, where we stayed at yet another Chinese hotel on the seafront. The following day was my twenty-fifth birthday so, at John's insistence, we celebrated it with a western-style breakfast at one of the more upmarket hotels in the city. We then parted company again, because John wanted to continue south along the East Coast, while I had decided to travel across the Malaysian peninsula in order to visit Kuala Lumpa. That was the last I saw of John, until my arrival in his home city of Auckland exactly a year later!

The road inland cut its way through lush jungle terrain. It was a fairly lonely ride, as settlements were few and far between now, and I missed John's company. The heat was quite oppressive as well and it was some relief when the daily monsoon downpour arrived to cool things down a little. It was a hard ride, but I made good progress to reach the town of Mantakap, which is right in the centre of the Malaysian peninsula. One of the highlights of Malaysia for me so far had been the quality and variety of food to be found in the night markets at almost every town. Mentakap was no exception, and the main street was completely closed to traffic from early evening, as numerous food stalls started to set up. As usual, I wandered around sampling several tasty snacks, before eventually selecting my main course from one of the stalls. After a full day's cycling, this was a great way to end the day.

The ride from Mantakap was even tougher, as I climbed steadily into the Genting Highlands. My efforts were amply rewarded, however, by the wonderful views across this hilly region of tea plantations. The final twenty miles was nearly all downhill, as I came down from the Highlands. It was an exhilarating descent, taking me right into the suburbs of Malaysia's capital city.

Kuala Lumpa is a bustling, cosmopolitan city, full of gleaming modern skyscrapers. However, I found it to be quite a 'down to earth' place, with plenty of character and colourful street markets. The International Youth Hostel in the heart of the city provided a good base from which to explore, but very little opportunity for sleep! The lights in my fifty-bed dormitory stayed on until at least 3am each night, and there was constant noise from the streets below, which were full of pubs and clubs. Fortunately, however, the city's main sights lie close together and I was able to visit all of them in an afternoon, necessitating a stay of just two nights. Perhaps the most interesting of these sights was 'Masjid Jame' – an old mosque, which is situated at the confluence of the Kelang and Golak rivers, where the city is said to have begun.

In Kuala Lumpa I was able to obtain an Australian working visa, valid for one year, from the Australian High Commission. This gave me a huge lift, as it meant that I could continue my journey through South-East Asia safe in the knowledge that there would be the opportunity to look for work, and hopefully build up my dwindling travel funds again, once in Australia.

From Kuala Lumpa I headed south along a fairly busy highway, which followed the West Coast. There seemed to be far more development on this side of the country, and much of it was quite ugly – drab concrete apartment blocks overlooking litter-strewn beaches. The first place of any interest that I reached was the quiet seaside resort of Port Dickson, where I checked into a surprisingly luxurious Youth Hostel. There were no other guests that night, so I had the whole place to myself! The warden seemed quite relieved to have some company, and invited me to join him for dinner at a seafood restaurant nearby. He introduced me to some of the locals gathered there, and we spent the evening playing a traditional Malaysian game called 'Chonka', which is played with marbles and a long wooden board.

In the morning, after a leisurely breakfast with the warden, I continued south. The highway was lined with palm trees, giving plenty of welcome shade, and the scenery improved considerably, with sweeping views across the Straits of Melacca. Passing a small, beautifully painted, wooden house, with a handkerchief garden that was bursting with colour, I stopped for a closer inspection. An old man was watering the garden, and he invited me in for refreshments. The interior of this traditional Malay home was just as impressive, with ornate decorations. I had barely sat down when the old man's daughter appeared with a plate of sliced mangoes, from the mango tree in the garden, home-made biscuits and a jug of mango juice. The old man told me that he had lived in the house all his life and that he often received tourists from the nearby beach resorts, who had stopped to admire the house as I had done.

That evening, I reached the famous old port of Malacca, which was once the most important trading port in south-east Asia. There was a good choice of travellers' hostels here and I eventually chose the Paradise Hostel. The name was slightly misleading – in fact, it was a messy, ramshackle kind of place - but the staff could not have been more welcoming and I felt at home straight away.

The next day I wandered around the ancient streets of Melacca, which were full of fine buildings and monuments, many of which were colonial relics from the times of Dutch and Portuguese occupation. In the evening I was invited out to dinner by one of the Malay staff at the hostel. We met up with some of his friends at one of the numerous seafood restaurants at the harbour. After the meal we visited some of Melacca's nightclubs, which were rather like school discos! One of his friends was a young, well-spoken, man called Ben, who lived in Singapore, and was in town visiting his uncle. He boasted that his uncle was one of the richest men in Malaysia and, as if wanting to prove this, invited us all back to his uncle's home for coffee. Approaching the palatial mansion along a very long driveway, I could see that Ben had probably not been exaggerating. It was quite late by now so, after coffee, I accepted an invitation to stay overnight. My en-suite quarters were quite luxurious and made a nice change from the rock hard hostel beds, with assorted 'creepy-crawlies', that I was accustomed to!

Ben's uncle was away on business, so I never did get to meet him. However, I was given a morning tour of some of the houses that he owned in the town. They were all built in the Chinese style, but with various colonial influences and full of amazing antiques. They were real treasure troves, and I felt quite privileged to see these private collections. After my tour, Ben had to leave for Singapore, and he offered to drive me there. However, I was enjoying my ride through Malaysia far too much to skip the last section.

My stay in Melacca was rounded off with a visit to the Melacca Sultanate Palace, which is one of the largest wooden constructions in Asia. Housed within this remarkable building was the Melacca Cultural Museum, containing artefacts from the ancient Malay kingdom that once flourished here.

I was blessed with heavy cloud cover on the morning of my departure, allowing me to make good progress along the coastal highway without having to contend with the energy-sapping tropical sun. By the time the clouds had began to clear away in the afternoon, I had virtually reached the seaside resort of Batu Pahat, which was my destination for this day, and was soon settled into a comfortable little Chinese hotel in the town. As usual, my evening stroll led me to the night market for an excellent seafood dinner.

With the port of Johor Baru, on the southern tip of the Malaysian peninsula, still eighty miles away, I set off at dawn the next morning. It was just as well because the sun was out early, and I had to make frequent stops to rest and drink as much water as possible. Approaching Johor Baru, the highway became increasingly busy and at times the noise of the traffic was deafening. Everyone seemed to be heading for Singapore!

A small Chinese hotel by the harbour in Johor Baru, with a view of the stone causeway that crosses the narrow Johore Strait to Singapore, was to be my last port of call in Malaysia. My journey across the Malaysian Peninsula had been extremely pleasurable. Though perhaps not as rich scenically as Thailand, the relaxed and friendly nature of the local people everywhere more than compensated, and the amazing variety and quality of the food had been an added bonus

Riding across the causeway onto Singapore Island was a rewarding moment, as it signalled the end of another major stage of my journey. Customs were swiftly negotiated on the other side, and it took just an hour to ride across the island to the city of Singapore. On this short journey, I was struck by the order and signs of prosperity in all that I saw around me. Even the highway was lined with neatly laid out flowerbeds.

The city of Singapore itself was a joy to ride around, as there surely cannot be a safer city in the world for cyclists. There were wide, clearly marked, cycle lanes everywhere and, when I did have to venture onto a road, the drivers could not have been more considerate and aware of me. I was soon in amongst the giant skyscrapers of the downtown area, where I found my way to 'Das Traveller's Inn'. This was one of Singapore's notorious 'crash pad' hostels, where as many beds are crammed into the building as possible. The place was bursting with backpackers, but immaculately clean, and there was a nice sociable atmosphere.

There was plenty to see in Singapore, so I spent five days relaxing and enjoying the city. Among the bustle of capitalism and modern structures, I discovered the ethnic neighbourhoods of Little India and Chinatown, as well as some impressive old colonial buildings. One of these was the General Post Office, where I collected my latest morale-boosting ration of mail.

My overall impressions of Singapore were quite mixed, although leaning slightly towards the negative. It is a spotlessly clean modern metropolis, whose inhabitants are extremely polite and well mannered. Society is well ordered, with numerous restrictions and hefty fines imposed for such offences as dropping litter, or failing to flush a public toilet. As a result of these firm measures – mainly imposed by Prime Minister Lee Kuan Yew, who had ruled since 1963 – it seems that a safe, clean and prosperous nation has arisen. This is some achievement, but I could not help feeling that there has been a huge cost. The city seemed to have a slightly sterile atmosphere – lacking the warmth and colourful chaos that one would expect of an Asian city. There also seemed to me to be a lack of individuality, particularly among the teenage generation. I learned that there tends to be great pressure on them to achieve academic success, in order to embark on a lucrative career as soon as possible. One that I spoke to seemed to be incredibly jealous at my freedom to travel the world without being condemned a failure as a result.

My plan was to travel from Singapore to Jakarta by ship – a journey that takes two days. Having checked that it would be no problem to take the bike on board the ship, I arrived at the port in plenty of time for the morning departure. While queuing for my ticket, however, I was approached by a smartly dressed man, who introduced himself as the Chief Port Authority Official. He informed me, in no uncertain terms, that it would not be possible to take the bike on the ship, due to a new rule that been introduced that morning. He could not offer a sensible explanation as to why my bike could not be accommodated on the huge ship that was docked just a few yards away, and our discussion soon developed into a heated argument. It seemed that there was nobody at the port in a position to overrule this man and, with a sizeable crowd having gathered round to watch, he was not going to back down. Realising that Singapore was not the place to risk being charged with disorderly conduct, I had no choice but to accept this rather arbitrary ruling and head back into the city. My only remaining option was to fly to Jakarta, and I managed to arrange a flight with Singapore Airlines for the next morning.

Early in the morning I wheeled my bike into the departure lounge of super-modern Changi Airport. The hall was virtually empty, apart from a lone backpacker. On seeing me, he jumped up and rushed over to greet me. At first I thought that he was just pleased at seeing another Westerner, but then I recognised him. It was Steve – the 'Geordie' cyclist that I had encountered on several occasions in Yugoslavia, some six months before! He had since returned home to Newcastle with his girlfriend Lily, worked there for a few months, and then come out to Asia alone. He had been travelling mainly in Indonesia, and had just popped over to Singapore to renew his Indonesian visa. The Port Official's harsh decision had led to the most unlikely reunion!

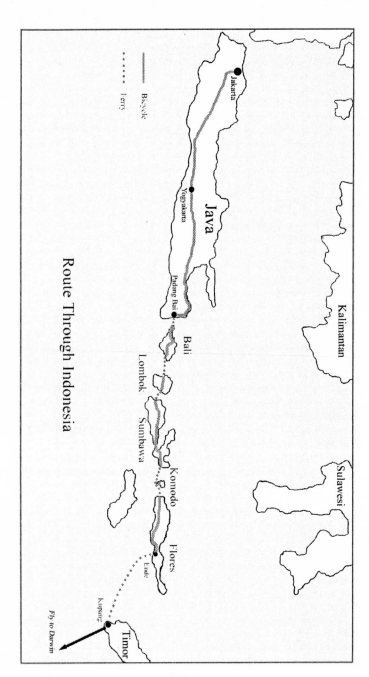

Route Through Indonesia

Bicycle

Ferry

Jakarta

Java

Yogyakarta

Padang Bai

Bali

Lombok

Sumbawa

Komodo

Flores

Ende

Kupang

Timor

Fly to Darwin

Kalimantan

Sulawesi

154

CHAPTER FIVE

A CIRCUMCISION AND A FUNERAL

Jakarta to Kupang

THE STREETS OF JAKARTA WERE A HIVE of activity, with people rushing about in all directions. After travelling through the relatively 'Westernised' countries of Thailand, Malaysia and Singapore, this felt like the 'real Asia' again. The unbelievable level of curiosity that my appearance seemed to generate was reminiscent of India. It was not easy weaving in and out of the traffic, while trying to respond to frequent shouts of encouragement and welcome! On my short ride into the city, from Java's international airport, evidence of the great extremes of wealth and poverty that exist here also reminded me of India. Gleaming white office and hotel complexes looked down on overcrowded shantytowns, while expensive Mercedes and BMWs shared the streets with rickety old 'pedicabs'.

155

With a population of over seven million, Jakarta is Indonesia's biggest city by far, and it was quite dark by the time that I reached the main hostel area, close to the centre. Having checked into one of the hostels, I wandered down to the local 'warung', which is the name given to the typical street cafés here. The makeshift shelter covered one long table, which made for a very sociable atmosphere. The regulars gathered at the 'warung' were happy for me to share their table and insisted on me sampling the contents of several steaming pans, before deciding on my choice of evening meal. Eventually, I settled for a vegetarian dish called 'gado gado', consisting of mixed vegetables in a delicious peanut sauce, which was to become my firm favourite while travelling through Indonesia.

Two nights in Jakarta was enough for me. The heat and humidity was quite oppressive and I was anxious to escape to the cooler hill country, which covers most of Java. The highlight of my brief stay was a visit to Merdeka Square, which lies in the centre of the city, surrounded by parklands. In the centre of the square stands the 433-foot high National Monument - topped with a gold-plated flame, symbolising national independence. From the top of the monument, the city suburbs stretched far away to the horizon in every direction.

The island of Java, which is about the size of England, has over a hundred million inhabitants. Most of these are squeezed into the valleys between the huge volcanoes that dominate the island. Travelling south towards Bogor, this great density of population was quite evident. The towns and villages seemed to merge into each other, and everywhere I looked there were several pairs of eyes staring back at me. The highway itself was clogged with heavy traffic, which frequently came to a standstill. It was not a comfortable ride, but at least the tall trees on either side of the road afforded some protection from the intensity of the sun.

Bogor was another dusty and humid city. I did not linger here for too long, as my sights were firmly set on making it up into the mountains before nightfall. Having negotiated the busy city streets, the traffic thinned out at last, and I embarked on a long, gradual climb into the beautiful Puncak region. Here the lush terrain of hillside tea plantations, waterfalls and lakes was further enhanced by the brightly coloured wild flowers in full bloom all around. That night I stayed at a small Youth Hostel in the village of Cisarua, close to the Puncak Pass. The altitude here was around 1500 metres, and it became wonderfully cool as the sun dropped. It was even too cold for mosquitoes, so I had a particularly good night's sleep.

The next day I rode a further fifteen miles up the valley to the village of Cibodas, which lies on the side of a volcano called Mount Gede. This short ride took several hours, as the lush, tropical countryside demanded numerous photo stops. The tea-picking season was well underway now, and pickers were hard at work in their bright red shirts and straw hats, adding a splash of colour to the rolling green plantations.

The hostel at Cibodas was idyllically situated on the edge of a deep valley, at the foot of Mount Gede. There were no other guests that night, but the warden advised me to enjoy the solitude as he was expecting a party of sixty students from Jakarta to arrive the next morning.

At dawn, as the sun was rising over the valley, I set off to explore the nearby Cibodas Botannical Gardens. The Gardens were very tranquil at this time of day and a blaze of colour. My intention to climb Mount Gede was dashed by one of the rangers, who warned me that this would not be safe, as the volcano was very active at the present time. He advised me to go no further than the Cirebeum Waterfall, partway up the mountainside, so I duly marched off in the direction indicated. The trail led through thick forest before suddenly opening up into a large clearing, revealing three great waterfalls plunging into a mountain stream.

Back at the hostel, the warden warned me to expect the atmosphere to be a little more lively that evening, as the students had arrived. They were a high spirited group, and the evening meal turned into something of a food fight. The ones that were not too busy throwing their food around seemed determined to grab the chance of practising their English on me, so I was kept quite busy!

The next morning, after another fairly chaotic feeding session, I quietly slipped away, and embarked on an exhilarating fifteen-mile descent to the town of Cianjur. My cycle computer indicated a speed of 48 miles per hour on the descent, which is not bad for a mountain bike! From Cianjur it was up and down for the rest of the day, as the road wound its way between huge volcanoes. Reaching one mountain pass, a fairly upmarket roadside restaurant unexpectedly appeared. A small, rotund man with a cheery, moustached face was standing at the doorway. He must have been the proprietor because he excitedly ushered me in and told me to choose anything from the menu - 'on the house'! Being ravenously hungry, as usual, I needed no second invitation, and was soon tucking into a large plate of fried noodles. True to his word, the proprietor refused my offer of payment, and even presented me with a street map of Bandung, the next big town on my route.

Bandung is Java's third largest city. Lying at an altitude of 700 metres, it was much cooler than Jakarta and less hectic! I stopped for two nights here, allowing me the opportunity to visit the nearby volcano Tangkuban Parahu. This was a very accessible volcano, with a road leading right up to its crater, but this accessibility can have its drawbacks. Stepping off the bus, I was quite disappointed to be faced with a line of souvenir stalls extending some distance around the rim of the crater. Despite this negative aspect, it was quite an experience to stand on the rim of a volcano crater for the first time in my life, as smoke billowed out from a pool of boiling sulphur deep within.

From Bandung, I followed the highway eastwards, across a landscape of forested mountains, green valleys and terraced rice fields, with dark smoking volcanoes looming in the distance. There were several mountain villages dotted along the route – including Leles, where I visited an old Hindu temple, lying on a small island in the middle of a lake. As the afternoon wore on, I began to feel the effects of a stomach virus, but managed to keep going to the town of Garut.

After a brief search for lodgings, I discovered a cosy little guesthouse, built around a stone courtyard. An elderly lady was in charge, and I had barely moved my things in when she appeared at my doorway with a pot of tea and some rice cakes that she had made. This was about as much as my stomach could handle, so there was no need to venture out again that evening.

In the morning the old lady was back again with some breakfast – coffee, bread, bananas, more rice cakes and some 'Indonesia Cake' (a delicious national speciality made of several thin layers and baked for hours). Though feeling slightly better, the thought of cycling anywhere did not fill me with enthusiasm, so I decided to spend the day resting up here. In the afternoon I did manage a short walk, and was greeted everywhere by shouts of 'Hello Mister!' and 'Where are you going?' This question is not easy to answer when you are just wandering around aimlessly!

The long climb out of Garut seemed almost effortless, as my mind focussed on yet more stunning scenery. The mountains were much closer now, and the road followed a steep-sided valley between them. Green rice fields rose in steps up the valley sides, while far below a bubbling stream snaked its way into the distance. As the road gradually levelled out I was able to sit back and really appreciate this beautiful island.

The ride ended with a descent into the lowland town of Banjar, where I found another homely little guesthouse. This one was perhaps a little too friendly though, as my sleep was disturbed by another guest, who knocked loudly on my door at around midnight. He explained that he had heard that there was an Englishman staying and wished to practice his English. At my polite refusal he just sighed and asked for my home address instead!

Despite the unexpected midnight visit, I had slept well and made good progress the next day. There were stunning vistas at almost every turn, as I peddled into the mountains of Central Java. The highlight though was reaching a high pass, towards the end of the day, from where a sea of firs stretched far away below me in every direction. From the pass, I descended into the sizeable town of Banyumas, to look for lodgings. On making enquiries, however, I was told that there were no hotels at all in the town. A small crowd had gathered around me, and one man suggested a visit to the 'Kepala Desa' (Headman), who may be able to arrange accommodation for me. Apparently he lived a couple of miles outside the town, which meant climbing back up the hill that I had just come down. As I wearily set off, another man called me back and suggested that it might be possible for me to stay at the local Muslim boarding school, where he was a teacher. This seemed a bit more promising, so I followed him to the school, and was soon being introduced to the Principal.

After giving a short account of myself over coffee and biscuits, I was warmly welcomed and shown to the guest room, which was next to the staff common room. One of the teachers, named Asman, invited me to dinner at his mother's house nearby. The family were already gathered at the table when we arrived, and we sat down to quite a feast. The Principal had asked me to speak to some of the students that evening, so as soon as the meal was finished we returned to the school. Around forty students were neatly assembled in a stone courtyard, and eagerly awaiting our arrival. After some brief introductions from the Principal, I gave a brief account of my journey through Java, similar to the one that I had given to the Principal himself a few hours earlier. The students showed great interest, although their slightly puzzled expressions suggested that they were not able to understand everything that I was saying. The next hour was spent trying to answer some of their questions, which were mostly aimed at establishing how it was possible for someone to spend so much time away from his home and family! The discussion may well have continued late into the evening, but the Principal drew proceedings to a close by insisting that I must surely be tired and should take rest. The evening was rounded off with a coffee in the staff room with Asman and some of his colleagues, before retiring to my quarters.

At 6.30am, Asman awakened me with coffee and pancakes. This, he explained, was not breakfast but just a snack! Half an hour later we were again seated in his mother's house for a 'proper' breakfast of rice, vegetables and omelette. We then walked back round to the school, where the students were just arriving for morning lessons. Asman soon had them lined up for a group photo to mark my departure.

Spurred on by this terrific send off, I rode out of Banyumas and embarked on a long steady climb into the mountains. The double breakfast had given me plenty of energy, and I climbed steadily for several hours to reach the cool mountain resort of Wonosobo early in the afternoon. This would be my base for a visit to the nearby Dieng Plateau.

The Dieng Plateau lies at an altitude of two thousand metres, within the crater of an ancient, extinct volcano. It has been a Hindu pilgrim site for over twelve centuries, and at one time there were over two hundred temples here, only eight of which remain. Arriving on an early morning bus from Wonosobo, I first visited the Arjuna Complex – a group of five temples that are believed to be the oldest in Java. Lying in the centre of the plateau, these temples were made of stone and of very simple design. Nearby was a more active part of the crater, where steam rises from hot sulphur pools. It was quite an experience to walk around the smoky cauldrons, listening to the sound of boiling water bubbling away beneath the surface. By midday the mist was starting to descend over the mountains. As I boarded the bus back to Wonosobo, the Arjuna Complex was just beginning to disappear in the mist.

My next destination was the world famous Borobodur Temple, just forty miles east of Wonosobo. Feeling adventurous, I decided to make this distance even shorter by following some minor roads through the mountains, rather than sticking to the main highway. It was not too long though before I was regretting this decision, however, as the mountain road soon deteriorated into little more than a track. The climbs were incredibly steep, and even my lowest gear did not seem low enough! I was determined to keep going, however, and received plenty of encouragement from the mountain villagers, as I passed by at the pace of a snail.

Eventually, I made it to the village of Borobodur, which is dominated by the temple complex on its outskirts. It was mid-afternoon, and the village was overwhelmed with tour buses and crowds of tourists, swarming back and forwards between the village and its great monument. A place like Borobodur Temple is usually best appreciated early in the morning, before the tour buses have arrived, so I decided to check into a guesthouse. Very few tourists choose to stay overnight in Borobodur, as it makes such an easy day trip from the main cities of Central Java, and the only other guests that evening were a couple of young German cyclists. They were coming to the end of a year-long journey through Asia, and looking forward to returning home the following week. In the evening, we went for a meal together in the village, which had turned into a quiet little mountain settlement again.

Borobodur Temple is the largest Buddhist monument in the world, and considered to be one of the wonders of the world. It is thought to have taken ten thousand men over a hundred years to build it, and this astonishing claim seemed quite credible to me as I wandered around at the first light of dawn. The huge structure is built on six levels, each symbolising a stage on the path to enlightenment. The terraces were decorated with numerous stone Buddhas, stupas and relief carvings, depicting the life of Siddhartha Buddha from childhood to his departure from the material world. Looking out over the surrounding mountains from the highest level, I was able to feel some of the inspiration that must have helped to create this grand and colossal monument. The achievement seems all the more remarkable when you consider that it was built before the age of machinery. Coach-loads of tourists were already starting to descend on the place, so it was time to make my way back to the village for breakfast.

After breakfast, I rode further up into the mountains. It was a misty day, so there was not too much opportunity to appreciate the scenery as I climbed higher and higher to reach a hostel in the village of Kaliurang, on the slopes of Mount Merapi – the most active volcano in Java.

The busy hostel was fairly basic, but had a lively and friendly atmosphere, which made me feel at home straight away. The manager, Christian, was a passionate mountaineer and a jovial character. That evening, I joined the other guests for his nightly talk entitled 'Climbing Mount Merapi'. It was an entertaining talk, full of stories from a lifetime of climbing and numerous mountain rescues that he had assisted with. Most of the backpackers gathered there were inspired to attempt the climb, which involved setting off from the hostel at around 1am, in order to reach the crater by dawn, and descend again before the whole mountain was cloaked in mist by about midday. Christian assured us that anyone who lingered at the crater for too long would probably get lost in the mist and end up spending several days on the mountain!

I was tempted to tackle the climb myself, but eventually decided on a shorter climb to an observatory platform partway up. I set off at 3.30am with a couple of others that had also ducked the main challenge, and we reached the platform in time for sunrise. It was a clear morning and the summit of Mount Merapi emerged gradually from the darkness, with huge amounts of smoke billowing from its crater. It was an amazing sight - well worth the early start!

From the heights of Kaliurang, it was a chilly descent into the city of Yodyakarta. Generally considered to be Java's cultural capital, Yodyakarta is something of an artist's 'Mecca'. Despite the large number of tourists milling around the city centre, I found the atmosphere quite relaxed. There was plenty of excellent street theatre and numerous galleries displaying the works of some of Indonesia's leading painters and sculptors.

The city is especially famous for its batik, and I visited one of the many open workshops where you can watch it being produced. Batik is a kind of cloth, on which designs are traced in wax. The un-waxed parts are then dyed, before the wax is boiled out, with the process being repeated for each colour of dye. It was fascinating to watch and the results were quite beautiful. I very rarely purchased souvenirs on my travels, but could not resist a piece of batik.

I could not leave Yodyakarta without attending a performance of the famous Ramayana Ballet – a traditional Javanese dance that was staged nightly in the city. Against a backdrop of the Sultan's Palace, the elaborate open-air presentation included a full orchestra and a troop of dancers dressed as monkeys!

A short ride east of Yodyakarta brought me to the Prambaman Temples, which are some of the largest and finest Hindu temples in the world. They date from the eighth century, when Hinduism replaced Buddhism as the dominant religion in Java. The temples were covered with reliefs depicting episodes from the Ramayana story, which was fresh in my mind from the previous evening. Prambaman was, apparently, intended to outshine Borobodur, which was some ambition. This may not have been achieved, but it was an impressive sight, nonetheless.

It was only a few more kilometres to the other great cultural city in Central Java – Surakarta. Approaching the city, a local man called Yono rode up alongside me on his bicycle. He invited me to stay at his family's new hotel, which was called 'The Happy Homestay'. Intrigued by the name, I followed him though a maze of alleyways to the hotel. The place was clean and reasonably priced, and everyone did indeed seem to be rather happy! Yono supplied me with maps and local information, together with a pot of tea, before setting off on his bicycle again to find some more Westerners.

Surakarta was quite similar in style to Yodykarta, although with fewer tourists.

That afternoon, I visited two royal palaces, belonging to different branches of the same family. The most interesting was the Mangkunegaran Palace, which was a complex of huge, carved teak pavilions.

Back at 'The Happy Homestay', Yono had managed to round up three more guests – a French couple and a Brazilian girl. He seemed pleased with this achievement, and celebrated by producing a bottle of 'arak' – a local brew - and some palm sugar cookies, which made for quite a sociable evening!

From Surakarta, there was a choice to make, between the busy highway that followed the valley floor or the more direct mountain route over the volcano Mount Lawa. The opportunity to escape from the stifling lowland heat was too good to turn down. It had to be the mountains.

As the volcano loomed ever larger in front of me, the road became very steep and I had to use the lowest gears. A couple of hours' tough climbing brought me to the town of Tawangmangu, where I rested for a while at the foot of one of Java's biggest waterfalls. It was just another six miles to the pass but, with the road became even steeper, it seemed like sixty! It was necessary to stand on the pedals to slowly force them round, until they just would not turn anymore. There was nothing for it but to climb off and walk the last couple of miles to the pass, where I nearly collapsed from exhaustion. There was a tea-stall at the pass, and it took several cups before my senses returned to normal, The views from the pass were largely obscured by cloud, although I did catch a fleeting glimpse of Mount Lawa's summit before beginning the descent.

The downhill road was bumpy and equally steep, with sharp hairpin bends, so the utmost caution was necessary. Without my heavy back panniers it would have been impossible to ride down without flying over the handlebars! A short way down, I came to the town of Sarangan, situated on the shores of a perfectly clear lake in the shadow of Mount Lawa's summit. This seemed like a good place to spend the night, so I checked into a small pension on the edge of town. My room had a balcony overlooking the lake and the valley below. My efforts to get here had been well rewarded, because it was a beautiful spot.

As the sun rose over the lake, I loaded up the bike and started the day with a twenty-five mile descent back down into the lowlands. After a late breakfast in the town of Maduin, I then followed a very busy highway along the valley floor to the city of Jombang. It was not the most scenic ride, but the previous day's tough climb seemed to have caused the old knee injury to flare up again, so it was a relief to be riding on the flat again.

My tiny hotel room in Jombang had a stone floor and was covered in cobwebs. There were quite a few co-habitants from the insect kingdom as well, but it was a place to sleep and that was all that I needed. The other guests seemed quite taken aback at my arrival. One of them spoke English and was able to explain the reason for this reaction. Apparently I was the first foreigner ever to stay at this hotel!

This was clearly not a 'touristy' city and I attracted plenty of attention on the streets that evening. It was all very good-natured though, and I felt quite at ease. At a crowded street corner café I was made to feel most welcome, and all offers of payment were adamantly refused! Much of the previous week had been spent rushing around the numerous tourist attractions of Central Java, so it felt good to spend an evening at such an 'ordinary' place, in the company of some genuine Javanese people. The experience was just as valuable to me as my visit to the great Borobodur Temple a few days before.

From Jombang, I reluctantly decided to stick to the lowland highway, rather than risk aggravating the knee again in the mountains. It was a fairly tedious ride, with the noise of traffic constantly ringing in my ears, but the miles gradually passed as I tried to keep my mind occupied by singing songs to myself and reflecting on my Indonesian experience so far. This was not a country that I had thought much about before leaving England, but it was turning out to be a fascinating place to explore - full of scenic and cultural riches.

That night I reached the large town of Probbolingo, on Java's north-eastern shores. This would be my base for a visit to nearby Mount Bromo, so I checked into a hotel next to bus station. Early in the morning, a local bus carried me up the steep slopes of Mount Bromo to the town of Ngadisari. From here it was a further two-mile climb on foot to the outer crater rim. The crater of Mount Bromo itself lies within an enormous outer crater, with a sea of sand lying between the two rims. It is a most unusual and spectacular volcanic landscape and the views from the outer rim were amazing. Across the sand, plumes of smoke were billowing from the inner crater of Bromo. Far away in the distance Mount

Semeru – Java's highest mountain – was also emitting puffs of smoke from time to time. Several hours were spent hiking around the outer rim and even venturing as far as the inner crater rim, where the smell of burning sulphur was almost overpowering. It was mid-afternoon by the time that the clouds started to roll in across the sea of sand, and within half and hour the whole scene was wiped from view.

My journey across Java was now almost complete. For the next couple of days, I rode into a gentle sea breeze on the eastern coastal road towards Ketapang, which is the ferry terminal for Bali. I broke the journey with a night at the beach resort of Pasir Putih, which lies in the shadow of Mount Ringgit. This laid-back resort seemed to cater mainly for the domestic holiday trade, and I met several Indonesian holidaymakers at the hotel and on the beach. One family from Jakarta invited me to join them for a fish supper at the local night market.

The Bali crossing takes just twenty minutes so, on reaching Ketapang, I jumped onto the ferry straight away. It was quite sad to watch the fascinating island of Java slowly disappearing away into the distance. However, with only a month remaining on my Indonesian visa, and still six islands to cross, it was time to move on.

We landed at the small port of Gilimanuk, where I checked into one of several 'home-stays' that were dotted around the harbour. Among the guests at the home-stay were a Japanese couple that had been cycle touring with their fifteen-year-old daughter for over two years now. The young girl had been diligently keeping up with her schoolwork by correspondence throughout that time. They had cycled right across Australia, on the famous Stuart Highway from Adelaide to Darwin, at the height of summer, when temperatures soar into the late forties most days. For anyone to manage this journey would be quite something, but for a fifteen-year-old girl to do it was almost beyond belief! After listening to their stories of this incredible journey, my thoughts started to turn towards Australia for the first time, and I looked forward to tackling the Stuart Highway myself.

Having heard that the south-western part of Bali is quite 'tourist-saturated', especially around Denpassar and Kuta Beach, I decided to head for the northern beach resorts instead. There was little traffic on the northern coastal road and it was a pleasant ride, with the blue ocean on one side and green rice-fields on the other.

Resting for a while by a roadside store near the village of Grokgak, I was befriended by a couple of local village girls named Sri and Minim. They spoke little English, but were eager to attempt conversation and asked where the rest of my group was. The news that I was travelling alone seemed to come as quite a shock them! Having digested the revelation, the girls seemed to decide that

I would make a suitable husband for Sri! This was suggested to me in a fairly subtle manner at first but, as I pretended not to follow their drift, the proposition was made quite bluntly! The situation became a little uncomfortable as I explained that the relationship would be doomed to failure, due to the fact that I was only planning to stay in Grokgak for a further twenty minutes! To soften the blow I bought them each a bag of peanuts (the store did not seem to sell much else). This worked surprisingly well, and we parted company on friendly terms.

That night I found excellent accommodation at a family guesthouse by the beach at Lovina - a quiet village surrounded by rugged, unspoilt countryside. It would be a perfect base from which to explore the northern half of Bali - an area was full of natural beauty and cultural attractions. Bali could not be more suitable for bicycle touring, with smooth, traffic-free roads and everything so close together. Over the next couple of days I visited a monastery, several waterfalls and hot springs all close to Lovina.

It was nice to come back to the friendly little guesthouse in Lovina each evening, in time to catch the nightly sunset from the beach. The northern coast of Bali is renowned for its sunsets, and each evening a small crowd of backpackers would gather on the beach to watch the big red sun slowly disappearing into the ocean.

Bali is dominated by three huge volcanoes – Batur, Abang and Agung – which lie close together in the centre of the island. Unable to resist the temptation to conquer at least one of these, I decided to head for a small mountain village called Tirta, at the foot of Mount Batur. It was a tough climb from the coast, but I was well rewarded by the spectacular mountain views. At Tirta I checked into a two-room guesthouse, owned by an elderly couple. The other room was taken by a couple of Swiss girls that I had previously met in Java, so there was a nice little reunion. Our Balinese hosts were incredibly cheerful and seemed unable to stop smiling! In the evening they took the three of us to visit the local hot springs, where some of the villagers were doing their laundry or having an evening wash. Nobody seemed the least bit bothered by our intrusion into their evening rituals, and we were soon relaxing in the warm volcanic waters ourselves.

At four-o-clock in the morning I set off with the Swiss girls to climb Mount Batur. The moon was full, so we were able to see the trail clearly and it was an easy climb. We were at the summit within a couple of hours, just in time for sunrise. A group of around twenty backpackers were already there, and we all sat down to watch the sunrise as if it was a piece of theatre! It was a great show, and we could even see Mount Rinjani (which lies on the nearby island of Lombok) rising above the clouds.

By mid-morning I was back down in Tirta, preparing to ride down into the southern part of Bali. Freewheeling down into the lowlands, I encountered a French couple, who were struggling uphill on heavily loaded bikes. They had been cycle touring for over five years, and were heading north from Australia. Over lunch we exchanged information on the areas that we were each heading towards. They had just come from the southern town of Ubud, and recommended a guesthouse there. There may have been an ulterior motive for this, however, as they also left me with their room key, which they had forgotten to return!

The town of Ubud is considered to be the cultural heart of Bali. The main street was lined with stalls selling artwork, textiles and other handicrafts. Despite the weight of tourism on this relatively small settlement, I found the atmosphere to be surprisingly relaxed, and the town made an excellent base from which to explore the central parts of Bali. There were numerous guesthouses, but I opted for the one that the French couple had recommended. They were delighted to get their key back!

The next day I visited the memorial temples of Gunung Kawi, near the village of Tampaksiring. The temples are carved out of niches in the face of two cliffs, at the foot of a lush, green valley of terraced rice paddies. According to legend, the giant Kebo Iwa carved these niches in one night with his own fingernails. Close to the temple, I stopped to rest by an old woodcarver's shop. The woodcarver was listening to Mike Tyson's latest fight on the radio, while patiently carving intricate designs on an elephant tusk.

On another day trip from Ubud, I visited the famous Besakih Temple (known as the Mother Temple), which is considered the most sacred of all Bali's temples. Situated high on the slopes of Mount Agung, the complex actually consists of thirty small temples – one for each Balinese district - built on seven terraces. Much of it was destroyed when Mount Agung erupted in 1963 – killing 863 worshippers – but restoration work has repaired most of the damage. Besakih was shrouded in mist that morning, but still looked magnificent.

From Ubud I rode a short distance to the town of Klungkung, which is a former dynastic capital. This seemed a refreshingly ordinary Asian market town, after the slightly artificial atmosphere of Ubud. It was not without its attractions though, and the old 'Water Temple' in the centre of town was a wonderfully tranquil place to relax for a few hours. While sitting in the small raised pavilion that overlooks the temple, I watched as the tourists came and went – most of them staying just ten minutes or so before dashing off to their next destination.

Continuing eastwards, I rode through the lush Kusamba region, which is speckled with the thatched roofs of salt-panning huts. At Goa Lawah (The Bat Cave) I had to run the gauntlet of eager souvenir sellers, and young girls who smile sweetly as they throw you a flower and then angrily demand payment a few moments later! It was worth the hassle though, because the sight of thousands of bats, clinging upside-down from the walls of the cave, was captivating!

The small fishing village of Padangbai is the ferry terminal for Lombok Island, and this would be my final base in Bali. I checked into a beach inn, with a loft that was converted into a 'bunk-room' for backpackers. The next day, I set out on a pannier-free bicycle to explore the eastern part of the island. Though attracting far less of the tourist trade than the rest of Bali, I found it to be a really beautiful area. Much of the lush terrain has been cultivated into terraced rice paddies, creating an unusual landscape. In the heart of this region was the ancient walled village of Tenganan, which is unique in its pursuance of original Balinese traditions. Most of the villagers here were engaged in traditional handicrafts, such as 'ikat' weaving, basket making and wood carving. They were most welcoming, and I was able to wander in and out of their homes to watch them at work, without feeling under any pressure to buy anything.

The highlight of my stay in Padangbai was the incredible spectacle of a Balinese cremation ceremony. To the Balinese, death is a time of passing from one life to the next, so this was a time of celebration. The day began with a lively procession from the village centre to a nearby cemetery. Everyone was in traditional dress, and the lavishly decorated coffins were carried on wooden platforms, supported by long poles. The coffins were proceeded by a marching band and dancers. Excitement reached fever pitch as the procession streamed onto the beach, and the coffins were actually carried into the sea! Many of the 'mourners' danced joyfully in the waves for several minutes, as the band played as loudly as possible on the shore.

With the procession finally reaching the cemetery, things quietened down considerably and the serious business started. Following some formal rituals, open fires were lit and the bodies slowly began to burn. Most people drifted away now and there was a general lull in the proceedings until the burning process was complete, some three hours later. Then followed another lively procession to the village pier. Here there were yet more speeches and rituals, before the ashes were finally lowered into a motor boat to be taken out to their final resting-place in the depths of the ocean.

The cremation ceremony had taken a whole day. I was told that the cost would be somewhere in the region of ten million rupiahs (around £3,500), which is a small fortune in this part of the world. It was quite a send-off though!

The morning ferry to Lombok Island was crammed full and I was lucky to get a seat for the five hour crossing, despite boarding an hour before departure time. As we set off, I recognised a group of Australian backpackers who were staying at Mac Long Teh's Guesthouse, in Malaysia, several months before. They told me that they had also spotted me twice from the coach windows, as they travelled down through Java. The journey passed quickly in their company.

Lombok (meaning 'chilli peppers') is a tiny island with a rural atmosphere, and is far less commercialised than Bali. The island is dominated by Mount Rinjani, which loomed large to the north, as I rode from the ferry port to the main town of Mataram. It was a short ride, and I arrived in plenty of time to explore the town before evening. The main sight was Narmada Taman – Lombok's most famous temple complex. It was built in 1727 and is notable for its man-made lagoons, symbolising the lakes of Mount Rinjani.

The next day, I was able to ride right across the island to the eastern ferry port of Labuhan Lombok. Along the way, I visited Lingsar Temple, which is unique in having an altar at which Hindus and Muslims can worship simultaneously. It was originally built in 1714, by the first migrating Balinese Hindus, and then reconstructed in conjunction with the indigenous Sasak Muslims, as a symbol of their unity. The two cultures do seem to co-exist in harmony on the island, although there is an annual festival at Lingsar Temple where offerings and prayers are followed by a mock battle between Hindus and Muslims. It was explained to me that the only weapons allowed are ketupat (steamed rice wrapped in banana leaf) missiles!

From Lingsar, I crossed the southern foothills of Mount Rinjani, which was largely obscured by clouds for most of the day. Besides horses pulling carts, there was little traffic on the highway, and nearly everyone waved or called out as I rode past. The sound of 'Hello Mister' was ringing in my ears by the end of the day! On reaching Labuhan Lombok, I jumped straight onto a ferry that was just about to leave for Sumbawa – the next island in the Nusa Tengara chain.

When we landed on Sumbawa, the other passengers were shepherded onto buses and whisked away in remarkably quick time, leaving me alone by the quayside. A short ride from the harbour brought me to a village of wooden houses on stilts. Here I received a rapturous welcome to Sumbawa by the people of the village. In no time at all everyone – it seemed – had come out of their houses to greet me. The children were especially excited and screamed for their photograph to be taken.

The road inland was little more than a bumpy dirt track and it took over two hours to ride just twelve miles, to reach the town of Alas, at the end of a very long day. Here I was again greeted by waving locals, who shouted encouragement as I rode into their town. It seemed that I was at last now discovering the 'real' Indonesia, away from the influences of mass tourism. The only hotel in Alas was a simple guesthouse next to the bus terminal. To my delight, the bus terminal turned into a lively night market that evening, and it was not long before I was able to track down a stall selling 'gado-gado'!

In the morning I set off on the bumpy road towards Sumbawa Besa, which is one of the two main towns on the island. The road runs from east to west, and is the only main road on the island, so at least there was little chance of getting lost! Great relief came when, after a few miles, the bumpy, pot-holed highway suddenly turned into a perfectly smooth, newly-laid tarmac strip. This was to continue all the way to Sumbawa Besa, with just the occasional gap (presumably to remind travellers how lucky they were!). With the sun beating down from a clear blue sky, I rode along in the best of spirits. The island of Sumbawa is sparsely populated and, once clear of the towns, there was very little sign of human habitation – quite a contrast to Java and Bali! The road followed the northern coast of the island and there were some fantastic views of Mount Rinjani, across the water on Lombok Island. It was a majestic sight, and I felt adequately compensated for hardly catching a glimpse of this giant volcano while on Lombok itself!

Reaching Sumbawa Besa, I quickly found lodgings and went in search of food. A market seller 'saw me coming' and tried to overcharge me outrageously for a bowl of fried rice, which annoyed me greatly as everyone else that I had met on the island so far had been so welcoming. She backed down with a smile, however, when I calmly asked her to come up with a sensible price!

The road east wound its way through some rugged hill country. It was a solitary ride, although there were a few tiny roadside settlements, where I was spurred on by shouts of 'Hello Mister!'

The small junction town of Empang marked the halfway point of my ride across the island, and there were lodgings to be found here. While taking my usual evening stroll, I noticed that a sizeable crowd had gathered in the market square. It did not take me long to discover the cause of the commotion – two more cycle tourists had arrived in town!

The new arrivals were Mike and Kilmany - a Canadian couple that had been on the road for several months now. They were as surprised to see me as I was to see them in this remote town in the middle of one of Indonesia's least-visited islands. Assuming that we were all together, the locals were directing them to my hotel where – they insisted – a friend was waiting! It was a funny situation, and I certainly enjoyed the unexpected company that evening.

My new companions were travelling in the same direction as me, so we rode together the next day. The pace was a little slow, with the Canadians favouring a multiple pit-stop strategy, but we gradually made our way over a ridge of mountains into the eastern part of the island. By the time that we reached the town of Dompu, it was late into the evening and our food supplies had long been exhausted. The guesthouses here were surprisingly expensive, but we were able to save money by sharing a room together for the night.

From Dompu it was a leisurely ride along the coast to the larger town of Bima. We stopped in one lovely seaside spot for a rest, but were frequently disturbed as virtually every vehicle that passed stopped to find out why we had stopped! In Bima we checked into the cheap and cheerful Losman Komodo, which was situated right next to the old Sultan's Palace. Here we were to stay for a couple of days, while waiting for the twice-weekly ferry to Komodo from the nearby terminal.

On my way to the night market for some supper, that evening, I walked passed a large open tent where some kind of gathering was taking place. Noticing that

I had stopped, a couple of those nearest the entrance invited me in. A space was made for me on the grass and refreshments laid in front of me. Attention was focused on a group of dancers in extravagant costumes that were performing with great passion at the front of the tent. It was explained to me that this dance was a kind of prayer, which was being offered in preparation for a circumcision ceremony, which would be taking place the following evening. Apparently, a young descendent of Sumbawa's last Sultan – who died in 1942 – was to be circumcised. On my departure, I was invited to attend the main ceremony the following night.

At about the same time the following evening, I duly returned with Mike and Kilmany. The proceedings began with a small procession, as the main participants entered the arena, wearing traditional costumes. At the head of the procession was a small boy of ten years, who showed no obvious signs of trepidation at what was to come. A group of four young girls, wearing bright red dresses, stepped forward to perform a slow, sombre, dance. An old man sitting next to me whispered that this dance was especially popular in the Sultan's times. The boy then bravely stepped behind a screen and there was silence for about fifteen minutes, as the operation was apparently being performed. A few readings from the Koran followed, and we were all served with light refreshments to round off a rather strange evening!

The following morning we loaded up and rode thirty miles or so to the island's eastern port of Sape. This last stretch was quite mountainous and took us most of the day. Passing through one mountain village, we were chased by a group of about thirty children – all screaming and waving knives (in a friendly way of course!). They kept up with us for a couple of miles, before reluctantly giving up the chase. We stopped briefly to reward their efforts by taking some photographs of them. This cheering mob of knife-waving children on the hillside would be my lasting memory of Sumbawa.

Every available space was accounted for on the 'Sumbawa to Flores' ferry, as we pulled out of the tiny harbour at Sape. We were seated cross-legged on the floor of the cargo deck, next to an ex-paratrooper from Aldershot and his Danish wife. He was also a keen cyclist, and admitted to feeling envious when he saw us boarding the ferry with our bikes. Much of the seven-hour passage was spent chatting with them and the time passed quickly, despite the cramped conditions.

Eventually, we passed close to Komodo Island, which is famous for its unique species of giant lizard, known as the Komodo Dragon. Most of the Westerners aboard the ferry were due to land here, so we halted about a mile from the coast. This was as close as the big ferry could get, due to shallow waters around the island, and a much smaller boat was waiting to transport us to the shore. About fifty passengers climbed down into the small boat, to be packed closely together on the floor of the vessel. The three bicycles were then lifted down onto the roof of the captain's cabin. Last to board were the Canadians and myself, and we had to perch precariously on the side of the boat for the short voyage.

The waves were riding high, as we made for the shore, and our little ferry rocked from side to side. At times it seemed certain to capsize, but somehow we made it to the rickety wooden pier that protruded from the shoreline. Unloading was a delicate operation, as we had to climb out one by one from alternate sides, in order to prevent the vessel from capsizing. Finally, the bikes were hauled up onto the pier, and the landing was complete.

We had landed on a sandy bay, enclosed by dark, rugged, barren hills – seemingly suitable terrain for dragons! Komodo Island is inhabited by only around one hundred people, and the only accommodation available to us was a government tourist camp. The camp consisted of thirty small wooden cabins, and one larger one, which served as a restaurant. All the huts were perched on stilts, so as to prevent unwelcome intrusions from the dragons.

The Camp Supervisor was in a foul mood, apparently because everyone had been complaining about the exorbitant cabin fees. When Kilmany politely asked if the three of us would be able to camp, he boiled over completely! He shouted that it was far too dangerous to camp and we would have to sleep on the floor of the Administration Hut, as there were no cabins left. This, as we later discovered, was untrue, but his feelings had been hurt and he seemed to want to punish us in some way

The arrangement suited us fine, as we would not be charged for sleeping in the Administration Hut. Mike and Kilmany set up their free-standing tent on the veranda, while I laid my sleeping mat on the floor inside. The only furniture in the hut was a wardrobe and a desk, and I received a nasty surprise when a snake popped its head out of a small hole in the wardrobe. I was beginning to realise why these quarters had been allocated to us, but the wardrobe was locked and the snake securely imprisoned, so there was no need to worry too much!

In the evening, everyone gathered in the large restaurant hut for dinner. There was some alarm at the huge number of rats that scurried along the rafters above us - occasionally dropping down on or near the tables as we were eating. This was one of those wild places that you sometimes dream about, but never realised actually exist on this planet!

Another large group of tourists arrived by charter boat the following morning. This meant that seventy-five of us – all armed with cameras – were gathered together for the grand safari. We were to be accompanied by eleven rangers – each armed with a big stick – and a live goat, which was to be slaughtered and fed to the dragons.

The Komodo Dragons belong to a group called monitor lizards. There were over three thousand of them on Komodo Island, and they apparently exist nowhere else in the world – except for a few on the nearby islands of Rinca and Flores. The Camp Supervisor – who doubled as Chief Guide – confidently informed us that they do not have their origins in pre-historic times, as is widely believed. He also warned us of the dangers of straying away from the trail – pointing to a small wooden cross, erected in memory of a German girl, who had been eaten alive the previous year.

It was a twenty-minute march to the feeding area, and we encountered one five-foot dragon along the way. Its skin was scaly, with small ridges along the centre of its back. Its appearance was most dragon-like, as if it had fallen straight out of a child's story book. The giant lizard seemed quite tame, however, as it ambled along slowly just a few feet away from us.

The feeding area consisted of a large pit, around which dragons of various sizes – the biggest perhaps ten feet long – were lumbering about fairly aimlessly. It was as though we had been transported back to the dinosaur age! The rangers ushered us all into a large pen, while keeping the animals at bay with their sticks.

With everyone safely enclosed, the screaming goat was then slaughtered, without ceremony, and slung into the pit, where four or five of the larger dragons were eagerly waiting. Next followed the gruesome spectacle of them fighting over and devouring the goat. The two largest dragons were having a tugging match with the main carcass, while the others were biting away at whichever part they could reach. This feeding session took place twice a week, apparently, in order to provide 'entertainment' for the tourists.

Back at the camp, most people seemed satisfied that the morning excursion had made their visit to the island worthwhile. With the big ferry not due to pass by until the following day, people divided into groups and chartered private boats for the four-hour trip to Flores. The Canadians and myself, however, decided to stay on Komodo for another night.

With most of the tourists now gone, the island seemed very peaceful. We spent the remainder of the day swimming in the crystal clear ocean, and exploring the area around the camp. Two baby dragons actually wandered onto the camp grounds in the evening, and ambled around the huts for several hours. They seemed quite tame, but we did not venture too close! There was also a wild boar and several deer for company, including one that we named Roy, for reasons that I cannot recall.

In the morning we enlisted one of the rangers as a guide, and returned to the feeding pit. We saw just as many dragons as the previous day, and it made us wonder why the need for the barbaric stunt with the goat.

Later on, we boarded the small ferry again to meet up with the big Flores-bound ferry that was due to pass by that afternoon. It was a great relief when the big ferry came into view, as we had been bobbing around at the meeting point for a couple of hours, and I was feeling quite seasick. The deckhands took great delight in rising to the challenge of hauling our loaded up bikes up onto the ship, and our little adventure on Komodo Island was over.

On the ferry we met a tall German cycle tourist named Olaf, who had been riding for almost a year on a rather unusual bicycle. The frame was designed with a cross right in its centre, which created extra strength, he explained. This was probably just as well, because he was carrying an enormous load.

We landed on Flores Island, at the small port of Labuahan Bajo. Olaf went off to camp in the local schoolyard, while I shared a room with Mike and Kilmany at Losman Sony, on a hill overlooking the harbour. I would have preferred to go with Olaf to the schoolyard, but had not yet been able to replace the camping gear that was lost in Pakistan. Fortunately the Canadian couple seemed happy for me to tag along with them.

Flores is a mountainous island and its roads were reputed to be the worst in Indonesia. In view of this, my Canadian friends opted to travel by bus - at least as far as the town of Ruteng, seventy-five miles inland. Preferring to cycle, I set off at the first light of dawn, in order to give myself a decent chance of reaching Ruteng before nightfall. Before long, I caught up with Olaf, who had been well looked after by the local schoolmaster. He had managed to set off even earlier than me, but had had to resort to pushing his heavily laden bicycle up the first long steep climb of the day. He was not intending to reach Ruteng that day so, not having the luxury of a tent, I pushed on ahead. An hour or so later, an overtaking truck pulled over in front of me, and I recognised Olaf's bike in the back. Olaf himself was sitting comfortably in the cab, and the driver offered me a lift as well. I was enjoying the ride through this lush, mountainous terrain, however, and the road surface was not too bad, so I declined the offer

On my first long descent of the day, it finally happened - I crashed! Rounding a bend, my front wheel skidded on a patch of loose gravel and I was sent flying over the handlebars. I landed on my chin, chipping one of my front teeth, but apart from that it was just cuts and grazes. The bicycle was undamaged as well, so I dusted myself down and climbed back on, rather gingerly.

The descent brought me down into a village called Majawa, nestling in the valley below. Olaf's truck ride had terminated here and I spotted his bicycle straight away, by the entrance to a roadside café. There were a few startled looks as I ambled into the café, not least from Olaf himself, and I realised that my injuries must have looked worse than they felt. A woman came running with a bowl of water to wash the blood away, and apply dressings to some of the abrasions. I then had lunch at the café with Olaf, who had decided to make camp in this village for the night.

Still determined to try and make it to Ruteng that day, I set off again early in the afternoon. However, the road out of the valley was incredibly steep, and it soon became apparent that I may have taken on a little too much. The road condition deteriorated rapidly, to little more than a gravel track, and I was managing barely five miles an hour.

By 6pm, the sun was disappearing behind the mountains, and I finally had to accept that there was no chance of making it to Ruteng before dark. It would be far too dangerous to try and ride on these narrow mountain roads in the dark, especially without lights. The only option was to try and flag down a passing truck, so I chose a suitably visible spot and settled down to wait. Within a few minutes a truck appeared, and the driver was happy to carry me the final eleven miles to Ruteng. He was also able to recommend a hotel, and set me down at the entrance. Soon after my arrival, the

Canadians turned up, having taken the afternoon bus from Lubuan Bajo. It was great to see them again at the end of an eventful day!

Lying at an altitude of 1100 metres, Ruteng is a pleasantly cool mountain settlement, surrounded by green hills and terraced rice paddies. Mike and Kilmany set off the in the morning, having decided to give the cycling a go, while I decided to spend the day here recovering from my exertions of the previous day.

The following morning, I rode on through the mountains towards the coastal village of Borong. The ride was mostly downhill, but it was tough going because the road was little more than a bumpy, muddy track. The worst part was a ten-mile stretch where sharp edged rocks had been used to corrugate the track, so that it would still be usable during the rainy season. Although it was an uncomfortable ride, the superb tropical scenery provided ample compensation, as I looked out over great expanses of green terraced rice paddies, covering the mountainsides all the way to the ocean. In the distance, I could even make out the outline of the island's most famous volcano – Kelimutu.

Arriving in Borong, I was greeted by some of the village children, who eagerly led me to the only guesthouse in the village. Already in residence were the Canadians, who had reached Borong the previous night. The terrible road surface had confirmed to them that this was not an island for cycling, and they had been waiting at the village bus stop all day for a bus to take them back up into the mountains to Bajawa. It had been a frustrating day for them, however, because all the passing buses had been full, and they were now resigned to another night in Borong.

In the morning, Mike and Kilmany joined me again for the ride to Bajawa. They had decided that the ride could not be worse than another day of waiting at the bus stop! Before long, however, we encountered yet more appalling road conditions, and had to walk much of the way over the rocky surface. It was quite exhausting, with the sun beating down from a cloudless sky, and it was some relief to reach the mountain village of Aijmere for lunch. As we were eating, a half-empty bus pulled up temptingly in front of us. It was bound for the eastern port of Ende, and it did not take Mike and Kilmany long to make up their minds. Their bikes were soon loaded onto the bus, and we parted company for the final time.

Ahead of me was a twenty-five mile climb to Bajawa. To my relief, the road surface improved considerably after Aijmere, and I was able to find a good climbing rhythm. Just before dark, I finally made it to Bajawa, after nine hours in the saddle. It was no problem to find lodgings in this sizeable town, and I just about had enough strength left to take a shower and eat a bowl of noodles before falling into bed. Riding across Flores was proving quite a challenge, but the worst was surely behind me now.

My legs were still aching when I awoke the next morning. It would have been nice to rest for a day here in the sleepy mountain town of Bajawa but, with only a few days left on my Indonesian visa, it was necessary to press on. My final destination on Flores was the port of Ende, some seventy miles away. The journey would be mostly downhill, so I did not think it would be too hard to get there in a day. This was to be my final cycling day on the journey between England and Australia, because from Ende I planned to catch the twice-weekly ferry to the island of Timor, from where I would fly directly to Darwin.

The day did not go quite according to plan however. Having cycled just a few miles from Bajawa, I noticed that my front tyre was about to burst. It must have been damaged on the rocky road surfaces, and I judged it highly unlikely that it could last all the way to Ende. If it burst on one of the steep descents, I might not make to Ende at all! While I was standing there trying to decide whether to risk a nasty accident by riding any further (I was not carrying a spare at this time), a bus that was bound for Ended pulled up behind me. Though clearly full, the driver took one look at my front tyre and insisted that there was room for me. The bike was tied onto the back of the bus, while I squashed into a small space that had been made for me on the back seat.

The bus moved slowly over the bumpy mountain road, and it was certainly not a comfortable journey. Through the mass of bodies around me, I caught occasional glimpses of a spectacular landscape that was dominated by a huge smoking volcano, which popped up regularly on either side of the bus, as we wound our way through the mountains. At one point, the back wheels of the bus got stuck in some muddy potholes, so we all had to get out and push!

Several hours later, we finally arrived in Ende. My search for lodgings seemed destined to end in failure, as each guesthouse that I tried was full. Apparently most visitors to Flores base themselves in Ende, in order to visit the famous Kelimutu Volcano nearby. However, I finally got a bed for the night when I was overheard at one hotel reception by an American geologist, named Jim, who was engaged on a three-month research project on the island. He had a spacious twin room at the hotel, and insisted that there was plenty of room for me, and even the bicycle!

The Timor ferry was not due to leave for a couple of days, allowing the opportunity for an excursion to

Kelimutu. This volcano is particularly famous for its three crater lakes, which are known to change colour from season to season. I learned that the best way to appreciate this natural wonder was to stay at the foothill village of Mone, and set off from there on a special bus which departed from Mone at four-o-clock each morning, in order to reach the crater by daybreak. The following evening, having left the bike, and the bulk of my luggage, with Jim, I set off on a local bus for Mone.

The tiny village consisted mainly of a string of backpacker hostels and guesthouses, all of which were 'full to bursting'. Eventually, I managed to negotiate for myself a rope bed in the kitchen of one of the guesthouses. This arrangement seemed fine for one short night, although I was forced to revise this assessment of the situation on being awoken after just a few minutes sleep by a small army of tiny rats! It was the last time that I would be bedding down in a kitchen in this part of the world!

It was standing room only on the 4am special bus service, but I was just glad to be out of the rat-infested kitchen. The road to the crater was amazingly smooth for Flores – it was apparently laid especially for a visit of the President of Indonesia, a few years previously. After being deposited close to the summit, I marched with a group of bleary-eyed backpackers to the lookout point, and settled down to wait for the sunrise. As the sun rose, the three crater lakes gradually came into view. On this morning the lakes were coloured light green, dark green and black, which made for quite a spectacle, and there was a general consensus that it was well worth the early start.

The walk back down to Mone was very pleasant, with sweeping views across the valley and all the way down to the ocean. About halfway down, hillside farmers directed some of us onto a very steep track, which would cut about three miles off the walk. The track was a bit too steep for me, however, and it was not long before I fell headlong into prickly bush!

Stumbling back into Mone, with my fresh collection of cuts and grazes, even the backpackers were staring at me as if I had just landed from another planet!

The ferry crossing from Ende to Kupang, in West Timor, was scheduled to take twenty hours. Boarding the ferry three hours early in order to secure a seat for this marathon voyage turned out to be a wise move, as the boat was already filling up fast. The sight of this huge ferry making its twice-weekly departure was obviously one of the highlights of the week in Ende, as hundreds of islanders had gathered on the pier to wave us off.

There were few Westerners among the several hundred passengers, although I did recognise a Dutch couple. They were touring Indonesia themselves, and we had already bumped into each other several times previously. We shared a bench and chatted for most of the journey, as well as exchanging reading matter. When night came there was very little space for lying down, but I managed to slide underneath the bench for a few hours sleep, allowing my friends some more room on the bench. It was an uncomfortable night, but everyone's spirits were lifted when a beautiful sunrise signalled daybreak. As we neared the shores of Timor, we were even treated to the sight of a school of dolphins swimming in the wake of the ferry.

With only a few days left on my Indonesian visa, there would be little time for exploring in West Timor. My first port of call was the Merpati Airlines office, where I was informed that all flights to Darwin were fully booked for the next six weeks. However, they put me on a standby list for the next flight, with an assurance that there were usually plenty of spare seats.

My last few days in Indonesia were spent soaking up the sun at the Taman Ria Beach Inn, a few miles outside Kupang. It was a sociable and relaxing place, which was just what I needed at this time. A strange inertia had come over me, and I did not feel my usual sense of enthusiasm for exploring the local surrounds. Indonesia is a truly beautiful place, with a fascinating culture, but I had seen enough for now.

Arriving at the airport in plenty of time, I found that there were at least ten others on the standby list. It was just half an hour before take-off when it was finally confirmed that there would be room for all of us. It had been quite a nerve-wracking wait, and I was relieved to have escaped the hassles that may have been entailed by overstaying my visa. All of a sudden, Australia was just an hour and a half away.

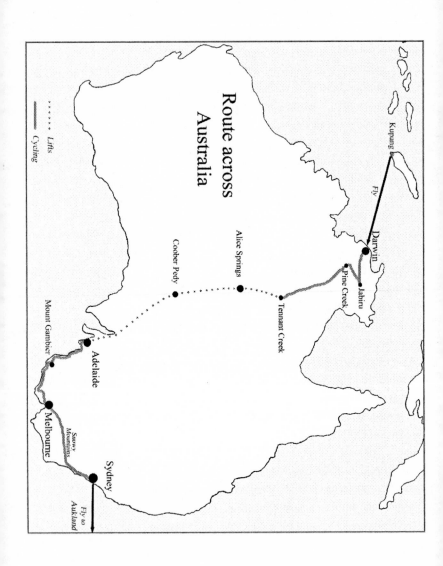

Route across
Australia

Kupang

Fly

Darwin

Jabiru

Pine Creek

Tenant Creek

Alice Springs

Coober Pedy

Mount Gambier

Adelaide

Melbourne

Snowy
Mountains

Sydney

Fly to
Aukland

······ Lifts

—— Cycling

CHAPTER SIX

INTO THE OUTBACK

Darwin to Sydney

HAVING BOARDED THE PLANE AT SUCH SHORT notice in Timor, it seemed just a matter of moments before the northern coastline of Australia came into view – a long jagged line stretching east and west to each horizon. Behind that line was a huge chunk of land known as the Northern Territory, or the 'Top End'. The vast, sun-baked plains below were coloured a mixture of deep reds and purples. On a small peninsula, jutting slightly out into the ocean, a cluster of white buildings could only be Darwin. As we flew closer, it became clear that the suburbs actually covered quite a large area. It was strange to think, however, that this bright-looking town, with a population of just over seventy thousand, was the largest settlement for a thousand miles in any direction.

Coming in to land, I was able to pick out a thin straight line leading south from Darwin across the desert - the Stuart Highway, or 'The Track', as the natives call it. Australians seem to have a nickname for everything! This historic road stretches two thousand miles across Australia to Adelaide on the south coast. It was named after an early explorer – John Stuart – who made one of the first south-to-north crossings of the country. I would be seeing plenty more of that highway over the coming weeks.

Being used to Asian prices now, the large Darwin Youth Hostel seemed very expensive. However, it was a comfortable place and the dormitory charge, of fifteen Australian dollars per night, included a free meal at the nearby Victoria Pub, so it was good value really.

Darwin is a modern city, which seems to have recovered well from the Japanese bombs, which nearly wiped it out during World War II, not to mention Cyclone Tracy, which had a similar effect in 1974. Much of the city was constructed after Cyclone Tracy and has been neatly planned, with tree-lined streets and attractive green parks. It was nice to wander around on that first evening without being constantly stared at or shouted at, and I began to appreciate that this was a completely new stage of my journey. Though I would miss the warmth of the Asian people and their rich cultures, it was some relief to be fairly anonymous again! My walking tour ended at the Victoria Pub, where I joined the long queue of backpackers that were waiting for their evening meal. This turned out to be quite a treat, as I had not tasted 'pie and mash' for a very long time!

Ten days passed very quickly in Darwin, as I grew accustomed again to the comforts of Western living, such as toilet paper! There was a good mix of travelling characters at the hostel, including a middle-aged Englishman named Midge, who was resting up after spending six months driving around the remoter parts of Australia. Prior to this, he had given up his job as a youth worker, due to stress, and it seems that his journey through the outback had been the perfect tonic for this.

With my travel funds now almost depleted, I arrived at the C.E.S. (Commonwealth Employment Service) early one morning to join a crowd of people that were queuing for casual labour. The doors opened at 7.30am and we were all registered. By 10am, however, no work had been found for anyone and people gradually started to drift away. Some that I spoke to told me that this was the usual pattern of events, and that the job situation in Darwin was worse than ever. Eventually, a few people at the front of the queue were given some work for the day, and the rest of us were told to go home. It seemed that my chances of earning money in Darwin were slim.

There was more success when it came to replacing the camping gear that I had lost on arrival in Pakistan, some eight months before. Darwin is the last stop in Australia for travellers that are heading north to Asia, and many of them are looking to shed excess luggage – particularly camping gear that may be of limited use in Asia. After trawling the hostel notice boards, I was able to purchase an excellent tent, a petrol stove and a large rear pannier - all for less than a hundred Australian dollars. I also gave the bike a good service, and replaced some of the parts that were starting to wear out.

Perhaps the highlight of my stay in Darwin was an evening visit to the weekly international market, held at Mindil Beach. There was an impressive array of food, clothes and handicrafts from all over the world. Local bands provided the entertainment and the evening sun turned the whole sky red, as I ate my supper on the beach.

With the job situation in Darwin looking so bleak, I resolved to travel south on the Stuart Highway to Alice Springs and try my luck there. Riding across the desert would be quite a challenge, and different to anything that I had experienced before. An Australian backpacker in the hostel dormitory did his best to put me off the idea, by telling me that I was crazy to even consider such a boring and uncomfortable ride. However, I wanted to experience the vastness and harsh isolation of the Australian Outback, and there can be few better ways to do this than to cycle across it.

My load was heavier than ever on departure from Darwin, on a hot Bank Holiday morning. For a start, I was carrying about eight litres of water – mainly in plastic cordial bottles – which would, hopefully, be enough to last me until evening. The Darwin Tourist Office had informed me that there was water available from roadhouses or water tanks at least every seventy miles between Darwin and Alice Springs, so I calculated on being able to obtain water every evening. Opportunities to purchase food would be less frequent, so I packed a five-day supply of basic food supplies. My recently acquired camping gear increased the load further, as it was considerably heavier than the super-lightweight equipment that I had used in Europe. My roommates at the hostel were convinced that it would be impossible to fit all this gear on the bike, but somehow I managed!

The pedals seemed to turn very slowly at first, as I made my way through the sprawling suburbs of Darwin. Once clear of the city, however, it was easy to build up momentum across the pancake-flat terrain. It was not long though before the first 'road-train' came hurtling past, reminding me that some caution was necessary even on this quiet desert highway. 'Road-trains' consist of three trucks joined together, and are only allowed to travel on the Outback highways. The driver had pulled right over to the other side of the road before overtaking me, but the tail-end truck swished around sufficiently to give me some cause for concern!

Twenty miles south of Darwin, I turned onto the newly laid Arnhem Highway, leading to the Kakadu National Park, 120 miles to the east. From there it would be possible to return on the Old Kakadu Highway, which joined up with the Stuart Highway again at the small town of Pine Creek, further south. It was a big detour that would add several days to my journey, but I could not leave the 'Top End' without visiting Australia's most famous National Park.

The smooth, straight Arnhem Highway cut like an arrow across a rugged, tropical wilderness, which was teeming with wildlife. In particular, there were all kinds of weird and wonderful bird species - some of which I had certainly not seen before. By lunchtime, I had already drunk six litres of water and realised that it would be necessary to carry even more in future. Fortunately, I was able to refill the bottles at the tiny settlement of Humpty Doo. There was a lot of holiday traffic on the highway, mostly heading back towards Darwin as the Bank Holiday weekend drew to a close, and most of the drivers acknowledged me with a wave or the occasional shout of encouragement.

Late in the afternoon, I reached the Mary River Crossing, where there was a small picnic area, which would make an ideal camping spot. Nearby was the Bark Hut Inn, where I was able to refill my water bottles again and take a shower, before returning to my riverside camp. Some of the locals at the Inn warned me not to swim in the river as it was full of 'big salties' (crocodiles)! With this being the dry season there was little chance of rain, so there was no need to set up the tent. I cooked my dinner over a small campfire, and the smoke from this was enough to keep the mosquitoes at bay. As it turned dark, I lay down on my sleeping mat and spent the rest of the evening gazing at the clear desert sky, which was full of more stars than I had ever seen before.

Despite setting off from my camp soon after dawn, it seemed like no time at all before the early morning sun began to beat down from a cloudless sky. Riding further east, towards Kakadu, an interesting new feature appeared on the landscape. Dotted about in fairly random fashion were several huge mounds of mud, known as 'magnetic anthills'. Apparently these were built by white termites and are always constructed on a precise north-south axis!

Two large stone slabs marked the entrance to Kakadu National Park. A plaque on one of the stones proudly declared that, in 1981, this Park became the first place in Australia to be added to the UNESCO list of world heritage and cultural sites. A smaller signpost nearby warned of the danger of crocodiles! The Park is essentially an enormous wildlife sanctuary, covering some 7,720 square miles. Its boundaries also protect a large system of rivers and creeks, as well as a rich Aboriginal heritage extending back to the earliest days of human existence.

Late that afternoon, I reached the Kakadu Holiday Village, by the South Alligator River Crossing, which was the first of several major holiday complexes within the Park. Another scorching hot day had left me drained of energy, and the lure of the swimming pool and Jacuzzi facilities was too much too resist! As well as being packed with holidaymakers, the camp seemed to be inhabited by a baby alligator, which strolled by as I was setting up my tent. The owner of the complex – a rugged old bushman called John – had invited me to join him and his wife, Minnie, for drinks that evening. Minnie was English, he explained, and would love to meet me. We ended up chatting late into the evening and they were able to pass on much useful advice, having travelled widely in Australia before choosing to settle in the Northern Territory. They also insisted that I should stay at the camp free of charge.

John had informed me that there were over 280 bird species inhabiting the Park, and that the best time to see them was at dawn, so I was up at first light the following morning. A stroll through the tropical rainforest surrounding the camp brought me to a large pond (known as a 'billabong' in these parts). There were several wallabies grazing around the billabong, as well as magpie geese, jacanas, kites and a sharp-beaked species known as darters. Back at the camp, the rest of the day was spent relaxing and chatting with some of the holidaymaking couples and families. Most of them were Australian and I was surprised at their readiness to furnish me with their home addresses - just in case I should find myself in their area!

John tried to persuade me to stay longer, but one day's rest was enough for me. Heading on towards the central area of the Park, I soon caught up with two young German cyclists that were just starting out on a six-month tour of Australia. We rode together to the Park Headquarters at the village of Jabiru, which is named after a large stork-like bird, which patronises the area. At Jabiru we were pleasantly surprised to find a well-stocked supermarket! After a picnic lunch with the Germans, I left them behind, as it seemed certain to take them the rest of the afternoon to figure out how to fit all of the food that they had just bought onto their bicycles!

The Arnhem Highway ends at Jabiru, so from here I turned onto the Old Kakadu Highway, which runs in a south-westerly direction towards Pine Creek. That night I camped at Muirella Park, which was formerly a safari camp for the first Europeans that visited Kakadu. Camp entertainment was provided by one of the National Park Rangers, who gave a talk and slide-show on the history of Kakadu right up to the present day. There were pictures of these early European visitors, who were mainly engaged in hunting crocodiles and buffalo for their hides and horns. Buffalo were still being hunted today, the Ranger told us, but this was due to a Government eradication program designed to limit the spread of tuberculosis.

From my base at Muirella, I visited Nourlangie Rock. This is a remnant of an ancient plateau that is slowly eroding away, leaving sheer cliffs that rise sharply above the floodplain. Arriving at Nourlangie, I discreetly attached myself to a group of British tourists that were about to embark on a guided tour. We walked around the base of the Rock, examining pictures that had been painted onto the rock-face – some of them more than a thousand years old. The more recent ones were simply painted on top of the older ones, as was the Aboriginal custom. One of the most intricate paintings depicted Namarrgon – the 'Lightning Man' – on whom many legends are based. With our tour of the gallery complete, the group were whisked away by minibus to another of Kakadu's highlights, while I made a short hike to the superbly-named Ambangbang Billabong, which lies at the foot of Nawarlandja Rock. Gathered at this idyllic spot were many of the unique bird species that reside in the Park, such as the distinctive jacanas and jabirus. From the top of Nawarlandja Rock, there was a panoramic view of Nourlangie and the forested plains surrounding it. Far away in the distance was a range of hills, which are known by the Aboriginals as 'Lightning Dreaming' – the home of Namarrgon.

Early the next morning, as the first rays of sunlight were shimmering on the floodplains and billabongs, I rode a short distance south to the campsite at Coinda, close to the Yellow Waters Billabong. The boat cruises on Yellow Waters were reputed to be 'unmissable', so I booked onto a late afternoon cruise.

The cruise certainly lived up to expectations. Yellow Waters Billabong snakes its way across a huge floodplain. Besides the numerous species of bird-life – all expertly identified by our Captain - we saw several saltwater crocodiles. Some were lazily sunning themselves on the banks, while others swam tantalisingly close to us. Arriving back at the jetty, a wonderful tour came to an end, as the setting sun turned the whole sky a deep orange colour.

Setting off from Coinda at dawn, I rode just seven miles further on the Old Kakadu Highway before the bitumen ended and the road was reduced to a gravel track. It was tough-going from here, particularly on the long stretches that were corrugated (which meant that metal bars had been laid across the road, beneath the gravel, so that the road would still be usable during the rainy season). I had to ride slowly over the ridges, enabling the flies to reach maximum irritation levels as they swarmed around me. The National Park was behind me now and it seemed that I would have to endure this torturous road for a hundred miles or so, before rejoining the Stuart Highway at Pine Creek.

Having bumped along the old highway for a couple of hours, the inevitable puncture occurred! The sun was blistering by now, so I pushed the bike a hundred yards or so to a clump of trees, providing in a tiny bit of shade for the repair to be carried out. As I was working on this, a battered old camper van pulled over. The four 'hippies' – two male and two female - that climbed out of the van were in a slightly drunken and dishevelled state, but seemed eager to help. They came from Darwin and had been touring the 'Top End' for a couple of weeks now. Having satisfied themselves that I was in control of things, they left me with the parting gift of a couple of cans of beer. The old van back-fired a couple of times as they slowly rolled away into the distance.

My original plan was to camp at the Mary River Roadhouse that evening, where I would be able to replenish my water supplies. However, as the afternoon wore on, it became clear that it would not be possible to get there before dark. 'Plan B' was to make a short detour off the highway to Barramundi Gorge where, apparently, the water was free flowing and safe to drink.

Barramundi Gorge was actually situated eight miles south of the highway, along a sandy 4WD track. Much of this had to be walked, as the sand was too deep to cycle through, so it was not such a short detour after all! It was worth the effort, however, because the Gorge was a beautifully secluded spot, with crystal clear, crocodile-free, waters fed by a gushing waterfall. After a refreshing swim, I set up camp in a small clearing close to the water's edge, which was already occupied by a large 'road-home' belonging to a family from Queensland. They were on a year-long tour of Australia, and the two young children were getting "the best education they could ever have" before they were even old enough to attend school! Why let the small matter of having a young family prevent you from making the journey of a lifetime?

The Queenslanders treated me to a terrific breakfast in the morning. They were planning to spend a couple of days fishing at the Gorge, so I left them there and set about pushing the bike back along the sandy track to the highway. It was strenuous work and when I finally reached the bumpy Old Kakadu Highway again, it seemed like a motorway in comparison! Back in the saddle, I trundled slowly along towards Pine Creek. It was not long before I reached the first of two river crossings. There was no bridge and the river literally flowed across the road! Fortunately - with the dry season well underway – the river was not too deep and it was quite easy to push the bike through.

The Mary River Roadhouse was an oasis of civilisation in the wilderness. The barman informed me that the Old Kakadu Highway was paved between here and Pine Creek. As I was celebrating this welcome news with a rather expensive sandwich, my 'hippie' friends rolled up in their instantly recognisable old van. They appeared to be sustaining themselves on a diet of mainly beer, and invited me to share a drink with them before heading off.

As promised, the gravel soon turned into bitumen, and I was able to ride fast enough to reach Pine Creek just before nightfall. There was a Youth Hostel at Pine Creek, but it took me some time to gain access. The manager was a rugged old man called Ron, who had lived in this outback town all his life. He looked after the hostel on a voluntary basis and had already locked up for the night, as there were no guests. On hearing my knocking, however, he ushered me in and told me to make myself at home. My clothes and camping gear were quite filthy, after a week of camping in Kakadu, so I decided to check in for a couple of nights, in order to wash the clothes and prepare for the long ride south.

Pine Creek began as a small mining community in the 1870s. Some of the old machinery used for mining was on display in a field behind the hostel, where an information board provided a brief history of the community. There was not much else to see in the town, however, which is probably why there was nobody else at the hostel! Ron was never far away though, so I spent much of the time chatting with him as he pottered around. He was a friendly old chap but - like many of the 'older generation' Australians that I had met so far – had a strongly nationalistic attitude. This was revealed mainly by his tendency to criticise others on the grounds that they were 'not from the Northern Territory' or, even worse, 'not Australian'. This was a trait that I would notice throughout my journey across Australia, and which was already starting to become quite annoying. He stopped short at having a go at 'Pommies', presumably out of politeness!

Although Ron was a little overbearing at times, he could not have been more helpful, and I am indebted to him for suggesting the addition of one valuable piece of equipment to my kit. On hearing that I was having trouble carrying sufficient water on the bike to last me through the day, he pulled the bladder out of an empty wine box and plonked it in front of me. This bladder would carry five litres and could easily be strapped onto the back of the bike, giving me the extra capacity required. It was a wonderfully simple solution, and later on I would discover another use for the wine box bladder. If you fill it up with water and hang it upside down from a tree, you have a functional, tap-controlled, shower!

It should have been an easy ride down to Katherine – just sixty miles south across flat terrain on the flat, smooth Stuart Highway. However, a strong headwind blew across the plains all day, making life difficult. Far away in the distance, a small dot on the road ahead gradually grew larger, as a cycle tourist approached from the south. He was the first Italian cycle tourist that I had met, and had cycled across the desert from the Queensland coast. He cheerfully went on to inform me that he had been riding with a strong following wind ever since joining the Stuart Highway at Tennants Creek, some five hundred miles south. As I was travelling in the opposite direction, this was not good news for me at all!

Progress was painfully slow and I stopped frequently to get my breath back. At one of these rest stops, a Melbourne couple pulled in behind me in their 'house-on-wheels' camper van. They had done some baking that morning and offered me a large slice of fruitcake with cold orange juice. This was gratefully received, but I did manage to resist their next offer of a lift with them down to Katherine. While we were discussing whether it was sensible to be cycling in these windy conditions, a particularly strong gust of wind caused the heavily laden bike to topple right over! However, Katherine was only twenty miles away now and I was determined to keep riding.

It was a good decision, as it was a wonderful feeling to roll into Katherine early that evening, after battling against the elements for the whole day. The large hostel here was comfortable and full of backpackers – quite a contrast to Pine Creek! The reason for Katherine's popularity with travellers and tourists is that it provides an ideal base for visiting Katherine Gorge National Park – one of Australia's natural wonders.

Deciding on just a day trip to the Park, I packed a lunch and set off early the following morning on a short ride to the Park's main entrance. Before long, the silence of the desert road was broken by the sound of loud hooting and familiar shouts of 'Hey Dave!', as I was overtaken by the four Australian hippies in their old camper van! Instinctively, I made ready to catch a can of beer as it came flying in my direction, but this time they invited me to throw the bike in and spend the day with them. There was not much room in the van, but these easy-going characters were like old friends to me now and they soon made space.

Katherine Gorge National Park consists of a series of thirteen spectacular gorges, created by the force of the Katherine River. We jumped onto a morning cruise that would take us through the first two gorges, which are the most accessible. It was quite an amazing trip, with the sheer canyon wall rising sixty metres above the water in some places. We also saw plenty of wildlife, including a couple of Johnston crocodiles, which are the fresh water variety. Like Kakadu, the area is steeped in Aboriginal heritage, and our guide pointed out several ancient Aboriginal paintings on the rock faces.

On the way back to Katherine, we stopped at some Hot Springs, which was the perfect place to 'mellow out' at the end of a great day. This was to be my last encounter with Mark, Steve, Colleen and Lisa, but I would not forget the welcome sight of their battered old van, bumbling around the 'Top End'.

Back on 'The Track', I was riding into a strong headwind again, towards the next settlement of Mataranka, eighty miles south. The landscape was an unchanging expanse of thick scrubby forest, all the way to the horizon in every direction. The road cut through the bush in a straight line, stretching far way into the distance, and I could see trucks heading towards me several minutes before they actually arrived. A rest area marked the halfway point between Katherine and Mataranka, and I was able to refill my various containers at a large water tank here. Swarms of irritating flies were milling around the tank, probably due to the large cattle trucks that frequently pull in, so I did not linger for too long.

The wind dropped in the afternoon and I was able to reach the small town of Mataranka quite easily. There was once a homestead in this area, which was the subject of the classic novel 'We of the Never Never'. The original homestead no longer exists, but a replica has been built on the site, just five miles east of Mataranka. The evening was still young, so I decided to ride out towards it and try to camp somewhere along the way. On the way, I passed by the Elsey Cemetery, where several of the real life characters, on whom the story was based, lie buried. Just a mile before the homestead, I set up camp in a shady meadow next to a fast-flowing river. It was an ideal camping spot, and there were several other campers already taking advantage of the natural site.

The Elsey Homestead Replica, together with some tropical Hot Springs nearby, formed the centrepiece of a large tourist complex, and I spent the next day relaxing here. Inside the large wooden building were drawings of the main characters from the story and a detailed description of life at the early homestead. To escape the afternoon heat, I joined a group of holidaymakers on the veranda to watch a showing of the film version of the story.

That evening, there was some drama back at the camp. A young man, that had been camping a little downstream, reported that all of his possessions had been stolen from his tent. Someone drove into Mataranka to fetch the local policeman and we were all questioned, apparently to no avail. The general consensus among the campers was that Aborigines must have been committed the crime, although nobody seemed to have any evidence or logical reasoning to support this assumption.

The next settlement marked on the map was Larrimah, fifty-four miles south. With the headwinds mercifully taking a day off, progress was fairly rapid and I arrived early in the afternoon. It was at Larrimah that a railway line from Darwin used to terminate, until it was abandoned after Cyclone Tracy in 1974. Besides the remains of the old railway station, however, there was little here now apart from a roadhouse with a camping area, a pub and a sprinkling of houses. The campground did have the luxury of a swimming pool, though, and the freezing cold water could not have been more refreshing! As evening approached, quite a few travellers pulled onto the campground in their camper vans, and we were soon gathered together around a big campfire. The nights were becoming cooler, as I rode south into the desert, and the fire was needed for warmth, as well as keeping the mosquitoes at bay.

Armed with yet more addresses of people to visit on the East Coast, I set off soon after sunrise, in order to take advantage of the cool early morning hours. The bushy landscape was as unchanging as ever, but the monotony was broken by frequent sightings of various colourful bird species. On one occasion, a swarm of eagles flew overhead, making it hard to believe that they were an endangered species. There were no shady rest areas en-route that day, so I stopped for lunch by the roadside, under the full blaze of the sun. The sun's intensity was quite bearable while riding, as the riding itself creates a breeze but, when stationary, it became extremely uncomfortable!

That evening, I reached the historic settlement of Daly Waters, lying a couple of miles west of the highway. The village boasted a caravan park, a petrol station and the Daly Waters Pub, which was 98 years old – the oldest pub in the Northern Territory. Next to the pub was a set of traffic lights, with an accompanying sign claiming that these were the remotest set of traffic lights in Australia! I am not sure how many tourists were attracted to Daly Waters by the traffic lights, but the caravan-park was pretty full!

For dinner that night, I splashed out on an excellent 'Barramundi Barbecue' at the pub, which made a nice change from the diet of lentil stew and porridge that had kept me going since Darwin. Barramundi is one of the Northern Territory specialities and it tasted delicious. Entertainment was provided by an outback band, playing traditional tunes such as 'Waltzing Matilda', so it was a real Australian evening!

The sun was high in the sky by the time that I made it onto the road in the morning, having consumed a little too much of the 'amber nectar' the previous evening! Fortunately, the next roadhouse at Dunmarra was only thirty-five miles down 'The Track', so there was no rush. On arrival, I set up camp behind the roadhouse, and spent the afternoon reading and drinking coffee in the truckers' café.

After a good sleep and a hearty roadhouse breakfast, I was ready for a longer ride down to the next service area at Elliot. Riding south that day, I noticed that the landscape was starting to become more barren, as the trees thinned out. The sandy desert plains became more visible through the trees, and I began to appreciate for the first time what a vast and empty country this is.

Elliot turned out to be a surprisingly large settlement. With a population of around 600, mostly Aborigines, it actually ranks as the fifth largest town in the Northern Territory! The caravan-park here was quite expensive, so I decided to camp in a public park. This was a bad move, however, because the ground was covered in tiny sharp thorns, causing both of the tyres to puncture almost immediately. There was nothing for it but to return to the caravan-park after all, and spend a therapeutic evening removing the thorns from the tyres!

Riding south from Elliot, the landscape became still more barren. Vegetation was now virtually non-existent, apart from a spiky desert plant known as 'spinifex', which massed itself across the plains. Shade was also virtually non-existent, and I was starting to get quite severe headaches from the sun. That evening, I reached another roadhouse at the tiny settlement of Renner Springs, which lies right on the dividing line between the seasonal wetland of the 'Top End' and the dry, desert 'Red Centre'. A Brisbane couple – Henry and Marie – parked their motor-home next to my tent and invited me for dinner. A fish supper was followed by prunes and custard, which was a real treat, as fruit and vegetables were so scarce in this region.

A severe gale struck up in the night, and my tent would surely have been blown away if it had not been secured to the ground with six-inch nails! Packing up camp in the morning, however, the tent somehow slipped from my grasp, and the caravaners were provided with some light entertainment as I chased it around the campsite!

With the gale force winds showing no signs of dropping, my options were fairly limited. I could either stay at Renner Springs for the day, sitting in the roadhouse café where food and drinks would set me back a fortune, or ride as far as possible and set up camp somewhere by the roadside. There was certainly no chance of reaching the next service area at Three Ways, eighty-five miles south, or Tennants Creek, slightly beyond that.

It was a pleasant surprise when Henry came over with a cup of tea, and added to my range of options by offering me a lift to Tennants Creek. It was a tough decision to make, but to ride in these conditions would have been little more than an endurance test, and that was not what my journey was all about. Though it felt a bit like admitting defeat, I graciously accepted the offer, and together we loaded the bike onto the motor-home.

It felt strange to see the Outback flash by so quickly as we drove south, but very nice to be protected from the gales and the glare of the sun. Henry and Marie treated me like an adopted son, feeding me at every opportunity and making me feel at home. We stopped for lunch at Churchill's Head – a large rock that is said to resemble the head of Winston Churchill. Someone had attached a stick, to resemble a cigar, and it did look quite convincing from a distance!

In seemingly no time at all, we reached the famous Three Ways junction. Here the Barkly Highway, which runs across the Nullabor Desert from the Queensland coast, meets the Stuart Highway. Hitchhikers have been known to wait for days on end at this junction for a lift across the desert, but today it was deserted. We stopped just briefly to have a look at the large memorial to the Reverend John Flynn, who founded the Royal Flying Doctors service.

Just fifteen miles further south, we came to Tennants Creek – a lively outback town with a population of three thousand. The town was given its name by John Stuart, who camped here on his famous journey north in 1860, but it really took off during Australia's last gold rush in the 1930s. Henry and Marie dropped me at the Youth Hostel, before heading off to the caravan-park. They would be continuing their journey to Alice Springs in a couple of days, and invited me to join them again then. It was an offer that I would seriously consider.

There was no sign of life at the Youth Hostel, but the keys were left hanging outside, so I checked myself in. The ride down from Darwin seemed to have taken a lot out of me, and it was time for a few days rest.

The next day was an important one for the town, with the arrival of the annual rodeo, and I spent much of the day experiencing this traditional part of outback culture. The local cowboys and cowgirls were out in force, and there were several events testing various skills, such as riding bucking broncos and lassooing. The atmosphere was fairly light-hearted, but I could not help feeling sorry for the horses and cows, that seemed to be subjected to a fair amount of trauma for the sake of this rather crude form of entertainment.

Early the following morning, as I was preparing to leave, the hostel warden finally turned up. He had been absent for the previous two days, during which time several people had come and gone without paying. He did not seem at all bothered by the loss of income – his only concern being that his football team had lost on Saturday. This, apparently, explained his absence!

Now that the ride from Darwin to Alice Springs had been broken, it made sense to travel with Henry and Marie all the way down to Alice. The experience of riding across the Outback on the Stuart Highway was one of the highlights of my whole trip, but I was feeling quite drained now and had little appetite for the remaining three hundred miles. Besides that, I genuinely enjoyed Henry and Maries' company, and it would be nice to travel across this next section of the Outback in a little more comfort! I rode around to the caravan-park and we set off together for Alice Springs.

The barren terrain that we travelled across was a rich mix of red dust and rocks, interspersed with tufts of spinifex, and some other hardy desert plants. Even from the comfort of the motor-home, it was easy to appreciate the inhospitable nature and stark appeal of this great empty land.

Henry and Marie were anxious that I should not miss any of the region's attractions, and we stopped first at the 'Devil's Marbles'. This is a scattering of huge boulders, some of which appear to be balancing precariously on top of one another. The strange formations were created by wind erosion over millions of years (unless you subscribe to Aboriginal mythology, in which case the Marbles were laid by the Rainbow Snake). We also stopped briefly at Central Mount Stuart – a small hill that is thought to be at the exact centre of Australia. The spot was marked by yet another monument to the much-revered John Stuart.

Approaching Alice Springs, we made the final stop of our tour at the Old Telegraph Station, three miles north of the town centre. Established in 1872, this was the base for the first European settlement in the area. The museum contained within gave some idea of the dangers and hardships that the early settlers had to endure. It was a haunting place which, like the vast empty desert surrounding Alice Springs, seemed to have a timeless quality about it. Next to the Telegraph Station was a small waterhole, which the early settlers named Alice, in honour of the wife of Charles Todd, who was the first Superintendent of Telegraphs.

We marked the end of our journey together with a drink at one of the cafes in Todd Street, the shopping mall in the centre of town, before going our separate ways. Henry and Marie were only planning to spend a couple of nights in Alice, while I hoped to find work and live here for a few months.

Once settled into the Youth Hostel, I phoned my friend Peter, who lived locally. Peter was the Australian cycle tourist who featured – along with Bob and Mike - in my journey from Thessalonika to Istanbul, described in Chapter One. We had managed to keep in touch since then via the 'poste-restante' system. On receiving my call, he came straight over in his pick-up truck, and we went for a drive around the town. He had been living here for several months now, and was working night shifts at one of the many hotels in town. It was great to see him again, and he was able to give me several contacts to help with the job hunt. Our short tour ended with a visit to the war memorial on Anzac Hill. From here the whole town was laid out beneath us, as well as much of its unique surrounding landscape. The

McDonnell Ranges run east and west from the town, stretching far away in a series of ridges to each horizon. At the southern end of town, the ridges are broken by the Heavitree Gap, which is just wide enough for the bone-dry Todd River and the Stuart Highway to run through on their way south. In every other direction lay flat empty desert – glowing red in the last rays of evening sunlight.

The employment situation in Alice Springs was much better than in Darwin, and I managed to find work in my own field, as a care worker at a local residential care home, and as an assistant teacher at the local school for children with special needs. Within a couple of weeks, I accepted an offer of a full-time job at the residential home. The home accommodated a group of five young adults with 'intellectual disabilities', which is the Australian equivalent of 'learning disabilities'. Over the coming months I was to find that attitudes towards disabled people in Alice Springs were amazingly positive, with plenty of provision made to ensure that even the most severely disabled were encouraged to play as full a part in society as possible. In fact, by trying to involve my clients in community activities, I became quite integrated into the local community myself!

With work secured, I went in search of some more permanent accommodation. My home for the next seven months was to be a rented room in a comfortable house on the southern edge of the town, right beneath the Mcdonnell Rangers. My landlady – Michelle – was a teacher at the local school for Aboriginal children, and her other lodger was a young nurse called Debbie, who had recently moved up from Adelaide. It seemed strange to be living in an ordinary house again and travelling to work each day, but I soon settled into this more conventional lifestyle.

The Todd River, which runs through the centre of town, remained dry throughout my time in Alice. Apparently it does flow after heavy rains, but these occasions are very rare. In fact, it is said that if you see the river flowing three times then you will never leave Alice! The sandy riverbed provided sleeping and living quarters for a very small proportion of the local Aboriginal population that have, apparently, become isolated from their communities, mainly for reasons of drunkenness. The vast majority of the Aboriginal population live in remote communities beyond the town limits, and invisible to the hordes of tourists that pass through Alice on their way to Ayres Rock and the McDonnell Ranges. For this reason, many of these tourists seem to head back to the East Coast under the common misconception that all Aboriginal people are 'layabouts and drunks'.

One of the residents at the care home was an Aboriginal man called Dennis, in his mid-thirties, who had no speech. It was necessary for me to visit Dennis's relatives at one of the outlying Aboriginal communities on several occasions, and this gave me a unique insight into their way of life. There was clearly some mistrust and an air of apprehension when I arrived on the first occasion. However, as soon as it became clear that I was not there out of idle curiosity, the family opened there home to me and could not have been more hospitable. I met several of their friends and neighbours, and learnt of their frustrations at not feeling that they have any place in modern society. There are very few genuine job opportunities even for well-qualified Aboriginal people in Alice Springs, due mainly to the lingering prejudices of employers, which means that most families are forced to survive on the benefits system. With the provision of benefits, young people no longer have incentive to develop their hunting and survival skills, as in the past, and many of them simply have too much time on their hands. Social problems are inevitable in these circumstances, but the people that I met were extremely dignified, and seemed to value family ties and traditions above all else.

In late August, a few weeks after my arrival, it was time for the annual Henley-On-Todd Regatta, which is one of the highlights of the Alice Springs social calendar. Improvisation was obviously required, due to the lack of water, and this came in the form of bottomless yachts and canoes, propelled by leg-power! Several local businesses were represented, and the day's racing program was finished off with a mock battle between ships representing Australia and the United States! This was one of numerous community events that seemed to take place most weekends, ensuring that there was never any shortage of entertainment in this vibrant desert town.

As summer progressed, the dry heat became quite oppressive, with temperatures frequently soaring into the mid-forties. However, I adjusted to the inhospitable climate and settled happily into the Alice Springs way of life, enjoying regular opportunities to explore the surrounding area with Peter and other friends. As often as possible, we would camp out in the desert and explore the gorges, canyons and waterholes of the McDonnell Ranges. We also made an unforgettable weekend trip to the Finke Gorge National Park, which contains Palm Valley. The red cabbage palms here grow nowhere else in the world, under natural conditions, and it seemed amazing that they could survive in such an arid region. Apparently the sand and silt on the dry river valley slopes retain just enough water beneath the surface for the palms to survive. It was a place of incredible beauty, and the experience was enhanced by one of the National Park Rangers, who gave an evening slide show and talk at the campground. He told us an old legend about the 'Punga Lunga' – a terrifying beast that lives in the hills and kills people at night. Apparently, the story was told to Aboriginal children at night, in order to deter them from wandering off into the bush on their own.

From time to time, cycle tourists would arrive in town – usually having cycled an enormous distance, and more than ready for a rest! One of these was a German fellow called Tillman, who had been touring by bicycle for the majority of the past fifteen years. He was a fascinating character, who made his living from writing travel books and testing products for various German producers of camping and touring equipment. Tillman stayed at our house for two weeks, during which time he worked on making a short video film on cycle touring for Italian television. Despite my protestations, and obvious lack of acting ability, I was persuaded to accept a brief starring role! We spent a whole day in the outback, with Peter behind the camera, making numerous attempts at filming the process of Tillman and I setting up camp and trying to make casual conversation around the campfire!

Perhaps the highlight of my stay in the Red Centre was a five-day camping holiday at Ayres Rock, with the residents from the care home. Ayers Rock and The Olgas are all that remain of a massive mountain range that is now virtually buried in the desert. It is a place of great beauty and mystery. It is also a place of great spiritual significance to the Aboriginal people who traditionally own the land, and I had no wish to join the hordes of tourists clambering up and down the steep sides of the Rock. In any case, Ayres Rock is most impressive when seen from a distance, surrounded by an endless expanse of flat, featureless desert. Each night, at sunset, the Rock changes colour from deep red to purple, and then to black, in one of the most amazing shows that I had ever seen put on by Mother Nature.

On the campsite, we slept in 'swags', which are pieces of thick foam encased in waterproof canvass, which can be zipped up around you to form a bivvy bag in the unlikely event of rain. Awoken one night by a cry of 'help me', I looked round to see our Aboriginal client, Dennis, battling to climb out of his swag. He appeared to have awoken in a state of confusion, having got slightly tangled up in the canvass. One of my colleagues had also awoken, and confirmed that the words 'help me' had come from Dennis. It was the first time that either of us had heard him talk, and I learnt later that he had not been known to utter a word since early childhood. We helped him to straighten out his swag, and he gazed around for a while before settling back to sleep. I never heard him speak again, but will never forget the moment when the barrier to his speech was momentarily removed on that desert campsite, in the shadow of Ayres Rock

Seven months passed quickly in Alice Springs. During this time I had made lots of friends, and grown fond of this close-nit community in the middle of the Outback. I had also worked hard and managed to build up sufficient funds to stay on the road for at least another six months - hopefully longer. With only seven weeks remaining on my Australian visa, I had decided take advantage of an offer to travel by car to Adelaide with my fellow lodger, Debbie, who was visiting relatives there. At the last minute we were joined by one of my work colleagues, Marnie, who jumped at the opportunity of visiting her own relatives in Adelaide. My plan was to spend a few days there with Debbie and Marnie, and then to ride northwards along the coast from Adelaide to Sydney – a journey of roughly two thousand miles. It was good to have spent so much time in the Northern Territory, which is perhaps the most unique part of Australia, but now it was time to explore the more temperate regions, where most Australians actually live.

It was hard to leave so many friends behind in Alice, especially knowing that I would probably never see any of them again. After the emotional trauma of a farewell breakfast with several of them, it was some relief to actually leave the town behind as we crossed the McDonnell Ranges, by way of the Heavitree Gap. We then followed the Stuart Highway across the golden desert plains, which extend virtually all the way to Adelaide, a thousand miles south. As we sped along in the car, to the sounds of Bob Dylan and Cat Stevens, I felt strangely detached from the vast, empty landscape, which seemed even more unchanging than the top half of Australia.

It was not until the evening, when we pulled off the highway onto a clay pan and set up camp beneath the setting sun, that I really felt as though we were in tune with our desert surroundings again. We were only a few miles north of the Marla roadhouse, but we had packed everything we needed for the overnight camp, so there was no need to go any further. We soon had a small fire going and dinner underway.

Soon after dawn, we were on the road again. We crossed the border into South Australia and continued south towards the opal-mining town of Coober Pedy, which lies midway between Alice Springs and Adelaide. The name of this town comes from the Aboriginal word meaning 'man who lives in a hole', and this is quite appropriate because most of the town's inhabitants do indeed live in holes! Summer temperatures here are so high that much of the town has been constructed beneath the ground. This unusual and remote settlement happens to sit on top of the world's largest known opal fields, and the mining operations have attracted a large number of European settlers. The 'over-ground' part of the town did have a suitably Continental feel to it, and we stopped for a 'souvlaki' at an open-air Greek café. We then ventured underground to visit a beautiful Catholic Church. It was comfortably cool underground, and this method of coping with the sweltering heat seemed a far more natural and pleasant solution than the usual alternative of air-conditioning. Apparently it is no more expensive to drill out a home in the rock than to build a home of similar size on the surface and, if you do it yourself, you might even discover enough opals during the process to pay for it!

A short drive out of town brought us to a hilly area known as the 'Breakaways', which is dotted with huge, conical, piles of white rock from the mineshafts. This slightly weird and wild-looking terrain was famously utilised by filmmakers as a setting for 'Mad Max II'. We also passed by the Coober Pedy Golf Course, where even the putting greens were brown!

Coober Pedy may well be the most bizarre place in Australia, and it was certainly an interesting place to break the journey for a few hours! As we continued south, the only features that broke the monotony of the unchanging landscape were the huge dry salt pans. Apparently, these filled with water in the seventies after some unusually prolonged rain. Now they were as dry as could be, however, and their white basins reflected the sunlight to give a blinding effect if you stared for too long.

It was terrific to see the ocean again at Port Augusta, and we celebrated reaching the end of the Stuart Highway with a fish & chip supper on the promenade. Continuing along the coastal highway, we finally arrived in Adelaide late in the evening. Debbie had arranged for us all to stay at an apartment belonging to her friend, Christina, who was away on holiday, so we went straight there.

Our apartment was nicely situated in the foothills of the Mount Lofty ranges, which form the backdrop to Adelaide. From the balcony, the city was neatly laid out beneath us in grid fashion, with large plazas and plenty of greenery, stretching all the way to the ocean. It was refreshing to be near the ocean again, after living in the heart of the Australian desert for seven months, and it was also good to feel cold again. With daytime temperatures dropping as low as 23 degrees centigrade, we all had to wear jumpers!

Debbie and Marnie had both grown up in this sedate city and were able to show me around, as well as introducing me to some of their friends and relatives. One memorable outing was a group cycle ride along the banks of the River Torrens to the Victorian-style resort of Glenelg for a swim in the sea and a picnic on the beach, which all felt very Australian!

A week flew past and the girls duly set off on their return journey to Alice. They had both become close friends to me and it was hard to watch them driving away. Their departure spurred me into action though, and I spent the rest of the day checking the bike over and collecting bits and pieces from the shops in preparation for the next leg of my own journey.

My route out of Adelaide took me over the Mount Lofty Ranges, so I had to find my climbing legs straight away. It was some time since I had done any serious cycling, so there was a price to pay that morning! My last view of Adelaide came from the summit of Mount

Lofty itself, from where I just about had enough energy left to fully appreciate how well-planned and attractively laid out this city is.

The rest of the day's ride was mercifully easy, as the road gradually descended through the wooded valleys of the Adelaide Hills. I had planned to camp somewhere in the hills but, feeling stronger as the day went on, rode late into the evening to reach the coast again at Wellington. The campsite here displayed a sign stating that cycle tourists could stay for the nominal fee of two dollars, apparently due to the fact that the owner was a keen cyclist himself.

The next day my whole body was aching and I felt quite lethargic. After a leisurely breakfast, however, I forced myself back onto the bike and rode slowly along the coastal road to Meningie. Here I had my first of several encounters with the Wayward Bus Tour Company, which ferries backpackers up and down the coast between Adelaide and Melbourne in a brightly painted minibus. The driver's name was Derek, and he invited me to join his group of high-spirited backpackers for a picnic lunch. It turned out that he knew an old friend of mine from England, who had worked for the Company the previous year, so we had an immediate connection. Over the next few weeks he would pass me several times as he travelled up and down the ocean highway. It was always a welcome sight, and he always stopped to introduce me to his latest group of backpackers.

Meningie lies on the edge of the Coorong National Park, which consists mainly of a sixty-mile long stretch of sand dunes, lying just off the coast and parallel to it. The narrow stretch of water between the dunes and the coast is home to an enormous variety of bird-life, attracting ornithologists from all over the world. Right on the edge of the dunes, just a few miles north of Meningie, lived a Dutch couple - Herman and Colleen. A friend in Adelaide had given me their address and promised me a warm welcome if I called in on them.

The house was easy to find, being the only one for some distance around. Colleen was at home and made me feel welcome straight away. Apparently my friend had phoned her the previous evening, so she had been expecting me all day. She seemed a real country girl and was very enthusiastic in describing the surrounding countryside. Herman turned up a while later after finishing the local school bus run. Despite being in his sixties now, this was one of several part-time jobs that he had taken on since retiring from his job as a Coorong National Park Ranger. He had to go straight out again to milk the cows at a local farm, so he invited me to join him.

As we drove along, Herman demonstrated his extensive knowledge of the area by pointing out various species of birds and giving me a brief history of every farm that we passed. It was starting to get dark when we reached our destination, and I was slightly alarmed at the sight of over three hundred cows waiting to be milked! However, we had the use of a very efficient rotary mechanism which enabled us to milk the whole lot in less than an hour, with Herman explaining the finer points of the process to me as we went along.

Back at the house Colleen had prepared a terrific dinner, and I spent the evening learning more about their life together here. They had bought their plot of land just a few years before, when it was nothing more than five acres of wasteland, overgrown with weeds. The two of them cleared the weeds by hand and then proceeded to design and build the house, using a simple mix of earth and concrete. Each section of wall was constructed by pouring the mixture into a mould. The home they had created was simple and spacious, blending in beautifully with the surrounding landscape. The main living room had an enormous window looking out across a small lake, which was frequented by all kinds of bird-life. Around the house, Herman had planted hundreds of trees, which served to break up the violent winds that tended to whip up across the lake very suddenly. They were both keen conservationists and seemed to live a virtually self- sufficient life here. Solar panels on the roof provided for all their energy needs, and their small plot of land produced most of their food.

Herman and Colleen really made me feel at home, and did not have too much trouble in persuading me to stay another day – "in order to get to know the Coorong a little better". The day began with breakfast at 6am, after which I accompanied Herman on his morning school bus run. We collected the bus in Meningie, and headed first for an outlying Aboriginal settlement. We picked up six Aboriginal children here, and then thirty or so white children on the way back to Meningie. It appears that racist attitudes are quite prevalent in these parts, and Herman explained that he only continued to do the school run because so few other drivers were willing to pick up the Aboriginal children. He seemed to have a great rapport with all the children and clearly worked hard to encourage harmony on the bus!

Herman had the rest of the day free, so we picked up Colleen and went on a tour of the southern end of the Coorong National Park. They both had a wealth of knowledge about the Park and its wildlife, so I could not have been in better hands. They seemed to lead incredibly active lives, and when we returned to the house I spent a couple of hours planting trees with Herman, while Colleen prepared another tremendous feast straight from the garden!

The coastal road leading north from Meningie followed the edge of the Coorong National Park. Strong headwinds blew across the dunes, blowing sand into my face almost constantly, so it was not an easy ride. On reaching Salt Creek, I called a halt to my battle against the wind and sand. Herman had recommended a camping spot here, so I followed a narrow track through the forest, which led to a sandy clearing close to the waters edge. It was just as he had described it, and I soon had my evening campfire burning.

The wind dropped overnight, which made for more comfortable riding conditions the following day. The landscape became drier as I rode north, and the flowing channel of water between the mainland and the sand dunes turned into a white shining desert.

That night I reached the quiet seaside town of Kingston, where I had arranged to stay at the home of Brian and Neila Densely, who were the parents of my former landlady in Alice Springs. There was nobody at home, however, so I deposited the bike in their back garden and went for a swim in the sea. There were still no signs of life on my return, but I eventually managed to contact them from a nearby phone box. Apparently, they had been expecting me the previous evening, and were now out of town for a few days. It seems that I had somehow lost track of the days, which can easily happen when you are on the road! They gave me permission to camp in their garden, however, so at least I had somewhere secure to spend the night.

My fitness was building up nicely now, and the next day I made good progress along the coastal highway. The landscape was a mixture of forest and coastal plains, with the ocean never far away. This seemed to be a popular route for cyclists and I encountered several along the way – including a Japanese couple that had

246

travelled down from Melbourne by tandem! By mid-afternoon I had reached my target for the day, which was the resort town of Beachport.

The seafront Youth Hostel was of the simple, traditional kind that I tend to prefer, as they always seemed to be more conducive to meeting people. There was only one other guest that night – an Australian girl called Schona, who followed up on the usual introductions by running through her entire life story! She was a real talker, but good company after a few days of virtual solitude on the road. We pooled our resources for dinner and managed to produce quite an evening feast between us.

Rain came for the first time since my departure from Adelaide, as I rode north from Beachport. It was quite refreshing at first, but the novelty soon wore off as it became heavier and heavier throughout the day. My sights were firmly set on reaching Mount Gambier, however, where I had an invitation to stay that night with another couple that had been contacted by my friends in Adelaide.

Eventually, Mount Gambier came into view. This town is roughly the midway point between Adelaide and Melbourne, and lies in the shadow of a volcano of the same name. The name was apparently chosen by crewmembers of the Lady Nelson, which was the first ship to sail the length of Australia's southern shores. I headed straight for Richard and Shirleys' house, and this time there was no mix up with the days, although they had wondered whether I would make it to them through the rain! Richard and Shirley were members of the local tennis club, and we spent the evening at the club's monthly social evening. The evening ended with a bowling tournament, which was one of the few sports that I still had enough energy left to participate in!

It was still raining the following morning, as we made our way up to the crater of nearby Mount Gambier. The volcano is famous for its crater lake, which turns bright blue when the sun shines on it. On this dreary morning, however, it looked very much like any other lake. As we walked back down into the town, Richard and Shirley told me of their plans for the future. It seems that they were destined to spend some time apart because Shirley was intent on spending a year travelling around Europe, while Richard was considering a move to Alice Springs in order to work with a friend that was setting up a bakery business there. He had lived in Mount Gambier all his life and had never been to Alice Springs, so he was very interested to hear my impressions of the place.

My hosts invited me to stay another night but, with the rain easing off after lunch, I decided to head off. This decision may have been a little rash, however, as I was barely out of town when the heavens opened again! It was tempting to turn back, and Richard and Shirley were probably half-expecting me again, but I kept going.

Within a few miles I reached the State border and crossed over into Victoria, which is considered to be the most 'British' of Australian States. My plan was to ride just thirty miles or so to the seaside village of Nelson, where a campsite was indicated on my map. However, it was still raining heavily when I arrived and the idea of camping had long lost its appeal. Instead, I rode a further twenty miles to Nioka Farm – a small country farm, which also operates as a Youth Hostel.

It was still raining in the morning, so this time I decided to do the sensible thing and stay put. The farmer and his wife had a great book collection, so I spent the morning reading, while my wet things were drying out around the stove – including a few five-dollar notes! The sun finally made an appearance in the afternoon, so I joined some of the other guests for a walk in the surrounding rainforest, where we spotted several Koala Bears. As well as being cute and cuddly, these little furry creatures have a reputation for being quite vicious, so we kept our distance!

It was a blustery day, but dry at least, as I rode steadily through the pine forests for several hours, before reaching the coast again at Portland. It was a lovely ride, which I was able to enjoy all the more after 'recharging my batteries' at the farm. Over lunch in Portland, I got into conversation with an elderly couple from Melbourne who happened to know a young disabled man called Jon, who was one of the residents at the care home in Alice Springs. They had lived on the same Melbourne street as Jon and his family many years before, but had long since lost touch with them. They were delighted to hear that he was in good health, and living life to the full in Alice Springs. It was a strange coincidence, and Australia seemed like a small place all of a sudden!

From Portland the road followed the shoreline, and I rode well into the evening to reach Port Fairy. This historic old town is home to Australia's biggest folk festival. The annual festival had taken place a couple of weeks before, but the large Youth Hostel was still packed with backpackers. Fortunately there was one dormitory bed available. Once settled in I ventured into the crowded kitchen to start preparing my evening meal. As I was waiting for the next available hob, a Swiss girl invited me for dinner, as she had accidentally prepared far too much pasta. Suzanne and her sister, Monica, were spending a month-long vacation travelling around Eastern Australia by hired car. We seemed to connect straight away, and spent the evening chatting in the hostel lounge. They were planning to head off in the morning but we exchanged addresses, and I would meet up with them both again four years later when they visited England.

Just north of Port Fairy, I made a slight detour inland to visit the Tower Hill Wildlife Reserve, which is an area of rainforest situated within a huge volcanic crater. After a short hike around the Reserve, I returned to the bike to find a couple of wild kangaroos searching through my panniers for food! Riding back towards the coast, I skirted the city suburbs of Warnambool, and then turned onto the Great Ocean Road. This famous road follows a particularly spectacular stretch of coastline all the way to Geelong – two hundred miles further north.

The first real beauty spot was Childer's Cove, where a golden sandy beach was backed by rugged cliffs. It had been another overcast day, but the sun burst through the clouds, just as I arrived, to light up the scene. A few miles further was the 'Bay of Islands', where the ocean has eroded the limestone cliffs into pillars of rock, scattered across the bay. It was nearly dark now, so I set up camp in a forest clearing just off the road. It was strangely comforting to hear the ocean continuously crashing against the rocks, as I nodded off to sleep in my cosy little tent.

The Great Ocean Road continued to snake its way over the cliff tops to the fishing village of Port Campbell. On the way, I stopped frequently to inspect various strange rock formations, including one known as London Bridge, where I returned from the lookout point to find an old lady posing by my bike for a photograph. She wanted to tell the folks back home that she had cycled the Great Ocean Road!

Port Campbell nestles in a lovely bay and, though it was still early in the day, I decided to stop for the night at the hostel here. It turned out to be a lively evening, as a group of students from Melbourne were also checked in for the night. Their bus driver provided the main entertainment with a fine demonstration of didgereedoo playing. I had a go on it myself, but without too much success!

The next day's ride was superb – with fine weather, fantastic scenery and thrilling descents! There were numerous opportunities to stop and admire the dramatic geographical features that make this stretch of coastline such a popular holiday destination for many Australians. Perhaps the most memorable sight was the famous 'Twelve Apostles' – a group of huge rock pillars that have been cut adrift from the shore by the wind and waves.

The Great Ocean Road then turned inland and started to climb through the pine forests of Cape Otway. At a rainforest reserve called Melba Gully, I had another encounter with the Wayward Bus Company. This time Derek was on his way back from Melbourne with a different group of backpackers. They were another lively bunch, and we had lunch together before they all piled back into the bus for the next leg of their journey south.

That night, I camped at a National Park site deep in the forests of Cape Otway. At first, the site seemed to be deserted, but as I was setting up my tent the site manager came over. He greeted me with the surprising news that John Major had just won the General Election in Britain.

From the forest camp I continued my ride across the rolling hills of Cape Otway, before rejoining the coast again at the busy resort town of Apollo Bay. From here the road was cut into the cliffs, as it followed the shoreline northwards. It was tough riding now, but the spectacular panoramic views at every turn provided ample reward. That evening I checked into a hostel at the pretty town of Lorne, which nestles in a deep bay, backed by steep hills covered in dense rainforest.

Early the next morning I set off on a hike along the Erskine River Valley. The first rays of sunlight brought to life a lush green haven of eucalyptuses, tree ferns and waterfalls. I walked as far as a small clearing, known as 'The Sanctuary', where several large, smooth rocks were arranged in a rough circle. Apparently, 'The Sanctuary' was used for church services, over one hundred and fifty years ago.

Riding north from Lorne, I passed beneath a huge timber archway, which marked the end of 'The Great Ocean Road'. The road was now simply called 'Highway One' - and the scenery less spectacular to match – as it turned inland. Without the scenic distractions, I was able to make steady progress to reach the big, industrial city of Geelong by late afternoon. It seemed an ugly place at first, but there was a pretty waterfront area in the centre, overlooking Corrie Bay, and I checked into a hostel here.

Melbourne was just a day's ride away now. Over breakfast, the hostel manager informed me that the Geelong-Melbourne freeway was open to cyclists. This was some relief, as there seemed no obvious alternative route on the map. Filled with anticipation of reaching one of the world's major cities that day, I rode hard along the bike lane in top gear. After a brief lunch stop at Werribee, I descended on Melbourne early in the afternoon, and headed straight for the southern suburb of Murrumbeena. My Great Aunt Pat lived here, having moved to Australia several years previously. She was expecting me, and welcomed me into her home.

A child surveys the war memorial at Gradisco, Italy

Tea-rooms were a focal point of village life in Turkey

Karachi buses could get a little overcrowded!

Spontaneous welcome committee in Bengali village

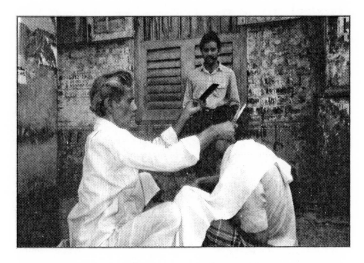

In 1991, a street haircut in Calcutta cost one rupee
(about three pence)

Balinese cremation ceremony in full swing!

The German cyclist, Olaf, on our first meeting in Flores, Indonesia

The Stuart Highway cuts across the 'Top End'

Bush crime was sometimes a problem in Australia

The Marlborough Sounds from Queen Charlotte Drive,
New Zealand

Local farmer, martin, delivers English newspapers and astonishing vegetables to the fruit stand at Malakwa, Canada

Bob and his dog, on tour in Oregon, U.S.A.

Masahira crosses the Golden Gate

Jubilation on reaching the Mexican border with
Annabel and Kate

Village market stall in the Western Highlands,
Guatemala

Melbourne is an elegant, cultural city, built on a coastal plain at the top of the horseshoe-shaped Port Phillip Bay. Its compact centre was sprinkled with fine Victorian buildings, which sprang up in the wake of the gold rush. Perhaps the most interesting feature, though, was the ramshackle old tram system. As well as adding a touch of character to the city streets, it appeared to be the best way of getting around.

Melbourne is also a city of parks and gardens, with more than a quarter of the inner city area set aside for recreational use. The Botanical Gardens, just across the river from the downtown area, was probably the most impressive city park that I had ever come across. Within its one hundred acres were twelve thousand species of native and imported plants and trees, arranged around sweeping lawns and ornamental lakes.

One evening I arranged to meet up with a girl called Sharon, who was a friend of Debbie – one of my travelling companions on the car journey down to Adelaide. She gave me a taste of Melbourne's cultural side by taking me to see a very funny play in a tiny backstreet theatre. Sharon was a keen cyclist herself and, the following day, we went for a ride around Port Phillip Bay. Our ride ended at the trendy Bay-side suburb of St Kilda, where the esplanade was brought to life by a colourful craft market and various street performers. It was like a seaside version of London's Covent Garden.

Easter week passed very quickly in Melbourne, with Aunt Pat making life very comfortable for me. It was a complete break from the rigours of the road. The home cooking was delicious, and she even prepared a variety of pies for me to carry with me on my journey. It was some job to fit them all into the panniers, but I managed it somehow!

Despite being weighed down by the pies, I rode quickly through the Melbourne suburbs, and soon found myself in the green foothills and valleys of the western end of the Great Dividing Range. It was good to be on the move again and I rode well into the evening, before stopping to camp at a roadside picnic area, complete with a barbecue area and plenty of wood lying around for a campfire. This was fortunate, as the evening had turned surprisingly cold.

The next day began with the sound of a car, noisily pulling in off the highway. When I emerged from my tent, the driver apologised for waking me, and passed me a coffee from his flask! There was a light frost that morning, so I rebuilt the fire and cooked some porridge.

It remained cold throughout the day but, with the sun shining brightly from a clear sky, it was a great day for riding. I peddled all morning through rolling, forested hills to reach a pretty little lakeside village with the even prettier name of Bonnie Doon. From here I followed the shores of the lake through several more villages, before heading into the hills again for another roadside camp, near the village of Swanpool.

The next day's riding was not so enjoyable, as I could find no alternative route to the busy Hume Freeway. It was a noisy and tedious ride, but fast-going at least. The freeway sliced through hilly terrain, which was made famous by the exploits of the outlaw, Ned Kelly. The highlight was a brief detour to the village of Glenrowan, where he made his famous 'last stand'. It was nice to turn off the freeway at Wangaratta and continue through the hills on much quieter roads. The autumn colours were in full abundance now and I became quite absorbed in my surroundings. Approaching the town of Beechworth, I even caught a brief sight of the Snowy Mountains, far away in the distance.

Beechworth was a well-preserved historic old town, with a wide main street lined with colourful wooden buildings with verandas. It had a real outback feel to it, and would not have looked out of place in an American western. An old hotel building on the main street now functioned as a Youth Hostel, so it was time for a long-overdue shower and a comfortable bed!

It was downhill all the way from Beechworth to the larger town of Wadonga, where I was entertained for a while by some soldiers that were practising their marching routines. Apparently they were getting ready for the Anzac Day Parade - Australia's version of 'Remembrance Day' – which would take place the following day. From Wadonga I rode north on the Murray River Highway, which followed the southern shores of Lake Hume, bringing me to the quiet lakeside settlement of Tallangatta. I set up camp close to the water's edge, on the town campsite, just in time to catch a beautiful sunset over the lake.

The mountainous alpine region, which contains the Snowy Mountains, really began after Tallangatta, and the ride from here to Corryong turned out to be really tough. I had carelessly neglected to stock up on food supplies before heading into the mountains, expecting to be able to buy food in one of the villages marked on the map. Unfortunately, these villages turned out to be nothing more than the occasional cluster of farmhouses, and hunger began to set in. Fortunately my emergency supply of cereal bars, buried deep in one of the rear panniers, gave me the energy to keep going.

By late afternoon I finally made it to the town of Corryong, which sits on a mountain plateau, close to the New South Wales border. The shops here were all closed for Anzac Day, so I treated myself to pie and chips at one of the pubs on the high street. This gave me a huge burst of energy, which I decided to utilise by riding a further twenty miles to the lakeside resort town of Kancoban. There is nothing like an Australian pub meal when you are really hungry!

Before long, I had crossed the State border and caught my first glimpse of Mount Kosciusko. With its summit at 2228 metres above sea level, this is Australia's highest mountain and it towered majestically above the smaller peaks of the Snowy Mountain range. The only disappointment was the complete absence of snow! The Snowy Mountains were not – apparently – snowy, at this time of year.

Reaching Kancoban, I checked into a simple Youth Hostel for the night. Already in residence were a group of anglers, who had been trying their luck in the lake that has been created at Kancoban by the damming of the Swampy Plain River.

The Anglers had warned me that the Alpine Way through the Kosciusko National Park, from Kancoban to Thredbo, was the steepest road in Australia, so I set off in the morning with some trepidation. Within a few miles, I reached the entrance to the National Park, which contains the Snowy Mountains, and began climbing across the heavily forested southern flanks of Mount Kosciusko. My attention was drawn to several colossal pipelines, rising steeply up the mountainside to form part of the famous Snowy Mountains Hydroelectric Scheme. Completed in 1972, this project is considered to be one of the engineering marvels of the modern world, and the scale of the pipelines was quite incredible.

Having remembered to carry food this time, I stopped for lunch at a shady picnic spot beside the Murray River.

From here the real work began, as the Alpine Way turned to gravel and climbed steeply through the mountains. Anglers have a tendency to exaggerate a little, but it soon became clear that these ones at Kancoban had not been exaggerating about the gradient of this road! It was bottom gear riding, and I had to stop every hundred yards or so to rest and get my breath back. By the time that I finally made it up to Dead Horse Pass, at 1582 metres, the day was almost gone. Nestling in the valley below was Thredbo – Australia's premier ski resort - and the steep winding descent brought me flying down into a cluster of Swiss-style chalets and hotels. With the ski season not yet underway, the town was fairly quiet and there was plenty of room for me at the Youth Hostel.

After six days of solid riding since leaving Melbourne, it was time for a rest day, and Thredbo was the perfect place to spend it. With the first snowfall expected any time soon, there was a lively air of expectancy about the place. After breakfast at the hostel, I set off with some of the other hostellers for the summit of Mount Kosciusko. It was not an arduous trip, as we took the Crackenback chair-lift to the upper terminal, from where it was a gentle two-mile hike to the summit. The skies were clear and you could see for miles across the highest section of the Great Dividing Range. At the summit, I chatted for a while with a middle-aged couple, Brian and Leslie, from Bulli – a coastal town just south of Sydney. They invited me to visit them on my journey north.

It was raining steadily, on my departure from Thredbo, and there was a touch of snow on the mountaintops at last. It was a miserable day for riding, so I just rolled a short distance down the valley to another resort town called Jindabyne, which lies on the shores of a lake with the same name. It turned very cold on the lakeside campground that evening, so I headed for the warmth of the local pub.

Soon after sunrise, I emerged from my tent to be greeted by the unforgettable sight of the early morning sun illuminating a wide rainbow across the lake. As the rainbow gradually disappeared, I rode slowly around the shores of Lake Jindabyne, and then up into the hills again towards Cooma. At the village of Berridale I could not resist the temptation of a huge 'mountain burger'. The café owner assured me that this was the biggest burger in Australia, and it certainly filled me up!

Cooma is a bustling mountain town, known as the 'Gateway to the Snowy Mountains', although for me it was really the back door. The Backpackers' Hostel here was virtually empty that night, so I had the luxury of a dormitory all to myself.

Snow was falling lightly as I set off from Cooma on another long hard climb up to the village of Nimmitabel. It was a bitterly cold day, so I warmed myself up with a few cups of coffee here, before heading across a bleak, snowy plateau. The skies cleared gradually as the afternoon wore on and, to my great delight, the long awaited descent to the coastal lowlands finally appeared before me. It dawned on me at that moment that I had made it across the Great Dividing Range. It would be coastal riding all the way to Sydney from here. The long descent brought me down into the East Coast town of Bega – known throughout Australia for its cheese! Again the Youth Hostel was empty, and I wondered how these places could afford to stay open at this time of year.

From Bega, the Princes Highway runs up the coast all the way to Sydney, some three hundred miles further north. It was pleasant riding, with the ocean to my right, sending me gentle sea breezes, and green rolling hills to my left.

Just north of the historic old village Tilba Tilba, which is also famous for its cheese production, a Japanese cycle tourist approached from the opposite direction. He became very animated at the sight of me - waving and smiling – and we both pulled off the road as our paths crossed. The reason for his excitement became apparent when he produced from his panniers a photograph of a possum sitting on the saddle of my bicycle! Apparently, he had visited Lorne, on the Great Ocean Road, a few weeks earlier and noticed the possum sitting on the bike as it was parked outside the Youth Hostel there. I must have been checking in at the time, unaware that my metal companion was providing this unusual photo opportunity! I thought for a moment that this cheerful character was going to offer me the photo as a memento, but it was clearly a treasured possession and he carefully tucked it back inside his panniers. As he cycled away into the distance, it occurred to me that I had not even got his name.

That night I found excellent accommodation at a Backpackers' Hostel in the resort town of Narooma, which lies at the head of a deep inlet. The hostel was set in fifteen acres of bush-land on the far side of the inlet. It was a very tranquil place, so I decided that it was time for a rest day.

In the morning, I swapped the bicycle for a canoe, and rowed across the bay to collect some groceries from the town centre on the other side. It was good to let the arms do some work and give the legs a rest! The remainder of the day was spent strolling and relaxing in the beautiful grounds of the secluded hostel. In the evening, the calm was slightly disturbed by the arrival of a young English guy, who lived in Sydney, and his parents, who were over on holiday from England. The parents seemed to be in a state of shock at having been persuaded to spend the night in a hostel. However, they could not have asked for a more gentle introduction to world of 'backpacking', and they soon realised that it was not going to be as uncomfortable as they had feared!

Riding further north, the Princes Highway became increasingly hilly. However, with Sydney firmly in my sights now, I relished the challenge and made good progress. The next town of any size was Bateman's Bay, where a young lad approached me on the seafront. He was keen to take up cycle touring himself and wondered if I could pass on any tricks of the trade. I told him just to load up his bicycle, climb on and keep peddling – everything else would fall into place! This seemed to satisfy him and he went away quite happy. A few miles north of Bateman's Bay, I set up camp for the night in a secluded forest picnic area.

As usual, when camping by the roadside, I was on the road soon after sunrise. It was a hard morning ride, with gusty winds blowing in from the ocean to hamper my progress. The pretty little fishing port of Ulladalla seemed a good place to rest for a while, so I raided the local bakery and sat by the harbour watching the boats come and go.

A few miles further north, the highway turned inland and became quite busy. Sydney was not too far away now, so the increase in traffic was only to be expected. I rode late into the evening to reach a Youth Hostel in the industrial city of Nowra. The hostel was run by an elderly lady, from England's Lake District, who seem pleased at the opportunity to reminisce with somebody about the 'Old Country'.

At an old farmhouse on the outskirts of Nowra, where I had stopped briefly to check the map, another elderly lady called me in for a coffee. This city seemed to be full of friendly old ladies! She lived with her son, Lawrence, who had a mild 'intellectual disability'. Over coffee, she showed me some photographs from a trip that the two of them had recently made to Kakadu National Park. My Australian journey was coming to an end now, but the photographs brought back memories of its beginning, some nine months and several thousand kilometres before.

The road from Nowra rejoined the coast again and there were some panoramic views over a seemingly endless stretch of golden sand, known as 'Seven Mile Beach'. Following the highway alongside this windy beach, I managed to link up with a group of racing cyclists who, helpfully, protected me from the sea breezes by slowing up a little, so that I could ride in their slipstream. It was the kind of supportive gesture that can give you a real lift when you are riding on your own all day.

My support team dropped out at Shellharbour, and the Princes Highway expanded to accommodate six lanes. It was virtually a motorway now, and I tried to just keep my head down and shut out the deafening traffic noise. After several hours of this, it was a relief to finally turn off into the city of Woollongong. After threading my way through the busy city streets, I rode a few miles further north to the small coastal town of Bulli. Brian and Leslie – the couple that I met on the summit of Mount Kosciusko the previous week – lived here in a small cottage, just a few yards back from the beach. They had been expecting me all day, and seemed genuinely pleased to see me again.

Brian and Leslie were in the habit of starting each day with an early morning swim and, not wanting to offend them, I agreed to join them. Their pet dog – an old brown Labrador called 'Charlie' – was obviously used to the routine, as he bounced into my room at 5.30am to wake me up! Half an hour later, we were all splashing around in the ocean. Not surprisingly, at this hour, the water was rather cold, but very refreshing! There can be no better way to set yourself up for breakfast, and we returned to the house for a hearty 'fry-up'. Although my hosts were probably in their late fifties, they certainly seemed 'young at heart' and intent on living life to the full. I would not forget their hospitality to a virtual stranger that they had met only once, very briefly, and would probably never see again.

Though Sydney was only fifty-seven miles away from Bulli, the ride was quite pleasant, as I had decided to avoid the Princes Highway and find my way in on the minor roads. My route took me north along the coast on a narrow road that was cut into the cliffs, affording spectacular views of the rugged shoreline and golden beaches. A long steep climb brought me to Stanwell Tops – a tiny cliff-top settlement, where hang-gliders were queuing up to fling themselves over the edge.

The hard riding was done now, and it was not long before I reached the outer suburbs of Sydney. Making my way towards the city centre, it seemed like no time at all before I was actually riding across Sydney Harbour Bridge. The instantly recognisable Opera House was glistening in the sun below me, as I stopped at the centre of the bridge to take in the scene. It was a moment that I had imagined many times, and the reality was no disappointment! My journey across Australia was finally over, and I still had a week left on my visa to explore one of the world's most glamorous cities.

Sydney is a glittering and trendy city, but I also found it to be a surprisingly warm and hospitable place. From my hostel on the north shore, it was just a short ferry ride across the harbour to the downtown area, where there always seemed to be a lively atmosphere and plenty of street entertainment to enjoy. My sightseeing included a walk around the harbour-side Botanical Gardens and a visit to the old inner suburb of Paddington, where rows of Victorian-style terrace houses have been beautifully restored. I could not resist popping into the lift at Sydney Tower, which was one of the world's tallest buildings at the time. From the viewing gallery at the top I was able to take in the whole city and could even see as far as the mouth of Sydney Harbour.

The highlight of my time in Sydney though was an incredible meeting with an old friend called Darren, who had been a work colleague during the year leading up to my departure from England. I had not been in contact with Darren and had no idea that he was now in Australia, so it was something of a shock hear him call my name as I boarded a bus to see where it would take me. He was sitting at the back of the bus, on his way to a downtown café where he had been working for the past nine months. I visited him at the café several times after that chance encounter and we spent many hours catching up on each other's lives, over cappuccino and cake.

My stay in Sydney was all too brief, but I managed to set a day aside for a visit to the Blue Mountains, which lie sixty miles to the west of Sydney. I had booked onto a backpacker tour, which meant squeezing into an old minibus, with young travellers from Europe, Canada and America. The driver gave an excellent commentary as we drove out of Sydney, and whetted our appetites for the day ahead with a brief history of the region that we would be visiting. As we approached, the Blue Mountains were shrouded in a thick fog. It was not long before rain set in as well, and it became apparent that the dismal weather was going to last all day. We only caught brief glimpses of the mountains through the fog but, despite this disappointment, it was a thoroughly enjoyable trip. The camaraderie within the group was excellent, and everyone seemed determined to make the best of the situation. The driver did his best to improvise as well and took us on a long rainforest walk. Rainforest seems to come alive in the rain and it was a strangely uplifting experience. We also had a ride on the world's steepest railway at Katoomba, which has a gradient of 52 degrees in places. The day was nicely rounded off with a pub stop on the way back into Sydney.

On my last day in Sydney, which was my 26th birthday, I paid a final visit to Darren at the café, where he quickly arranged an impromptu party! A birthday cake was produced and the staff took a break from their duties to sing to me! It was a great send-off, and I headed off to the airport in the best of spirits. My flight to New Zealand was not until early the following morning, so I had a night in the departure lounge to reflect on a long and eventful journey across Australia.

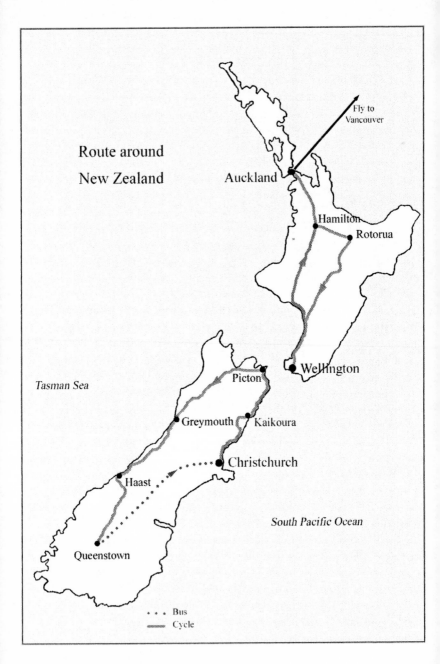

Route around
New Zealand

Fly to
Vancouver

Auckland

Hamilton
Rotorua

Wellington

Tasman Sea

Picton

Greymouth
Kaikoura

Christchurch

Haast

South Pacific Ocean

Queenstown

· · · Bus
~~~~~ Cycle

Chapter Seven

A Winter's Tale

Auckland to Queenstown

The plane dipped below the clouds to reveal the city of Auckland, sprawling across a narrow strip of land between two harbours and surrounded by numerous islands. We came in to land on a crisp, frosty winter's morning.

The city centre Youth Hostel was situated in Parnell Village, a thriving district of old Victorian timber villas that have been transformed into antique shops, designer boutiques and street cafes. On arrival, I made a phone call to my old travel companion, John – the Auckland dock worker who had cycled with me for a few days in Thailand and Malaysia, almost exactly one year previously. He seemed delighted that I had finally made it to New Zealand, and invited me to stay at his home in the Herne Bay suburb. It was already late in the evening, so I promised to come the next day.

John's home sat right on the waterfront, close to the Harbour Bridge. It was great to see him again and we spent several hours 'catching up' over a leisurely breakfast, the following morning.

With John working long shifts at the docks, I had the house to myself most of the time. It made a convenient base from which to explore the city and plan my trip around New Zealand. It was just a short walk around the harbour to the downtown area, which had a surprisingly easy-going and tranquil atmosphere for a city of this size. From the summit of Mount Eden, close to the city centre, I was able to appreciate just how kind nature has been to Auckland. There is plenty of greenery, and nobody lives far from the water's edge. The two big harbours were filled with yachts, and it was easy to see why Auckland is sometimes known as the 'City of Sails'.

New Zealand's national sport is rugby and John had a passion for it. He managed to finish work early one evening, so that he could take me to a match at Eden Park, which is the national stadium. John was able to explain some of the finer points of the sport to me as we watched the all-conquering Auckland team – consisting of most of the current All Blacks squad – trouncing their opposition from Wellington. This knowledge would come in useful as I was to get caught up in numerous conversations about rugby while travelling around the country!

Before leaving Auckland, I booked a flight to Canada, allowing me a couple of months to ride around New Zealand. With winter starting to set in now, I was not sure how far south it would be possible to travel on the bicycle, but hoped to make it at least as far as the famous skiing and hiking resort of Queenstown, on the South Island.

On my way out of the city, I caught up with a rather elderly cyclist who was out on an early morning training ride. We rode together for around twenty miles and the conversation helped the miles to pass quickly. Cycling is a popular pastime in New Zealand and, despite the cold weather, there were plenty of bikes on the road that morning. In fact, it was not long before another rider rode up alongside me! This time it was a young female rider and she accompanied me as far as the town of Huntly, where we warmed ourselves up with coffee and a bag of chips.

After lunch, I pressed on alone towards the city of Hamilton, which is the largest inland city in New Zealand. The Waikato River passes through the city and, on arrival, I checked into a hostel on its banks. Youth Hostels in New Zealand have a very good reputation on the travellers' grapevine, and this one was certainly very comfortable. With night temperatures dropping well below freezing at this time of year, I would be doing my best to reach one each night!

Heading further inland towards the centre of the North Island, I reached Cambridge, where a lake in the town centre was packed with so many ducks that they could hardly move! Beyond Cambridge, the rolling green fields, dotted with sheep, reminded me of England, so I felt quite at home. The village of Tirau marked the beginning of a long gradual climb to the Mamuku Plateau. The landscape became much more barren and desolate now, and gusty winds whipped up rather suddenly across the plateau to slow my progress. Daylight was rapidly fading as a chilly descent finally brought me down to the edge of Lake Rotorua, and it was just a short ride around the lakeshore to Rotorua itself.

The town of Rotorua lies in an area of much volcanic activity and is the main tourist magnet of the North Island. I was fortunate to have some contacts here – friends of my Aunt Pat in Melbourne – that had invited me to stay with them. Bruce and Sarah were a young couple with a two-year-old son called Logan. They made me very welcome and invited me to stay with them for a few days, in order to see something of the area. Bruce's father – Ray – suggested that I start with a trip to nearby Mount Tarawera. The idea sounded good to me, so he booked me onto a tour for the next day and even lent me his hiking boots!

Mount Tararewa last erupted in 1886, covering an area of five thousand square miles with ash, lava and mud. We drove right to the crater in a 4WD truck, and then hiked around the rim and down inside. The track leading down into the crater looked impossibly steep, but it was covered in a layer of tiny stones, which made it possible to descend by digging your heels into the stones and leaving the rest to gravity. The stones provided just enough braking power to enable a gentle slide down to the bottom. We then hiked along another trail, which eventually brought us back up to the rim. The tour concluded with a visit to the site of the village of Te Wairoa, on the lower slopes of the volcano, which was buried in lava during the 1886 eruption. Some of the buildings had been partly excavated - including the hut of an old Maori High Priest called Tohunga, who had prophesied the eruption. At the age of 110 (reputedly) he was buried in his hut for four days, before being unearthed alive!

A further three days were spent visiting other local attractions, usually in the company of Bruce and Ray, who were anxious for me not to miss anything. Ray had worked for many years at a large animal sanctuary called Rainbow Springs. He took great pleasure in showing me around and explaining how the sanctuary had developed, over the years, from a small trout farm to a home for numerous rare and endangered species of fish and bird life.

Strangely, my lasting memory of Rotorua would be the many paintings and drawings of the 'Pink and White Terraces' on display around town. These glistening silica formations on the shores of Lake Rotomahana were considered to be one of the natural wonders of the world, before they vanished forever during the eruption of Mount Tarawera. It would have been nice to be able to turn the clock back 106 years, in order to see the real thing!

Twenty miles south of Rotorua, I stopped to rest at the entrance to a small National Park called Waiotapu Thermal Wonderland. My attention was drawn by the slightly curious behaviour of a young Park Ranger, who was loading his 4WD truck with bags of soap. Alex explained to me that he was about to drive to the Lady Knox Geyser, where he would pour the soap into the geyser. This would produce a small eruption, to entertain the tourists that would be gathered there waiting for him. He insisted that it was a spectacle not too be missed, and invited me to leave the bike at the Ranger Station nearby and join him for the ride.

Before long we were bumping along a dirt track which followed the base of a volcanic valley into the depths of the National Park. Arriving at Lady Knox, a handful of tourists were duly gathered around a hole in the ground, awaiting our arrival. It was time for the daily 10am eruption! Alex gave a short geography lecture before ordering everyone to stand back at least twenty yards, in order to view the eruption from a safe distance. Having emptied three bags of soap into the hole, he barely had enough time to scramble back himself before a thin column of boiling water shot up to a height of at least fifty metres, before fanning out into the largest fountain that I had ever seen. It was an impressive spectacle, which lasted for several minutes and delighted the assembled onlookers.

As we drove back to the Park entrance, Alex kindly took the time to give me a brief tour of some of the other weird and wonderful volcanic features of the Park, including the famous Champagne Lake – a turquoise natural hot spring with steam rising from the water's surface. Back at the Ranger Station, we had a cup of tea together, before I went on my way.

Following my unplanned stop at Waiotapu, I rode hard the rest of the day in order to try and reach the lakeside town of Taupo, in the centre of the North Island. A few miles short of Taupo, there was narrow dirt road on the right leading to a lookout point, from where it would be possible to view a local geothermal power station. There was still plenty of daylight left, so I decided to make the diversion.

At the lookout point, I was amazed to encounter my old German cycle touring companion, Olaf! Our paths had crossed almost a year previously on the Indonesian

Island of Flores, when we arrived together on the ferry from Komodo, and then passed each other several times on the road to Ruteng. He was riding now with a German girl called Eva and they were heading north towards Auckland, having almost completed their tour of New Zealand together. We shared a meal together at the lookout point, while a bus-load of Japanese tourists took it in turns to have their photos taken with us. The power station was colossal, and made quite an impressive spectacle, but seemed rather irrelevant in comparison with this incredible chance reunion.

By the time that we climbed back on our bikes again it was starting to get dark, so we rode just a couple of miles to the nearby Huka Falls, on the Waikatu River, and set up camp together there. Olaf's tent was big enough for all three of us to huddle together around a candle and spend the evening exchanging stories from the year that had elapsed since we were in Flores. Olaf had spent most of that time travelling alone in Australia, before meeting Eva at a Melbourne hostel. The two of them had teamed up straight away, and now seemed to make a great couple. It was into the early hours by the time that I finally retired to my own tent, and drifted off to sleep to the sound of the gushing Huka Falls nearby.

Olaf and Eva continued their journey north at first light, while I headed in the opposite direction into Taupo. The town was just waking up on a bitterly cold morning, and I treated myself to a cooked breakfast at one of the lakeside cafes.

Lake Taupo is the largest lake in New Zealand, covering some six hundred square miles. Across the water were the snow-capped peaks of the Tongariro National Park, and I spent the rest of the day riding around the shores of the lake towards them. On the far side of the lake was the smaller town of Turangi, where I checked into a hostel for the night.

My roommate at the hostel was a middle-aged American called Steve, who was coming to the end of a two-week trout fishing vacation. He tried to persuade me to join him for his final day's fishing, but this has never been one of my favourite sports. Instead, I set off early in the morning to cross the Tongariro Plateau, by way of the Desert Road. Fortunately, there was no sign of the strong winds that are said to sweep across the plateau most days, and I was able to climb steadily to the highest point at 1074 metres. The surrounding mountains were mostly obscured by clouds, on a bleak winter's day, although I did catch occasional glimpses of snow-covered Mount Ruahepu, before descending into the town of Waioru, on the southern edge of the plateau.

From Waioru it was a much more pleasant ride across gentle rolling hill country, and the clouds cleared a little to reveal the rugged Oruahine Mountains away to the east. That night, I reached the tiny historic settlement of Mangaweka and found lodgings at a quaint little hotel called Puha Palace. This old building was once the home of the famous New Zealand poet Sam Hunt, but the present occupiers were a young couple that had moved down from Auckland to start a new life in the country. I was their only guest that night, and they could not have done more to make me feel at home.

The hard terrain was behind me now and I made rapid progress across lowland agricultural plains the next day. At the busy market town of Levine, I decided to try a night at the town campsite. The site was very well equipped, with facilities including a large kitchen and common room. With winter well underway now, however, it was virtually deserted. This suited me fine, because it was another bitterly cold night, so I brought my sleeping bag inside and slept on the couch.

The last stretch on the North Island was a blustery ride along the coastal highway, as high winds swept in from the ocean. With heavy traffic and drizzling rain thrown in, it was not the most comfortable ride! It was some relief to arrive in Wellington, which is the nation's capital city and the terminal for the Inter-Islander ferry. Passing the terminal, somebody shouted to me that the ferry would be leaving for the South Island in ten minutes. There would be an opportunity to explore

Wellington on the return journey, so I quickly purchased a ticket and rode straight onto the ferry.

The three-hour crossing between New Zealand's two major islands is reputed to be very scenic but, with appalling weather reducing visibility to almost zero, I retreated to the video lounge for the entire journey. We docked at the picturesque South Island port of Picton, which lies in a deep bay, surrounded by lush, forested mountains. There were several guesthouses dotted around the ferry port and a small Youth Hostel, where I was allocated a dormitory all to myself. The warden helpfully explained that he was not expecting anyone else, as most sensible people tend to avoid the South Island during winter, unless they are heading straight for the ski resorts!

The skies cleared dramatically overnight and I set off from Picton on a crisp, sunny morning. The coastal road towards the north-eastern city of Nelson was called Queen Charlotte Drive – named after the Queen of England in Captain Cook's times. It turned out to be a spectacular ride, with the road rising and falling steeply along a rugged stretch of coastline, and affording panoramic views over the deep inlets of the Marlborough Sounds at almost every turn. It would have been a crime to rush such a journey, so I stopped frequently to take in the incredible vistas.

It took all day to ride just twenty-four miles to the sleepy village of Havelock, which nestles beneath Mount Takorika. The Youth Hostel here was Havelock's original primary school, built in 1881. This school was attended by Ernest Rutherford, who later achieved fame by splitting the atom at Manchester University in 1932. My thoughts went back to the physics lectures that I had attended a few years previously at the Rutherford Lecture Theatre in Manchester, where the feat was actually accomplished. I never imagined then that I would spend a night at Rutherford's old primary school on the other side of the world!

There was a heavy frost overnight, and my cycling clothes froze solid on the washing line that was strung across the old playground. It took some time to thaw them out around the fireplace, before I could set off that morning. It turned out to be another very enjoyable ride, on a bright, sunny day, as the road veered inland through forested hills towards Nelson. On arriving in the city, there were several hostels to choose from, but I had to try one that went under the name of Dave's Palace!

Nelson was the first city to be established in New Zealand by the English colonisers. It has an ideal situation and was now a thriving tourist centre. To the north were the sandy beaches and snow-capped peaks of the Abel Tasman National Park, while to the south were the rivers and glacial lakes of the Nelson Lakes National Park. The atmosphere at Dave's Palace was wonderful, and huge meals were served each evening. The resident cook was a Dutchman with a familiar face, but I could not place him at first. He seemed equally baffled at the sight of me, and we chatted for some time before managing to work out that we were both staying at the Salvation Army Hostel in Calcutta at the same time, some eighteen months previously! Syd had been plying his trade as a cook at various hostels around the world, in return for his lodgings and the modest sums that he charged his fellow backpackers for what could only be described as top class cuisine.

I spent a few days at Dave's Palace, taking short walks in the surrounding hills during the daytimes, and coming home to Syd's delicious and exotic meals in the evenings. It was one of those places where it would have been nice to stay for much longer but, with winter settling in now, I knew that it was important to get down to the south before some of the roads were blocked off by snowdrifts.

On another bright, frosty morning, I rode out of Nelson, on a route that would take me through the Nelson Lakes National Park to the West Coast. The highway followed a river valley through lush forest to the village of Mokutipo, where lunch was a slightly stale meat pie and packet of crisps from the village store.

A long climb up to Hope Saddle was well rewarded with a panoramic view of the surrounding forests and lakes. Feeling a bit adventurous now, I decided to make a detour along the Braeburn Track. This dirt road would take me through the forest to Lake Rotorua (another one!), before rejoining the highway again at the town of Murchison, about twenty miles south.

It was a slow, bumpy ride, with just the sound of the wind rustling through the trees to break the tranquillity. Just before the lake, there was a rather rough-looking campsite, consisting of a very bumpy field and a couple of brick buildings that were still under construction. It was evening now, so I decided to investigate further. Turning into the driveway, however, I had to swerve suddenly in order to avoid an old station wagon that was hurtling towards me. The bearded driver gave a slightly apologetic wave, as he flashed past me and out of the gates.

Having regained my composure, I ventured further down the drive. At first, the site seemed to be deserted, but then an elderly man emerged from one of the buildings, wearing an old lumber jacket and bobble hat. He was of Swiss descent and spoke only broken English, but managed to explain that he was the owner of the project, which would be completed in time for the following summer. The nearby lake was very popular with anglers, he explained, and this luxury campsite was sure to attract plenty of visitors. It was clearly not ready for visitors yet, however, but he invited me to spend the night in the workman's cabin, which was occupied by a German builder that was working for him. I could only assume that this was the guy that had nearly run me down a few moments ago, but accepted the invitation anyway!

The cabin was actually an old railway carriage, and the old fellow got the stove burning before leaving me to settle in. Before long, the German worker duly arrived. His name was Mike, and he was quick to apologise for his erratic driving – explaining that he had not been expecting a cyclist to appear on the driveway at that moment! Mike had been labouring here for the last three weeks, with only his eccentric old boss for company, and seemed very pleased to have somebody else to talk to. As we chatted away into the night, he explained that the Swiss man actually owned much of the land in this region, despite his rather humble appearance.

Mike had advised me that the Braeburn Track was in a terrible condition beyond the lake, and would be virtually impossible to ride on. In view of this, there was nothing for it but to double back the way that I had come and take the highway instead. It had been an interesting diversion nevertheless, and another little adventure to store away in the memory banks.

Back on the highway, I rode down to Murchison, and then continued along a road running parallel to the broad Buller River, which carves a gorge through some rugged mountain country. Turning off at Inangahua Junction, I started to look for a roadside camping spot, as the evening drew in. This proved difficult, however, with most of the land fenced off privately, and I rode until just before nightfall to the village of Reefton, where there was a campsite. The site was closed for the winter now but, on making enquiries in the village, I received permission to camp there.

The next morning it was a much easier ride along the Grey River Valley, which cut through gently rolling farmland to the coast at Greymouth. This may well be a thriving resort town in the summer, but now it seemed a rather dull collection of motels and timber mills. The Youth Hostel was a welcome sight though, and it was nice to escape from the cold that evening.

The West Coast of the South Island is known for its high levels of rainfall, but I rode south from Greymouth on another clear sunny day. The highway was never far from the coast, as it crossed lush farmland on its way towards the Southern Alps. It was not too long before the mountains appeared on the horizon, with their snowy peaks glistening in the sun. That night, I camped behind a village pub at Hari Hari. It was far too cold for the camping experience to be remotely enjoyable, but at least I was able to spend the evening in the warmth of the pub. The locals were most welcoming, although a little bemused as to why I should want to ride around New Zealand in the middle of winter. (It was a question that I had asked myself several times!)

The expected rain arrived overnight, so I stayed wrapped up warm up in the tent until mid-morning, when it finally started to ease off. A rare puncture caused another brief delay, but I eventually made it back onto the road. It turned out to be a thoroughly miserable day, with the mountains making only brief appearances through the cloud and drizzle. The highlight was probably a rest stop at the village of Whataroa, where a sympathetic shopkeeper made me a cup of coffee! By evening, I had made it to a hostel at the township of Franz Josef, which is situated close to the famous glacier of the same name.

Never having seen a glacier before, I was determined to visit Franz Josef on a clear day, which meant waiting at the hostel for a couple of days. This was no hardship really as it was a comfortable place, and there were even a few other backpackers around the place for company. One of these was an East German girl called Birgit, who was hitchhiking around the country on her own. This might sound a little foolish, but she had recently hitched across Africa, from Cairo to Cape Town, and seemed more than capable of looking after herself! When the blue skies finally reappeared, I seized the opportunity and set off on foot along the Waiho Valley towards the glacier.

Approaching the glacier, I was made aware of its close proximity by the tormented sound of creaks, groans and gurgles, not to mention the occasional crash, as huge chunks of ice fell from its melting face into a pool of water below. When it first came into view, it looked like a thin smooth slither of ice, grinding its way down through the forested mountainside. On closer inspection, however, I was surprised to see that the face of the glacier was actually formed into steep pinnacles, arches and chasms, some of which were over thirty feet deep. A guided group of hikers were actually climbing on the glacier itself, but I was content to spend the day hiking in the surrounding mountains.

Before leaving the village of Franz Josef, I paid a visit to St James's Church, from where there was a beautiful view of the glacier and the Waiho Valley, through a plate glass window from behind the altar. Apparently, this view was chosen for the ninth stamp in the 1946 'Peace Issue', to mark the end of the Second World War.

Anxious to make the most of the clear skies, I jumped on the bike that evening and rode a few miles further south to the next hostel, close to Fox Glacier. This was to be my base for the next couple of days, as I sheltered from more inclement weather, while taking every opportunity to make short forays into the mountains and valleys. The Fox Glacier itself was very similar to Franz Josef, but the real highlight of this stop was a visit to Lake Matheson, just a few miles from the village. This is a beautiful and secluded spot, where New

Zealand's two highest mountains – Cook and Tasman – are perfectly reflected in the still glacial waters. It was an image that I had seen on tourist posters many times since my arrival in New Zealand, but the tranquillity of this place on a clear winter's day was something that a poster would never quite be able to capture. It was such an enchanting place that I actually rode out there three times!

It was eighty miles from Fox Glacier to the next settlement at Haast. I made an early start in miserable weather, which only deteriorated as the day progressed. This stretch of the West Coast is particularly rugged, and there were very few places to shelter from the rain, so there was little option but to try to ignore the discomfort and soldier on. The rain was quite torrential at times and my waterproofs were fighting a losing battle to keep me dry. There comes a point, however, when you are so wet through that you hardly notice it any more, and I actually started to enjoy the ride! The rough seas and dark skies contributed to a rather forbidding atmosphere, which only added to the sense of adventure.

The settlement at Haast was a welcome sight, although it was little more than a small cluster of buildings dotted around the highway. There was just one hotel, which looked fairly upmarket, but I would have paid anything to escape from the elements that evening! It turned out, however, that the hotel had a backpackers' bunkroom, so there was no need to blow the budget after all. Not surprisingly, the bunkroom was empty that night, so I was able to make full use of the space and hang out all my wet clothes to dry.

The skies cleared overnight and I set off from Haast in the best of spirits. The highway followed the Haast River Valley as it wound its way inland, through snow-covered mountains. The first real climb of the day was a steady one up to the Haast Pass, which, at 560 metres, is the lowest crossing point in the Southern Alps. The weather had remained fine and the mountain scenery was at its best, as I slowly made my way up towards the pass. From the pass, the road descended into the southern province of Otago. I stopped for the night at the village of Makaroa, which consisted of a Ranger Station, grocery shop, campground and a couple of farms.

Almost inevitably, the rain was back again in the morning! From Makaroa, the road followed the steep-sided shores of Lake Wanaka and quickly deteriorated into little more than a dirt track, that was just about wide enough for vehicles. When the track turned away from the lakeshore, I started to wonder whether I had somehow missed the main road altogether! The South Island is very sparsely populated, especially down in mountainous Otago, so it was unlikely that there would be any opportunity to ask for directions. I decided just to keep going and hope for the best.

It was a steep climb from the lakeshore and the track was quite slippery, so I had to push some of the way. Eventually, on reaching the pass, another huge glacial valley opened up before me, with a vast blue lake contained within. This was Lake Hawea, and a thin strip along its shoreline could only be a sealed road. Before long, I was safely down onto the tarmac and confident, once more, that I was heading in the right direction!

The highway skirted Lake Hawea, before criss-crossing the mountains again to rejoin Lake Wanaka at the pretty town of Wanaka itself, on its southern edge. This was the first sizeable settlement that I had seen for ten days, and it was a relief to be able to replenish my dwindling food supplies at the supermarket. The town had an ideal lakeside situation in the heart of the Southern Alps, but seemed completely unspoilt by tourism. This was probably because the growth and popularity of nearby Queenstown has enabled Wanaka to go virtually unnoticed, as the majority of tourists head straight for the South Island's most famous resort. There were a couple of hostels in the town, however, and I checked into one for a couple of nights.

From the dormitory window, I had a clear view of nearby Mount Roy. It was a majestic sight and the temptation to climb it was impossible to resist. This was the most ambitious hike that I was to attempt in New Zealand, and turned out to be one of the best. The trail started from the edge of town and wound its way up towards the summit. It took about an hour to reach the snowline, after which progress was rather slow. When I finally made it to the summit, about three hours later, the snow was more than a foot deep. My feet were numb from the cold, but the views across Lake Wanaka and the Southern Alps were incredible. The jagged, snowy peaks looked like an over-decorated Christmas cake glistening in the sun. I had barely reached the summit, however, when the skies suddenly turned grey, and the distant roar of thunder signalled an approaching storm. I hurried back down through the snow as quickly as possible, and had just about made it back to the town when the heavens opened!

Setting off from Wanaka at dawn, I battled hard all day against freezing winds that blew against me as I rode along the Kawarau River Gorge, through another chain of mountains, towards Queenstown. It was a tough ride, but there was some light relief on reaching the Kawarau Gorge Suspension Bridge – New Zealand's main venue for 'bungy-jumping'. Apparently this craze originated in New Zealand, and Queenstown now claims the title 'Bungy Capital of the World'! I had arrived just in time to witness the spectacle of six tourists enjoying their 'thrill of a lifetime'. Feeling no desire myself to jump off the bridge with my feet tied to an elastic cord, and having satisfied myself that the six daredevils were still alive, I continued with my own (slightly less thrilling!) business of riding into the headwinds. Half an hour later, the bungy-jumpers came hurtling past me in a minibus, on their way back to Queenstown. Eventually, with the light fading and snow falling heavily, I arrived in Queenstown myself.

Queenstown is considered to be the all-year-round adventure capital of New Zealand, with its ready access to the ski-fields and the glacier-carved coastline of Fjiordland National Park to the south. The town has a spectacular setting on the shores of Lake Wakitupo, across the water from a jagged mountain range called 'The Remarkables', which are shaped like an upside-down saw blade.

It continued to snow throughout the night, and Queenstown was buried under a foot of snow by morning. This first winter snowfall was referred to locally as 'The Big Dump' – signalling the start of the ski season. The ski-fields had to remain closed for another day, however, due to blizzard conditions on the slopes. This caused some frustration among the would-be skiers at the hostel, but I was more than happy to relax in the warm hostel lounge and rest my aching limbs! One of the backpackers there was an English girl called Jill, whom I had already bumped into four times during my journey around New Zealand. It was nice to see her again, although she did ask me whether I was stalking her!

The skies were clear in the morning and Queenstown was glistening in the snow. Most of the backpackers headed straight for the ski slopes, while Jill and I set off on a hike. From the town we made our way through deep snow towards the summit of Queenstown Hill. The trail was invisible, but we were able to follow a set of footprints that seemed to head in the right direction. The freshly fallen snow was hanging delicately from the branches of pine trees, creating something of a winter wonderland. As we neared the summit, spectacular vistas across the mountains and lakes of the Southern Alps opened up beneath us. It was like being in a dream at times and I took numerous photographs – only to discover later that none of them had come out, as I had loaded the film incorrectly!

On another clear and frosty morning, with temperatures hovering around minus seven degrees, a radio announcement warned that all roads leading south from Queenstown were blocked by snowdrifts, and that roads north were in a treacherous condition. I had already accepted that it would be impossible to ride further south at this time of year, but now it seemed that riding in any direction would be fairly tricky. With conditions predicted to deteriorate even further, I decided to choose a different form of transport, at least as far as Christchurch – three hundred miles to the north-east. Fortunately, some minibuses were still running, and I booked myself onto an afternoon departure. This left me time for a stroll around the town, and one last look across the water at 'The Remarkables'. Queenstown deserves its reputation as a world-class holiday destination, and my stay here was probably the highlight of my trip around New Zealand.

There were only two other passengers on the bus, so there was plenty of room for the bike. The first twenty miles were painfully slow, as we slid over a sheet of ice, but conditions gradually improved as we moved further north. The whole region was covered in a blanket of snow, making it quite unrecognisable from when I had cycled into Queenstown on the same road, four days earlier. We needed snow chains for the climb up to Lindis Pass, from where the summit of New Zealand's highest mountain, Mount Cook, could be seen towering above the other peaks. Then we skirted Lakes Pukaiki and Tekapo, before finally leaving the snow behind as we began to cross the intensely cultivated Canterbury Plains. At this point, I was tempted to jump out and start cycling again! However, I resisted the temptation and tried instead to join in with a discussion about sheep farming, which had lasted for most of the journey. Late in the evening, we finally arrived in Christchurch, where I was deposited at the Rollaston Youth Hostel.

Christchurch is New Zealand's second largest city, and is claimed to be the most English city outside England. It was named after Christchurch College in Oxford, which was attended by one of the early settlers. I began my explorations by climbing the tower of the large stone Cathedral in the main square. The narrow city streets beneath me were full of 'Old World' character, while the Canterbury Plains in the distance looked like a patchwork quilt. A couple of days were happily spent bumbling around this pleasant city, relaxing by the River Avon, and catching up on world news at the library.

It was nice to get back on the bike again, and I enjoyed a comfortable ride north on the coastal highway to Amberley, where the flat Canterbury Plains give way to gentle rolling hills. During the afternoon, the weather started to deteriorate so, on reaching the small town of Cheviot, I decided to look for lodgings. There was just one motel in the town, which was fully occupied by railway workers, but they allocated me some tent space and invited me to make use of the kitchen and lounge. Temperatures dropped to well below freezing overnight, so I had to sleep in five layers of clothing!

The next day's target was Kaikoura, which lies about forty-five miles north of Cheviot on the East Coast. I was well over half the way towards my destination when a motorist, who was travelling in the opposite direction, stopped to warn me that the highway was closed a few miles south of Kaikoura, due to an expected avalanche. My only way of reaching Kaikoura was to cut inland on a minor road, in order to link up with another highway at the village of Waiau. This was a big detour, and the inland road turned to gravel in places, so progress was slow. On reaching Waiau, it was already late afternoon and Kaikoura was still over fifty miles away – even further away than when I had started out from Cheviot in the morning! This was rather demoralising, so I decided to call it a day and spend the night in Waiau. The village campsite was deserted, but a sign on the gate directed me to the general store, where I was able to obtain the key. As usual, the site facilities were quite impressive - including a large kitchen, dining room and a comfortable lounge, equipped with snooker table and piano. I had landed on my feet yet again!

There were more problems the next day. It was raining heavily from early morning, and the 'highway' to Kaikoura turned out to be nothing more than a boggy dirt road. It was extremely hard work just trying to keep my balance at times, and Kaikoura seemed further away than ever. I ploughed away through the mud for several hours, before finally accepting a lift from a truck that had overtaken me twenty miles short of Kaikoura. The driver was from Blenheim, further north, and said that he had seen me in the morning when he was driving the other way to Christchurch. Now he was on his way back to Blenheim, and was surprised at how far I had managed to get!

At last we reached Kaikoura, which is a pretty, seaside resort, surrounded by rocky cliffs. The driver dropped me off at the Youth Hostel, just as the rain was finally easing off and the sun threatening to make an appearance. Kaikoura is also a renowned whale-watching venue, with sperm whales seen off its coast in greater numbers than anywhere else in the world. Apparently, the reason for their concentration in this area is the abundance of squid – their favourite food – in a deep trench less than a mile from the shore. The whale-watching trips were a little outside my budget, however, so I settled for a short walk along the cliff tops to visit a colony of seals that were basking in evening sunlight.

Back on the coastal highway, it was a much easier ride to Blenheim – not least due to fine weather! The landscape seemed to be a microcosm of New Zealand, with rich farmland, rugged coastline, snow-capped mountains and plenty of wildlife. Close to Blenheim, my front gear changer snapped on a steep incline, but this inconvenience did not prevent me from clocking up eighty-five miles by the end of a very satisfying day.

The apple-picking season was underway in the region, and the Backpackers' Hostel in Blenheim was full of itinerant labourers. It would have been a good opportunity to work for a few days and boost my travel funds but, with my flight out of Auckland just two weeks away now, I decided against it. That night, I slept in the middle tier of a three-storey bunk bed – sandwiched between an Israeli and a Maori. You never know who you will end up sharing a bed with in a hostel dormitory!

After a visit to the local bike shop for a new gear changer, it was a short ride north to Picton, and I arrived in time for the midday ferry back to Wellington. It was a pleasant three-hour cruise through the Marlborough Sounds, and across the narrow stretch of water that separates the two islands of New Zealand. For much of the way, we were trailed by a shoal of dolphins, diving and playing in the wake of the ferry. My tour of the South Island was over now and I reflected on a tough journey, in the middle of the harshest winter that this country had seen for over twenty years. The South Island is a special place though, with an immense variety of dramatic landscapes from the Marlborough Sounds in the north to the Southern Alps. Despite the hardships, it was a journey that I would not have missed for the world.

Wellington is known as the 'Windy City'. It lies on the western shores of Port Nicholson, squeezed between the sea and a range of steep hills. Behind the bustling central area, suburbs of quaint timber houses spill down the slopes and overlook the harbour.

One of these quaint timber houses was a Backpackers' Hostel, called Beethoven House, which had been recommended to me by several different people. Standing at the door was Mr Goh, the Chinese Proprietor, about whom I had also heard plenty! He was most welcoming, if a little overpowering, and sat me down straight away for a cup of tea and a kind of introductory chat. After eliciting a few details from me – mainly confirmation that I was not a Catholic or a smoker – he proceeded to entertain me with a barrage of non-stop 'jokes' and anecdotes, mostly on the subjects of – you guessed it – Catholicism and smoking! It was hard to know whether his dislike of these two pursuits was really genuine, or whether he was just playing out a role to see how I reacted. Next came a grand tour of the strangest hostel that I had ever come across. There was a bust of Beethoven in the hallway and almost every room contained some memorabilia relating to the great composer, including framed old newspaper articles from around the turn of the century. Being an occasional piano player myself, I happened to be carrying a piece of Beethoven sheet music in my luggage, and this pleased him no end! Competing for wall space with the Beethoven memorabilia were numerous typed notices, mostly containing derogatory remarks about Catholics and smokers. The one that really sticks in my mind, however, was attached to a door leading into one of the dormitories. It read:

> *'Please feel free to kick the head in of anyone who starts rearranging their backpack at five 'o' clock in the morning!'*

I allowed myself just two nights in the capital city, and it is this bizarre hostel that always springs to mind when I think of Wellington. Though not the most comfortable hostel I had stayed in, it was certainly the funniest! We were awoken at 7am each morning to the sound of Beethoven's Fifth Symphony, piped at high volume into each dormitory. This did not please everyone but at least produced some entertaining reactions! For breakfast we all sat around a long table, where we were forced to endure Mr Goh's morning sermon as he was preparing toasted sandwiches and tossing apples in our general direction. Despite being extremely eccentric, he looked after his guests well, and the modest overnight fee was well worth paying just for the experience.

With my flight to Canada less than two weeks away now I decided to take a fairly direct route to Auckland through the centre of the North Island. A strong tailwind blew me northwards towards Levin, where I returned to the same campsite that I had stayed at on the way down. The bottom bracket on the bike had become quite loose, despite repeated attempts at tightening it, so I popped into the bike shop for a replacement. The mechanic there was amazed that I had managed to cover over thirteen thousand miles on the same bottom bracket, and insisted on replacing it free of charge. He said that it was a small contribution to my round-the-world trip on behalf of New Zealand!

From Levin I continued north to the town of Bulls, before veering eastwards towards the coastal city of Whanganui, where I checked into a quiet riverside hostel for the night. The nights were a little warmer on the North Island, but it was still quite a relief to be indoors.

The highway from Whanganui passed through a hilly river gorge to the town of Raetihi, in the mountainous central part of the North Island. Here I turned off onto a narrow mountain road towards the small ski resort of Ohakune, which lies at the foot of Mount Ruapehu – the highest mountain on the North Island. With the ski season well underway now, all accommodation in Ohakune was fully booked, but I managed to persuade one of the hostel managers to let me sleep on a dormitory floor.

The weather was so bad overnight that the ski-fields had to be temporarily closed in the morning. This created a gloomy atmosphere in the hostel, with the would-be skiers not really knowing what to do with themselves. Leaving the despondent skiers behind, I rode north through the Tongariro National Park, which is dominated by the peaks of its three active volcanoes – Ruahepu, Ngurahoe and Taupo. My ride was cut short that day by a sudden torrential downpour, which made the mountain road very slippery. Although it was still early in the day, I decided to seek refuge at another ski resort, which was strangely named 'National Park'.

Again the hostels were mostly full, but I managed to get a bed for the night at one called Howard's Lodge.

Though it was raining heavily again in the morning, the ski-fields were declared open again. This was a cause for great rejoicing, and by the time I had got up the other hostellers were already busy shovelling down breakfast and cracking skiing-related jokes. Before long the hostel was deserted, and I enjoyed a leisurely breakfast with the hostel owner, Sue, who was relieved to have everyone out of the way so that she could clean the place at last!

With the rain easing off towards lunchtime, I collected my things together and started out on a pleasant ride through the northern section of the Park. The big climbs were behind me now and the road meandered across rolling hill country to the town of Tauramanui. This was the last town marked on my map for some distance, so I decided to check into a 'modest looking' hotel, called Grand Lodge, on the main street. There was nobody at the reception area, and I waited there for some time before one of the guests – a young Maori called Joe– invited me into the lounge. There was a lively atmosphere in the lounge, with thirty or so hotel residents – nearly all Maoris – enjoying a rugby match on the big screen. By the time the match had finished, it was well into the evening and there was still no sign of any hotel staff materialising. Joe suggested that I move my things into a room that he knew to be empty, and make full use of the facilities. He explained that most of the guests, including himself, were long term residents of the hotel, and that it was quite unusual for newcomers to turn up unannounced – hence the unmanned reception area.

There was a communal kitchen next to my room, so I set about preparing my dinner. It was not long, however, before a heated debate broke out in the lounge next door. It was not hard to hear what was being said, and I soon realised that the row was about me! One of the older guests was complaining bitterly that I had no right to use the hotel's facilities until the management had checked me in. He claimed that this was a typical example of the white man taking advantage of the Maoris. He was directing his complaints at Joe, who was arguing back vociferously on my behalf, explaining that I had nowhere else to go, and would gladly pay for my room as soon as someone turned up to take my money. The voices were getting louder and the two may well have come to blows, if it had not been for the sudden timely arrival of the Manager, who was also a Maori. He quickly calmed things down, and then came round into the kitchen and apologised to me for his absence. He even insisted on moving me to a bigger room. The older man retired to his room, sending me a fairly hostile glance as he passed by in the corridor!

Another rainy day followed, but I was becoming fairly immune to the drizzle by now and did not let it bother me too much. I rode north to the town of Otorohanga, and then went in search of the Youth Hostel. The hostel was included on the list of Youth Hostels that I had carried with me around New Zealand, but nobody in the town seemed to know of its existence. Eventually, a lady in the 'Milk Bar' managed to locate it for me by making several local phone calls. She sent me to the home of an elderly lady on the outskirts of town, who had converted her two large spare bedrooms into hostel dormitories! One of the rooms was occupied by three young English girls, while I shared the other with a typically polite Japanese traveller.

Not far from Otorohanga were the world-famous Waitomo Caves. These were formed from an ancient seabed that has been lifted and then eroded into a surreal landscape of limestone caves, some of which are still unexplored. Only two of the caves were open to the public, and I arrived just in time to join a tour of one of them. The Waitomo River flowed through the cave into the hillside, and the tour ended with a short boat trip through a part of the cave that was brightly illuminated by thousands of glow-worms. The glow-worm is the larva of 'Arachnocampa Luminosa' – a member of the gnat family. They are tiny creatures but, massed together in huge numbers in a dark cave, the effect was quite electrifying!

After spending a day at the caves, I returned to the hostel to find that the other guests had all moved on, to be replaced by six young lads from London. The old lady sensibly went out for the evening!

The Waitomo Caves were the last scheduled 'place of interest' on my tour of New Zealand, and there was little on my mind now besides getting back to John's house in Auckland as soon as possible. Riding north, the weather was terrible again and I started to look forward to the Canadian summer that awaited me. The road from Otorohanga joined up with Highway One at the village of Ngaruawahia, which I made no attempt to pronounce. Highway One cut across rolling farm country to the city of Hamilton, which had been my first stop on the way down. There were still a few hours of daylight left, so I kept going to the smaller town of Huntly. There was a campsite here, where I was able to escape from the elements by renting a cabin for the night.

The final leg of my New Zealand tour was yet another tough one, as I battled against strong headwinds and steady rain. Auckland was firmly in my sights now though, and I was determined to keep going. It was just starting to get dark when I finally arrived back at John's house in Herne Bay. We celebrated the end of my New Zealand tour with a night out at the Gluepot Inn – one of Auckland's most famous pubs – where the entertainment was provided by a local blues band.

There were a couple of days to spare before my flight to Canada, giving me a chance to recuperate and spend some time with John. While I had been away, he had been dreaming up another bicycle journey of his own, which he was anxious to discuss with me. His plan was to fly to Turkey and ride across Europe to England - more or less following the same route that I had taken through Europe, only in reverse. These plans would come to fruition a couple of years later, by which time I was back in England and able to return his hospitality!

On the day of my departure John took the day off from work and introduced me to several of his neighbours, including a young couple that had recently emigrated here from England. I was able to assure them that the country that they had chosen to live in was full of natural wonders, and just waiting to be explored! In the evening, John drove me to the airport, and I said goodbye to one of the best friends that I had made on my travels.

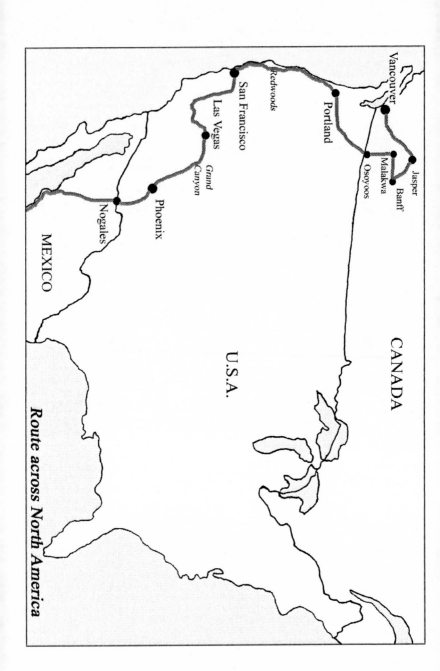

Route across North America

CHAPTER EIGHT

CALIFORNIA DREAMING

Vancouver to Nogales

SURROUNDED BY OCEANFRONT AND HUGE forested mountains, the beautifully situated city of Vancouver came into view, signalling the end of an eighteen-hour flight. It was 5pm on Sunday 12th July, 1992 – three hours earlier than when we had set off from Auckland. This was proving to be a long Sunday!

One of the Airport Customs Officials was quite unimpressed at my lack of an onward plane ticket, and did not seem at all happy with my explanation that I was intending to cycle out of the country. The officious young lady stood there shaking her head in disbelief as she flipped through the pages of my passport, and asked repeatedly where all the money was coming from to visit so many countries. My cause was not helped by the fact that both my credit cards had expired, even though I tried to explain that I would be receiving the replacements by 'General Delivery':

"What is General Delivery?" she asked

"I will be receiving my new credit cards at the post office"

"But there are many post offices in Vancouver"

"Yes, but only one is nominated for General Delivery. This is how I have been receiving my post for two years now"

She seemed entirely unconvinced by my arguments, but I did at least have enough money in travellers' cheques to cover my stay in Canada and her colleagues had found nothing offensive in my luggage. She eventually relented and stamped my passport for six months.

It had taken nearly three hours to escape from the airport and I was feeling extremely tired, both mentally and physically. Having been used to riding on the left hand side of the road in New Zealand for the past couple of months, I wearily climbed onto the bike and set off on the left hand side of the busy freeway that runs between the airport and the city centre. Within seconds, a huge juggernaut had almost flattened me, as it hurtled past me from the opposite direction - alerting me to the fact that they drive on the right in Canada! Pulling myself together, I made my way across the freeway, and rode carefully into Vancouver. It was 11pm when I finally arrived at the huge Youth Hostel in the Jericho Beach suburb.

The hostel was crowded and noisy, but this did not prevent me from sleeping like a baby until well into the next day. Having been finally awoken by the cleaning lady, I took a bus into downtown Vancouver, which occupies a small peninsula jutting into the Burrard Inlet. My first port of call was the General Post Office, where I collected my new credit cards, as planned. Then I paid a visit to the home of Mike 'The Bike' Berube – the Canadian cyclist with whom I had travelled for several weeks in Greece and Turkey. His home was an old mansion-type building called 'The White House', which he shared with six others. Unfortunately, Mike was away in Europe again, but two of his housemates – Sam and Christina – were home, and they invited me to make use of his room for a few days.

I soon settled into my 'White House' accommodation, which was right in the heart of the downtown district, and just a 'stone's throw' away from the oceanfront. The city had a truly cosmopolitan feel to it, with the second largest 'Chinatown' in North America and a lot of European influence. As well as the rich cultural mix, Vancouver has a vibrant music scene, and three of Mike's housemates combined part-time jobs and studying with membership of various rock bands. They all seemed to enjoy city life to the full and insisted on taking me out every night that week to different music venues.

In the daytimes, everyone was busy working or catching up on their sleep, giving me plenty of time to explore the city on my own. I particularly enjoyed walking and cycling in nearby Stanley Park, which is a beautiful inner city park, with a five-mile sea wall promenade providing stunning views across the harbour. The highlight of the week though was a visit to the Vancouver Folk Festival, across the bay at Jericho Beach. It was an amazingly diverse event, with representations from all corners of the globe.

My plan was to head north-east to the mountain resort town of Jasper, five hundred miles away in the Rockies. From there I would turn southwards again and ride through the mountains on the famous Icefields Parkway to Banff, in Alberta. My travel funds were starting to run a little low again, so I hoped to pick up some work along the way – perhaps in the resort town of Banff.

Most of the inhabitants of the White House honoured me by emerging from their bedrooms well before their usual getting up times to see me off! I would miss these easy-going people who had made me feel so welcome, and enriched my stay in Vancouver.

It was an uncomfortably hot day but, after two months of winter riding in New Zealand, I could hardly complain! Before long I was clear of the suburbs and riding eastwards through the Frazer Valley on the Lougheed Highway. As the afternoon wore on, the effects of several late nights out in Vancouver started to take their toll on me. Looking around for somewhere to camp, I soon discovered an ideal spot just a short distance from the highway. It was a sheltered patch of sand just a few yards from the banks of the Thompson River. Camping had been something of an ordeal in the harsh New Zealand winter, so I really appreciated being able to cook in the open again and relax by the river on a warm summer's evening.

Temperatures were already up into the forties when I set off the next morning. The road followed the Fraser River to the historic town of Hope, which dates back to 1848, when a Hudson's Bay Company outpost was established here. At Hope, I turned onto the Fraser Canyon Highway, which would take me north towards the high country.

A young man called Rudi rode up alongside me. He was out on a short ride from a nearby holiday camp that he managed, and invited me to join him there for lunch. The turn-off to the camp was just up ahead, so before long I was sitting down with his family for a buffet lunch by the poolside. These Canadians seemed to enjoy their food, and it turned out to be a terrific feast. The camp was virtually empty, with all the children away on their daytime activities, so it was a very relaxing place to while away the hottest hours of the day. I could not resist a dip in the pool before leaving, and it was late afternoon by the time that I was back on the road.

The Fraser Canyon was spectacular, with enormous, sheer cliffs bearing down on a gushing river. The highway was something of a roller-coaster, but I was feeling strong now, as temperatures dropped towards evening, and decided to keep going for as long as possible. It was nearly 10pm by the time that the sun finally started to disappear behind the mountains and I had to look around for somewhere to camp. A half-built wooden house by the roadside looked promising. There were no windows in place yet, and no signs of life from within, so I hauled the bike in and settled down for the night. Despite spending several hours at the holiday camp, I had covered ninety-two miles that long summer's day.

At first light I was on my way again, in order to take advantage of the cooler early morning hours, and to avoid the wrath of any construction workers that may have decided to make an early start on the house! The town of Lytton marked the end of the Fraser Canyon, and I turned onto the Carriboo Highway, which follows the Thompson River Valley. The previous day's long ride had left me feeling quite lethargic, so when the temperatures began to soar again around lunchtime I decided to call it a day. Near the settlement of Cache Creek, I checked into a large forest campsite. There was a group of small tents already set up on the site, belonging to some tree-planters, who were working nearby. When they returned to their camp in the evening, I enquired after work myself, but the boss was reluctant to take on someone that had no tree planting equipment of his own, and could only remember planting one tree before in his life!

The next morning I rode thirty miles before treating myself to a typical Canadian breakfast of fried eggs, pancakes and maple syrup at a café in the town of Savona. Riding on towards the Rockies, I was overtaken by an increasing number of enormous motor-homes. The Canadians seem to like to take home with them when they go on holiday!

Late that afternoon, I arrived in the city of Kamloops, which lies roughly halfway between Vancouver and Jasper. This city is one of the major trading and route centres in British Columbia, but there was something of a 'Wild West' atmosphere about the place - even the bank clerks were wearing cowboy hats! Enquiring after accommodation, I was told that there were no campsites in the city, and no hotels charging less than fifty dollars a night. However, one person suggested that I try the local short-stay hostel for homeless people. This was something that I had not thought of before, but it seemed worth a try. It was a bit cheeky, but the Manager seemed quite amused at my request, and agreed to let me stay for up to three nights. Most of the guests were elderly folk, who seemed to live almost entirely for the next drink and showed no apparent interest in my arrival, despite my excessive amount of luggage making me feel a little conspicuous. With three nights being the maximum stay, however, there were plenty of spare beds, and it was nice to sleep in clean sheets for the first time since leaving Vancouver.

It took a long time to break through the imaginary barriers that seem to exist between the other residents of the hostel and myself, but I did gradually get to know a few of them. There was one, in particular, that made an impression on me. He was a highly decorated army veteran and was able to show me several of his medals. On leaving the army, however, he had been unable to adjust to civilian life and developed a drink problem. His wife left him and things spiralled out of control, to the point that he had to sell most of his possessions. Now he was spending the last few years of his life with little more than his medals and the drink for company.

At a set of traffic lights on my way out of Kamloops, a young man waved his arms frantically as he rushed across the road towards me. He quickly explained that he was a cycling enthusiast, and hoped that I had time for a chat. He actually owned a bike shop nearby, so I accompanied him there for a cup of coffee. He told me that it was his dream to cycle around Canada one day, and was interested to know what my impressions were of this vast country. He would not let me leave without allowing him to make a contribution to my journey, and asked me to choose anything I liked from the shop.

All I could think of was a new pair of handlebar grips, so we selected a pair and he fitted them himself before seeing me off with an envious smile!

There were no more diversions that day, and I rode steadily until evening on the Thompson River Valley Highway, which sliced its way through rolling hill country towards the Rockies. The river was my constant companion, and I set up camp close to the water's edge, in a rest area just outside the village of Clearwater.

The sun came up at 5am, and I was on the road again shortly afterwards. It was blissfully cool in this early part of the day, and I breezed along the highway for a couple of hours before treating myself to breakfast at a café in the village of Avola. It turned into another very hot day again and by mid-afternoon I was running out of energy. A campsite on the shores of Lake Eleanor was too tempting to pass by, so I checked in for the night. An American family were 'camping' in their huge motor home close by, and one of the children was sent over with some blueberry pie and ice cream to go with my evening stew!

With the Rocky Mountains staring down at me now, I continued northwards to the town of Valemount and then turned east onto the Yellowhead Highway. It was mostly uphill riding now, but the awe-inspiring mountain landscape in front of me helped to make this seem almost effortless. That night, I set up camp in a picnic area right in the shadow of snow-capped Mount

Robson, which rises to 3954 metres – the highest peak in the Canadian Rockies.

There was still a long climb ahead of me to the Yellowhead Pass, which marks the State border between British Columbia and Alberta. Setting off at first light, I was able to settle into an easy rhythm and slowly gained altitude. Things became much harder, however, as temperatures soared, and the road seemed to go up and up forever. It was late afternoon by the time that I finally reached the pass, having climbed for over fifty miles! I stopped to rest for a while, and take in a stunning array of jagged, forest-clad mountains. I was over the Continental Divide now, and the hard work was done for the day. The highway followed the Miette River as it wound its way down to the resort town of Jasper, and I rolled into town just as the sun was starting to disappear behind the mountains. This would be my base for exploring the northern section of the Rockies, so I checked myself into a large Youth Hostel, just out of town on the slopes of Whistler's Mountain.

My first excursion from the Jasper hostel was a twenty-mile ride to Medicine Lake, which nestles between steep-sided mountains. 'Medicine' comes from the Indian word meaning 'magical', and the lake was so-named because of its annual disappearing act.

Each autumn, the water disappears through a network of underground tunnels, only to return in summer as the snows melt. On the way back, I made a detour to visit Malign Canyon, which is a spectacular limestone gorge with turquoise pools and cascading waterfalls. The final highlight of the day came when a black bear darted across the road in front of me, as I was riding slowly back up the hill to the hostel.

Another day, I rode to nearby Mount Edith Cavell - named after an English nurse, who was executed in 1915 for assisting Allied soldiers to cross the frontier at Brussels. I managed to ride a good way up the mountainside on a narrow track, before locking the bike to a tree and continuing on foot across the Cavell Meadows. The meadows were ablaze with colourful wild flowers, while ahead of me was the famous Angel Glacier, hanging dramatically from the steep face of the mountain.

On a sunny July morning, I set off from Jasper on the Icefields Parkway, which snakes its way through the Rockies between Jasper and Banff and is reputed to be one of the world's most scenic highways. There are numerous lookout points along the way, and my first stop was the Athabasca Falls, where the entire force of the mighty Athabasca River is funnelled through a narrow gorge, creating a thunderous waterfall. Adding to the dramatic effect was a rainbow, which seemed to rise out of the waterfall.

The Parkway is immensely popular with cycle tourists of all kinds. A group of twenty or so were part of a 'downhill cycle tour', with a large truck gathering them up at the bottom of each descent and transporting them up to the next pass. This seemed a strange concept to me, as I always felt that part of the joy of downhill riding comes from the effort that you have made to earn the descent. Another unusual sight was a backpacker who had temporarily turned into a cycle tourist, and rode along with his backpack precariously strapped to the rear rack!

The hardest part of the day was a steep thirty-mile climb to Sunwapta Pass, which marks the boundary between the National Parks of Jasper and Banff. Just before the pass, the road bent slightly to the left to reveal the magnificent Athabasca Glacier, glistening in the sun beneath the summit of Mount Athabasca itself. This is one of six enormous glaciers that hang from the Columbia Icefield – a vast blanket of ice, which is 300 metres thick in places, and covers an area of 375 square kilometres. A brief detour along a narrow track brought me right to the toe of the glacier for a closer examination of its deep crevasses.

Just over the Sunwapta Pass, I stopped for the night at a simple, 'Wilderness Hostel' which consisted of nothing more than a couple of huts, serving as a bunkroom and kitchen. There was no washroom, but the nearby Hilda Creek compensated for this! The evening was chilly at this altitude, and I huddled together with half a dozen hardy travellers – mainly cyclists – around the campfire, discussing everything from politics to gear ratios.

Waking up to the awesome sight of glaciers and snow-clad mountaintops all around was amazing. It seemed a shame to rush on, so I decided to spend the day hiking with a couple of Taiwanese girls who had shared their fried chicken breakfast with me. We followed the Parker Ridge Trail, which ascended above the tree line and across an Alpine meadow to a crest, from where we were able to look down on the Saskatchewan Glacier - the largest tongue of the Columbia Icefield. Returning to the hostel late afternoon, I jumped straight on the bike and rode a further twenty miles along the Parkway to the next Wilderness Hostel at Rampart Creek.

The Rampart Creek Hostel was larger than the one at Hilda Creek, and quite crowded that evening. On arrival, I was immediately invited to join in a game of volleyball, which was the last thing that I wanted to do after a day of hiking and cycling! I joined in for a few minutes, however, and then cooled off with a quick dip in the icy waters of Rampart Creek.

It was another clear, sunny morning as I embarked on a long climb to Bow Summit. At 2085 metres, this is the highest point on the Icefields Parkway, and I was rewarded with a stunning, bird's-eye view of turquoise Peyto Lake, shimmering in the valley below. Apparently, these Rocky Mountain lakes change colour with the seasons, as the melting glacial waters pick up silt on their way in. The descent brought me down to the shores of Bow Lake, whose tranquil waters provided a near-perfect reflection of the surrounding snow-capped peaks.

As the Parkway continued to wind its way through the Rockies, revealing spectacular mountain vistas at every turn, I started to become a little 'blaze' about the scenery. However, I could not fail to appreciate the 'Gem of the Rockies' – Lake Louise - that evening. The blue-green waters of this lake are framed by Beehive Mountain on one side and Fairview Mountain on the other, with the majestic Victoria Glacier in the centre, creating a perfect picture. The large International Youth Hostel at the nearby tourist settlement was to be my base for the next few days.

It was the start of the long Bank Holiday weekend, and Lake Louise was engulfed by hundreds of tourists in the morning. Many of them were Japanese, busy posing for group photographs on the shores of the lake. To escape from the crowds I retrieved my bike from the hostel store room and cycled a few miles to Moraine Lake, which is almost as famous as Lake Louise, since it is featured on the back of the Canadian twenty dollar note. The ten glaciated summits of the Wenkchemna Peaks give this lake a stunning backdrop. Leaving the bike fastened to a tree at the lakeside, I spent the rest of the day hiking through the Valley Of Ten Peaks to Sentinel's Pass. A thin pillar of rock protruding from the mountainside close to the pass could only be the 'Sentinel'.

The Icefields Parkway ends at Lake Louise, but I continued riding east on the Bow Valley Parkway to Banff. The climbs were easier now, but the mountain scenery was still magnificent. One short detour from the highway brought me to the Johnstown Canyon, where a gushing waterfall plunges through a narrow gap into the bubbling river below. Arriving in Banff late in the evening, I made my way to the Youth Hostel, which was situated on a hillside overlooking the town. Fortunately, there was one dormitory bed left!

Encircled by five towering mountains, Banff is a bustling little resort town. The numerous hotels and lodges have long attracted travellers in search of casual employment, and I made an extensive tour of them over the next couple of days. Though there was plenty of work available, my lack of a working visa proved a major stumbling block. The immigration authorities required proof of a definite job offer, before a working visa application could be processed, and none of the employers that I spoke to were willing to provide one. They only seemed to be interested in hiring somebody that could start immediately. My travel funds needed a boost, and it seemed that my best chance of earning some money was to look for casual fruit-picking work. With this in mind, I decided to ride back across the

Great Divide into British Columbia and head for the Okanagon Valley – Canada's main fruit-growing area.

Feeling a little demoralised at my lack of job-hunting success in Banff, I rode back along the Bow Valley Parkway to Lake Louise, where I could not resist paying another visit to Canada's most photographed spot. The day was still young, so I continued west by way of the Kicking Horse Pass, whose name comes from an incident that occurred in 1858, when the explorer Dr James Hector was kicked by a packhorse. It was a gentle climb to the pass, followed by a steep descent into British Columbia. On the way down, I passed the entrance to the Canadian Pacific Railway's famous spiral tunnels, which enabled trains to cross the Great Divide at low gradient.

These south-western slopes of the Rockies are part of the Yoho National Park. At the Visitor Centre in the village of Field, there was an eye-catching display entitled 'How to Behave in Bear Country', including several gory photographs of tourists that had been severely mauled because they were not observing the rules. That night, I set up camp in a forest clearing by the Kicking Horse River, taking care to ensure that any tasty bear treats were secured high up in a tree at a safe distance from the tent!

The next morning it began to rain heavily, as I was tucking into a hearty breakfast at a café in the town of Golden. When the rain eased off a little, and I could drink no more coffee, I climbed back into the saddle and embarked on a long climb up into the Selkirk Mountains. This is an ancient range of mountains that were formed millions of years before the Rockies. Straddling the range is Glacier National Park, containing over four hundred glaciers! Just within the Park boundaries, I discovered a lovely sheltered camping spot beside the Beaver River. The sun made an appearance at last and, after a refreshing evening swim, I washed my clothes on the rocks, just as nomadic Indians had probably done years before.

The next day began with a twenty-mile climb to Roger's Pass. It was a misty morning, and I could hardly see more than a few feet in front of me, let alone appreciate the scenery in what is reputed to be one of Canada's most attractive National Parks. It was mid-morning by the time that I reached the pass, which was marked by a small hotel. A sign outside advertised an 'all you can eat' breakfast for $8, and this was too tempting to resist!

Two hours later, full of muffins, pancakes, scrambled eggs and other breakfast delights, I embarked on a forty-mile descent from the heights of Roger's Pass to the large town of Revelstoke. The mist continued to deprive me of scenery, and I managed to cycle through Glacier National Park without seeing a single glacier! There was another black bear sighting, however. It jumped out of the bushes onto the road, just a few yards in front, and took one look at me before scurrying away.

From Revelstoke - a fairly industrial town in the shadow of Mount Revelstoke - I continued west across rolling plains to the village of Craigellachie. The campsite here was right next to the very spot where the symbolic 'last spike' of the Canadian Pacific Railway was driven in on November 7th 1885. This marked the completion of the Canadian Pacific Railway – the nation's first transcontinental railway.

Early the next morning, I rode a few miles further west to the tiny village of Malakwa, on the edge of the Okanagon Valley. There was a large fruit-stand here, so I dropped in to enquire after work. The farmer, Walter Sprado, had just finished setting up the stand for the day, and he cheerfully hired me on the spot. Walter owned a small berry farm behind the fruit stand, and purchased all kinds of fruit and vegetables from other local farms to supplement his own produce on the stand.

There was only one other worker at the farm – a local lad called Dale, who had a simple, but kind, nature. Within an hour of my arrival, we were picking strawberries together. Later on, I set my tent up on the edge of the strawberry field, and was given the use of an old trailer containing cooker, fridge and a radio. There was no running water in the trailer, but an outside tap and hose served as a shower. The conditions were basic, but more than adequate, and I looked forward to learning all about life on a country fruit farm.

During the first week of my stay, I was kept occupied with all sorts of jobs besides berry picking, including weeding and chopping wood for our nightly barbecue. The financial rewards were not great for such backbreaking work, but a new opportunity arose when the sixteen-year-old girl who worked on the fruit-stand decided to elope to Toronto with her boyfriend. Apparently, she was trying to escape the wrath of her parents, who had just found out that she was pregnant. This left a vacancy on the fruit-stand, which I jumped in to fill.

Working on the fruit-stand suited me, and before long I was able to organise it more or less how I liked. Walter was away collecting fruit most days, while Dale picked the berries and I operated the stand. There was a steady stream of customers, including tourists from all over the world that were on their way to the Rockies, and they nearly always had time for a chat. The favourite question was "What's an Englishman doing working on a fruit-stand out here in the middle of nowhere?"

There were few distractions besides the work, so I put in as many hours as possible over the next couple of months. In the evenings, Walter would sometimes invite me to accompany him on a trip down the valley to collect fruit from the other farms. Payment for these trips usually came in the form of a big meal in Kelowna or Vernon on the way home. Walter had spent much of his life travelling the world, before settling here in the Okanagon Valley, and we struck up a great friendship.

For additional company, there was always the faithful old farm dog, Albert. He would wait for me to emerge from my tent each morning, and then follow my every move until evening. I was also charged with looking after two wild kittens, rescued from a nearby farm, and three ducks that waddled around all day - never failing to entertain the customers down at the fruit-stand.

Some other travellers called in from time to time to pick berries for a few days, before heading for the more lucrative fruit picking opportunities further down the valley. I learnt that apple picking was particularly well paid. One of these pickers was a student from Argentina called Santiago, whose arrival was very timely as I had just started to learn Spanish. As well as helping me with my pronunciation, he furnished me with several addresses of friends and relatives down in South America.

Mention should also be made of some interesting characters that lived in the village, and helped to make me feel part of the small community. These included Dick - a retired Dutch farmer who was still a prolific gardener and supplied the fruit-stand with sweet corn and massive sweet onions. Martin was another retired farmer who had once lived in London. He produced excellent honey for the stand, and also regularly passed on to me his copy of the Times newspaper, which he received from England each week. Then there was Clary – an old man, crippled by arthritis - who often dropped in at the stand to buy a handful of plums and leave some food for the kittens.

The fruit business was an interesting one to be involved in, as there was so much to learn. At our stand we were able to develop an excellent reputation for apples, by collecting as many different varieties as possible. At one stage, we had a sign on the highway boasting seventeen different varieties, and people were stopping just to see if it was true or not! As the season drew to a close, we also collected some huge pumpkins, including one weighing over 130lbs that we kidnapped from a neighbouring fruit-stand during the night as a joke. It was recaptured the following night!

Sadly, an early frost signalled the end of the fruit-growing season in late September, and there was no longer enough produce to justify my continued employment. As a leaving present, Walter invited me to the annual Wine Tasting Evening, at the Capri Hotel in Kelowna – the main town in the Okanagon Valley. He assured me that this was the social event of the year in these parts, and even lent me some clothes so that I could look vaguely respectable.

Kelowna lies a hundred miles south of Malakwa. There seemed little point in me coming back afterwards, so I loaded the bike into the back of Walter's truck. Leaving the little farm behind was a sad moment, but I would carry some happy memories of the place, and the money earned would certainly come in useful.

The wine tasting event was surprisingly enjoyable. Fortunately, Walter had given me some prior education on the subject of wines, so that I did not make a complete fool of myself. When the function ended, we visited a couple of nightspots in Kelowna, before 'crashing out' in the back of the truck.

In the morning, it was time for a farewell breakfast courtesy of 'Old Clary', who had dropped a few coins into my hand the previous day for my first meal on the road. Then Walter dropped me off at the local Backpackers' Hostel, and headed off back up the valley.

Kelowna (whose name is derived from an Indian word meaning 'grizzly bear') processes one third of all apples harvested in Canada. Even at this late stage of the season, there were plenty of apples to pick in the surrounding orchards, and the hostel was full of itinerant labourers. I received several offers of work during my stay there but, with summer almost gone now, decided that it was time to start riding south towards warmer weather.

My legs were a little out of practice, so I began my journey south with an easy-paced forty-mile ride down the valley to Penticton. The lakeside highway passed through familiar territory, as I had been up and down the valley with Walter on numerous occasions. The lush hillsides were covered with orchards and vineyards, which produce all kinds of delicious fruits through the summer months, but were now starting to look a little forlorn, with the season drawing to a close. It felt strange to be travelling through the valley for the last time, and I could not resist stopping at a couple of Walter's favourite cafés, in the prosperous little lakeside communities of Summerland and Peachland. I also kept an eye on the lake for any sign of 'Ogopogo' – the Okanagon Valley's answer to the Loch Ness Monster – but he proved as elusive as ever!

It was mid-afternoon when I arrived in the pretty lakeside town of Penticton, whose name is derived from an Indian expression meaning 'a place to stay forever'. For me it was to be just one night though. After checking into the Youth Hostel, I decided to prepare for the next day's border crossing by going for a 'short back and sides'. It always helps to look reasonably respectable at borders! The Slovenian hairdresser got quite emotional when he learned that I had cycled through his home village in Yugoslavia. He refused to take any money, and asked only that I send him a postcard from South America in exchange for the haircut. When I got back to the hostel, the Manager did not recognise me, and tried to book me in again. I requested the same bed as the long-haired cyclist that had checked in earlier - leaving him rather confused and worried!

My legs were aching the next morning, but the stiffness soon disappeared as I rode onwards towards the border. The roadside orchards were still bearing juicy 'Red Delicious' and 'Macintosh' apples, which were just about within grabbing distance at times. After lunch in the border town of Osoyoos, which lies on a sand spit that almost bisects Lake Osoyoos, I joined the queue at the border. There was not long to wait, and I was waved across into the United States of America with just a cursory glance at my passport. The haircut obviously made a good impression!

The Okanagon Valley extends deep into the state of Washington, in the north-western corner of the U.S.A. Washington is known as the 'Apple State' and orchards continued to dominate the landscape as I rode south.

The small Youth Hostel at Tonasket was contained within the home of an elderly couple, who had converted their large basement into a bunkroom, complete with bathroom and kitchen. They seemed pleased to see me, as they had not had any guests for several days now, and went out of their way to make me as comfortable as possible. There was an old piano in the basement, so I took the opportunity to practise the five or six pieces of sheet music that I had purchased in New Zealand, and carried with me ever since. The first few notes brought my hosts rushing down the stairs to listen, so it turned into an impromptu concert!

On another bright, autumn morning, I rolled further down the valley on Highway 97. A week had passed since my departure from the fruit farm, and my fitness levels seemed to be back to normal now. I made good progress that day to reach the riverside town of Brewster, where the road signs were in Spanish, and most of the cafes were serving Mexican food. There was a trailer park on the edge of town, which did not look too busy, but my request to camp there was bluntly refused. This was a little puzzling, and I wondered whether I should have tried asking in Spanish!

Feeling a little 'put out' by this rejection, I climbed back onto the bike and rode hard towards the next town of Chelan, thirty miles further down the valley. Along the way, I kept a lookout for somewhere to pitch the tent, but the land on either side of the highway was either fenced off or too rocky. It was late in the evening when I finally made it to Chelan. It had been a long ride that day, but the campsite here was very nicely situated, on a grassy ledge overlooking the lake, so the day had a happy ending.

From Chelan, the highway climbed high up the valley sides, affording sweeping views of this southern section of the Okanagon. The terrain was a little more barren now, but there were a few orchards still in blossom and the occasional vineyard to add a splash of colour. Dropping back down towards Wenatchee, which is the main commercial centre for the American end of the Okanagon Valley, the highway was jammed with queues of apple trucks, slowly moving in and out of enormous packing houses with their end of season produce. After threading my way between the trucks, I finally left the Okanagon behind and turned west onto Highway Two. Ahead of me was a rather indirect route around and across the mountains to the West Coast.

After climbing steadily for a couple of hours on a narrow road, hemmed in by thick pine forest, I started to look around for somewhere to camp. A mud track into the forest led me to a secluded clearing next to a mountain stream. The evening was starting to draw in, so there was just time to set up the tent and get a small camp fire going before it turned dark. It had been another long day's ride, and I was just falling into a deep sleep, when a pair of headlights suddenly illuminated the whole tent. This was quite a shock, as I had thought myself to be well hidden from the world! Emerging hurriedly from the tent, I was greeted by a voice from the dark:

"Hi, I'm a Forest Ranger. Did you have a camp fire tonight?"

"Yes, but I doused it" was my response.

"O.K. fine. Sorry to disturb you. Somebody called us about a forest fire that they had seen from the highway, and we have to investigate all these reports."

With that he revved the engines, and the lights slowly disappeared as he reversed back down the track.

After a fitful sleep, in which I dreamt that my tent was engulfed by flames, I rode further up into the Wenatchee

Mountains. It was a steep climb up to the Swauk Pass, followed by a long, straight descent through the trees and then across open farmland. The road widened into a busy freeway as it left the mountains behind and cut across the plains towards the town of Ellensburg. Here I turned onto another narrow, winding road that would take me through the rocky Yakima Canyon. The Canyon is thirty miles long, and snakes it way through some rugged hills, which glowed orange in the evening sun. This part of the day's ride was so enjoyable that it seemed like no time at all before I was through the Canyon and back on the highway again, just outside the town of Yakima itself. The trailer park on the edge of Yakima was luxurious, with an indoor swimming pool and Jacuzzi among its facilities, and the off-season rates were quite inviting as well!

From Yakima, the highway crossed more open farm country to Toppenish, where I stopped for a late breakfast at one of the saloon bars on the main street. The charming young Indian waitress seemed anxious to feed me up for the road ahead, as she kept reappearing at my table with her coffee jug and extra slices of toast. Reluctantly dragging myself away, I headed out across the Toppenish Ridge. The landscape was becoming increasingly barren now, and riding was hard work as swirling winds swept across the plains. To make matters worse, I punctured twice that morning! The back tyre was starting to disintegrate and I just hoped that it would last me to the city of Portland, a couple of days away.

That night, I camped close to the Satus Pass at a State Park Camping Area (which is an area set aside by the authorities for free camping). An American family pulled up alongside for the night in their motor-home, and invited me to join them on a visit to a nearby Observatory. Here we were given an astrology lecture by America's first and only 'State Park Interpretative Specialist' (or, as he put it, 'a man who is paid to share his hobby with anyone who happens along'). We then filed into the telescope room and took it in turns to view the moon, Saturn and various star constellations.

It was a surprisingly cold night back at the Satus Pass and a thin layer of ice covered my tent in the morning. In record time I packed everything up and wrapped up in several layers, including the old balaclava that had served me well in Turkey and New Zealand, for the long descent ahead. After flying downhill for twenty minutes or so, I caught up with another cycle tourist just outside the town of Goldendale. He had long hair, an even longer beard, and was travelling extremely light. As I rode up alongside him, he introduced himself as Paul – a travelling Christian, who was riding around America to spread the word of the Lord. He then reeled off a string of bible quotations in order to consolidate his introduction, finishing with "Amen!" I was quite taken aback at this barrage of biblical quotations, but could not help admiring his enthusiasm. As we rode along together, Paul announced that he was very pleased that we would be cycling to Portland together (a rather heavy assumption, I felt). He also suggested that one day we should cycle around Africa together, feeding all the starving people. I tried to keep a straight face as I imagined us riding from village to village with panniers stuffed full of rice and biscuits!

We stopped briefly at a rest area to view the distant volcano, Mount St. Helens, which caused great destruction when it erupted in 1980. When a couple of elderly tourists pulled into the rest area to admire the same view, Paul immediately got to work on trying to convert them. Meanwhile, I was squirming with embarrassment in the background, and trying to figure out how to lose this guy! As it turned out, I did not have to wait very long.

Ten miles further on, we reached the huge Columbia River Gorge, which runs all the way to the West Coast at Portland, and defines the state border between Washington and Oregon. I had planned to follow the old highway through the hills on the Washington side of the Gorge, rather than crossing over and taking the more direct freeway route on the Oregon side. Paul, who had reached the gorge ahead of me by virtue of having virtually no luggage, had a different plan. Without waiting to consult with me, he turned off down a long steep hill, leading to a bridge across the Columbia River to the Oregon side. On reaching the junction a few moments later, I could just see him disappearing away down the hill – an ever- diminishing blob in the distance. Not wanting to follow him down there, only to have to climb back up again, I dutifully waited at the junction to see if he came back for me. He did not reappear, however, so I continued my journey alone, following the old highway as planned.

The old highway was cut into the north side of the valley, just beneath its rim, and almost devoid of traffic. Relieved to have given my overbearing missionary companion the slip, I was reassured further about my choice of routes by the panoramic views across the gigantic Columbia River Gorge, which were spectacular from my high vantage point. Besides the Gorge itself, conical Mount Hood was a dominating feature, rising above the Gorge on the Oregon side. The road was surprisingly level, but my stamina was put to the test late in the afternoon as I ran into some terrific headwinds, funnelling down the Gorge towards me. Judging by the large proliferation of wind-surfers on the Columbia River below, these strong winds were probably not an uncommon occurrence.

With my strength diminishing rapidly, and forward momentum virtually non-existent, I started to look anxiously around for somewhere to camp. As if by magic, a small roadside lake - with a grassy, well-sheltered, patch of land on one side – suddenly came into view.

It was the perfect place to set up camp for the night. It seemed that someone else had got here first though, as there was an old trailer parked up by the lake. As I set up my tent close by, a weather-beaten, bearded old man emerged from the trailer. He seemed quite pleased at the unexpected company, and invited me to make use of his stove. It turned into a pleasant, moonlit evening as we sat chatting by the lake. The old fellow's name was Jim. He had been through three divorces, the most recent one coming at the start of that year, and had decided to spend the summer 'getting his head together' in this peaceful little lakeside hideaway. He had a job just down the road at a fruit-packing house, and spent much of his spare time fishing in the lake. He was very apologetic that he hadn't caught any fish that day for my supper!

Waking up as the sun rose over the lake, I saw that Jim had already left for work. He had left the trailer open though, so I cooked porridge on his stove to warm me up and give me some energy before setting off. The winds had dropped completely overnight and it was a nice easy ride, as the old highway gradually dropped down the valley side to the riverside settlement of Stevenson. A few miles further on, I crossed over the mighty Columbia River on the 'Bridge of the Gods'.

On the Oregon side now, I rode a short stretch on the busy freeway before making a diversion onto the Historic Columbia Highway, which climbed sharply up the steep southern side of the valley. This highway was considered an engineering marvel in its day, but only this short section at the western end of the Gorge was now open to traffic. It was a tough climb, but a worthwhile one as the highway took me close to the Multnomah Falls, which are the highest in North America. At the Crown Point lookout, the Pacific Ocean came into view, and the entire city of Portland was laid out beneath me.

Known as the 'City of Roses', Portland is an attractive city, with fresh sea breezes keeping the air clean. There were numerous parks dotted around the city centre, including one called Mill Ends Park, measuring just 24 inches across! The Youth Hostel was located in a central district that was full of second-hand bookshops, health stores and alternative-style cafes. After spending a morning exploring the city on foot, it was nice to let the afternoon drift away while reading and sipping coffee at one of these cafes, as some extraordinary hairstyles came and went!

On a sunny October morning, I headed south out of Portland on Highway 99. Once clear of the sprawling suburbs, the highway cut across farming plains to the village of Lafayette, and then climbed over a narrow ridge of forested mountains, separating the plains from the coast. High up in the mountains, a 'hiker/biker camp', which is a campsite set up by the Government for the sole use of walkers and cyclists, was sign-posted. A narrow trail through the forest led me to a woodland campground with toilet block, picnic tables and a barbecue area – all for the sum of two dollars, to be deposited in a wooden box. Apparently, there were several of these hiker/biker camps down the West Coast, and it seemed an excellent idea to me.

It was raining heavily in the morning, so I quickly packed up camp and rode a few miles down the highway to a café. The small café was full of locals, all tucking into plates of huge pancakes with cream and maple syrup. There were no free tables, so I sat with a group of farmers, who took great interest in my travels and insisted on paying for my breakfast.

When I finally left the café, the rain had stopped and the sun was just beginning to burst through the clouds. It was just a few more miles to the highest point of the ridge, from where the Oregon coastline could be seen stretching away into the distance. A sharp descent brought me down into the small seaside resort of Lincoln City. From here, I turned south onto the coastal highway and climbed steeply again for several miles to reach the Cape Foulweather lookout point. It was here that Captain Cook landed on a stormy March day in 1778. It was his first sight of 'New Albion' (the North West Pacific Coast) and his account of this voyage aroused great interest around the world. A sign at the lookout warned that winds of 100 miles per hour were not uncommon here, but today there was little more than a gentle ocean breeze.

The highway continued to hug the rugged coastline of rocky capes and sandy beaches, with estuaries frequented by wading birds. It was an exhilarating ride and I kept going until late evening to reach another hiker/biker camp, which was sited in the corner of a deserted bay, just south of Newport. This one even had hot showers, which was quite a luxury!

The next day's ride was just as good. I covered seventy-five miles of coastline, which was mostly unspoilt – largely due to it being preserved as part of the Government State Parks. In the afternoon, I caught up with a very large man called Bob, who was riding on a rickety old bicycle pulling a small trailer. The trailer was loaded up with everything short of the kitchen sink, including a large radio! His travelling companion was a lame, ten-year-old sausage dog, which he carried on his shoulders for the downhill stretches. On uphill stretches he let the dog run along behind, as he slowly pushed his heavy load along. I rode alongside for half an hour or so, as we shared our impressions of the county. He told me that this trip was the fulfilment of a lifelong dream to tour his home State of Oregon, and that the opportunity had arisen when he was made redundant at the saw mill where he had worked for several years. It would have been nice to travel with this unusual twosome for longer, but they were only covering a few miles each day, and this would not get me down to Mexico! He kindly posed for a picture, with his four-legged friend on his shoulders, before I pushed on ahead.

A forty-mile stretch of flat road, alongside the famous Oregon coastal sand dunes, provided welcome relief from the hilly riding. I rode until just before sundown again to reach yet another hiker/biker camp on the southern edge of the dunes.

The next day there was an inland detour, through forests of Douglas Firs, before the highway returned to the coast at the old port of Bandon. This was a pretty little town, full of beautifully restored historic buildings. The day was still young, but it seemed a shame to just pass through quickly, so I checked into a ramshackle old hotel by the waterfront.

Among the other guests at the hotel was a Japanese cyclist called Masahira, who had cycled down from the northern tip of Alaska and was on his way to the southern tip of South America. He was a cheerful character, with a quiet determination about him. We would meet up several times on the road ahead, and form a bond of mutual respect and friendship as we travelled together. However, we were not to ride together immediately because I had decided on a rest day at Bandon, while Masahira was ready to move on the next morning. We were both heading for San Francisco on Highway 101, and he was carrying a much heavier load than me, so I expected to catch him up along the way.

My rest day was spent exploring the old port of Bandon, and giving the bike a good clean and tune up.

In the evening, I wandered down to one of the harbour-side cafes, where I managed to score a free dinner by playing the piano. The diners were mostly tourists, who seemed to appreciate my short classical repertoire, and I even earned a few tips!

The sea air was invigorating on another clear, sunny day, as I glided over forested cliff-tops and past long white beaches. At one rest area, a group of people were pointing and staring out to sea. Following their gaze, my eyes rested on the thrashing tail of a sperm whale, no more than fifty metres from the shore. It was a captivating spectacle.

Towards evening, a thick fog rolled in from the ocean, reducing visibility to little more than a few feet. I rode on tentatively, but had to pull off the highway at the sound of every approaching vehicle. It was some relief to finally reach a hiker/biker campsite near the town of Brookings, just north of the Californian border. I had covered eighty-four miles that day, and the sight of a solitary green tent in the corner of the campground told me that I had caught up with Masahira already.

It took just half an hour for us to reach the State border, during which time I managed to think of at least five songs about California. This seemed to impress Masahira no end, unless he was just being polite!

A few miles south of the border we came to the seaside town of Crescent City, which is known as the 'Gateway to the Redwoods'. Heading on into the forest, we were soon riding through a fantasy land of Giant Redwoods. The Redwood is the world's tallest tree, and the oldest living thing on the planet. A fierce conservation effort, dating back to the mid-1800s, has saved them from being wiped out by the logging industry, and the Redwood National Park covers more than a hundred thousand acres of forest land. Some of the trees were three or four metres wide at the base and over a hundred metres tall, so we certainly felt rather small as we made our way through them on Highway 101. That night, we set up camp on another hiker/biker camp, which was tucked away in a secluded forest clearing. Masahira seemed to take his road catering seriously and was carrying an impressive array of pots and pans on his bike, so we dined in style that evening.

Riding on through the forest, we caught up with an easy-going Dutch cyclist called Henry. He had purchased his mountain bike in Crescent City for the ride down to San Francisco. Having completed the introductions, we rode together to Eureka, where Highway 101 joined the coast again. This is another of the region's old logging towns, and the smokestacks rising from the lumber mills on the outskirts of the town indicated that logging is still an important industry here. Henry had been to Eureka before, so he guided us through the streets to the 'Old Town' area. Among the Victorian buildings here was an exquisite green and gold mansion, complete with turrets and verandas. It was like something out of a fairytale. We camped that night a little further down the coast at the village of Ferndale, which had its own fair share of beautifully restored Victorian buildings.

The next day we turned off Highway 101 onto the 'Avenue of the Giants' – a famous scenic route through the Humboldt region of the Redwood National Park. With the holiday season over, there was virtually no traffic and it felt like a dream, as we meandered slowly through this spectacular part of the forest. Some of the trees were uprooted, allowing us to clamber over them, and make a closer examination of their incredible root systems. A wonderful day turned into a memorable evening as we set our three tents up among the giant redwoods, deep in the forest. A small camp fire was enough to take the chill out of the air, on a moonlit night, and my two companions were able to provide some musical entertainment, as they both carried harmonicas!

With his laid-back attitude, Henry had not gone overboard on preparations for this cycle tour and had even forgotten to carry a water bottle! We were able to look after him though, and his sense of humour kept as entertained as we rode along together. Another leisurely day's riding brought us to a hiker/biker camp near the small town of Leggett, on the southern edge of the Redwood National Park. There were six other cycle tourists already camped there – all Americans - so we raided the local village store for supplies and had a cyclist's party. The others were heading north, so we would not be forming an army the next day!

Leaving the forest behind, we rejoined Highway 101 and breezed down the coast to the town of Fort Bragg, which is virtually owned by the logging company, Georgia Pacific. The firm's logging trucks hurtled past us at regular intervals on this stretch, making the narrow, winding road quite hazardous. The ride seemed rather disjointed that morning, with frequent stops breaking up the rhythm, as one or another of us needed to stop for various reasons. After lunch, we decided to ride separately, so that we could each go at our own pace and not feel as though we were holding the others up if we wanted to stop for some reason. We arranged to meet up in the evening at the next hiker/biker camp near Mendocino, in Russian Gulch State Park, and we all arrived within half an hour of each other.

Regarded as an 'Artist's Colony', the village of Mendocino is situated on a headland which juts out into the ocean. It is full of quaint old cafes and galleries, so we spent a relaxing morning mooching around and sampling delicious coffee and pastries – which Henry had a particular liking for - before continuing south the next day. We had barely set off from the village when the riding conditions suddenly deteriorated and we were shrouded in the famous Californian fog. It began to rain as well, making the narrow highway quite treacherous, so we decided that it would be safest to ride together. San Francisco was temptingly close now and nobody suggested turning back. Fortunately, the fog cleared soon enough and we were once more able to appreciate the scenery, as the highway followed a golden shoreline of idyllic beaches and rugged cliffs. We set up camp that night on the beach at Salt Point.

Henry was not the most organised of people, especially in the mornings, but we managed to set off reasonably early from our beach camp. Highway 101 rose and fell more sharply now as it cut along the edge of the cliff face, affording sweeping vistas of the endless sandy beaches and white surf. The morning mist gave this spectacular landscape a magical quality. Henry had decided to take a longer route into San Francisco, in order to visit a friend along the way, so we parted company at the village of Jenna – arranging to meet up again at a hostel in the city. Masahira and I continued south along the coastal highway, before cutting inland across a range of hills that separated us from the city. At the town of Olemna, we dropped into a grocery store for provisions and encountered a couple of young American lads, who were on a weekend cycling trip. We spent the evening with them on a campsite nearby, where we were able to reduce costs by cramming all four of our compact tents onto one official tent space!

We were only thirty miles from the city now, but there was still a long, winding climb over Mount Tamalpais to negotiate. Masahira always went slower on the climbs, so I rode on ahead and waited for him at the pass. It was some time before his small, stocky form came into view, patiently peddling away on the heavily laden bike. San Francisco was laid out beneath us now, but it was another misty morning, so it was hard to make out much of the city. After allowing Masahira a few moments rest, we dropped down into the northern suburb of Sausolito, on San Francisco Bay. Only the majestic Golden Gate Bridge separated us from one of America's great cities now. There was a cycle path across the famous bridge, so we were able to linger in the middle for a while and savour the moment.

Once over the Golden Gate, we were suddenly thrown into the chaotic downtown area of the city. It was hard to cope with all the noise and frantic activity, after riding on lonely roads and camping in the forest for several days, and it was some relief when we finally arrived at the European Guesthouse, where we had arranged to meet Henry.

The hostel had an extremely relaxed atmosphere, and more than its fair share of 'spaced out' travellers, who seemed to be making the most of what seemed to be a 'no rules' environment! There was one large dormitory, resembling an aircraft hangar, and the constant comings and goings throughout the night made sustained sleep virtually impossible, but at least there was plenty of room for the bikes! It was not long before Henry showed up, and we celebrated our reunion with a meal out in North America's largest 'Chinatown' district.

San Francisco was the one American city that I had really wanted to see, and my main reason for taking the West Coast route, rather than the more direct route through the central States. Its name conjures up visions of the swinging sixties, and I started my explorations by riding across town, with Masahira and Henry, to the Haight-Ashbury district. Once a neglected slum, these streets became the adopted capital for the 'Flower-Power' movement, which spread throughout America during the sixties and seventies. The area still seemed to have something of a 'hippie' feel to it, with plenty of colourful, alternative-style cafes and shops. At one of these cafes we got talking to a couple of 'messenger bikers', which are the American equivalent to 'courier bikers' in London. They seemed quite fascinated by our three touring bikes and invited us to a biker's party that evening.

The party was already in full swing when we arrived. The venue was a disused, backstreet warehouse, but most of the action was taking place in the streets outside, where a makeshift ramp had been set up. Cheered on by a noisy crowd of onlookers, the messenger bikers were trying to outdo each other by performing increasingly dangerous stunts, such as hitting the ramp at high speed and spinning around in mid-air before landing. It was quite a little cycling carnival, and there were some incredible home-made bikes of various shapes and sizes, including one that had motorcycle tyres. We enjoyed trying out some of these machines, which involved adopting some unusual riding positions! The local bikers seemed anxious to welcome us into their 'cyclist's union' and encouraged us to have a go at some stunts ourselves, but we all managed to resist this temptation. I was pretty sure that my travel insurance did not cover mountain bike stunts!

Ten days passed very quickly in this vibrant city. As well as taking in the sights, I managed to give the bike a complete overhaul and replace several of the components. The local bike shop took great interest in my journey and sold me everything at trade price. It was yet another generous gesture, which would help to keep me on the road for just a little bit longer. I also took the opportunity to update my vaccinations, with Mexico and South America not too far ahead.

Henry's tour was over now and he caught a plane to Australia, where he planned to meet up with his girlfriend and return to the carpentry trade. His bike had been stolen the night before, when he locked it up outside a shop for a few minutes. He always tended to look on the bright side of things, however, and consoled himself with the thought that at least he would not have to pack it up for the flight. I would certainly miss his company on the road ahead.

Just as Masahira and I were preparing to move on as well, I was laid low with a virus, which was probably a reaction to the vaccinations. We were planning to ride across the Sierra Nevada range by way of the Tioga Pass, which lies at an altitude of 9,000 feet and was likely to be closed for the winter very soon now. To delay our departure any longer could mean a huge detour, so I persuaded to Masahira to ride on alone.

It was a few days before I returned to something resembling full health and climbed back into the saddle for a final tour of the city. I rode around the massive Golden Gate Park, with its numerous species of plants and trees, as well sweeping views across the city and the Bay area, not to mention the Golden Gate Bridge itself. Then I rode up to Fisherman's Wharf, which is a waterfront area of museums and seafood restaurants, and the embarkation point for trips to the old prison island of Alcatraz. I tried to book myself onto a tour for later in the day, but all the trips were fully booked, so it was not to be.

San Francisco lived up to all expectations, and remains one of my favourite cities. I may just have to return one day to visit Alcatraz!

On a typically misty West Coast morning, I loaded the bike up and crossed the San Francisco Bay by catamaran to reach the Oakland suburb, from where my inland journey would begin. Oakland is really a city in itself, and a fairly notorious one at that time, having been the scene of major race riots a few months previously. The riots were sparked by the acquittal of four police officers who had been tried for the alleged racially-motivated beating of Rodney King – a black man who had been trying to resist arrest at the time. Several white people had been murdered during the aftermath of these riots, and I did feel a little nervous as the other boat passengers sped away in their cars, leaving me alone with my bicycle. There were plenty of signs of the urban decay and economic depression which may also have contributed to the riots, and I rode past several derelict buildings and closed-down businesses, scrawled with graffiti. There were plenty of smiles and friendly glances from the pavements, however, as I weaved my way through the traffic, and I soon felt more at ease. At one set of traffic lights a Rastafarian man shouted out "Man, you're loaded up and ready for everything!" while from another direction came "All right, man, go for it!"

After Oakland came Berkeley – where Jimi Hendrix made one of his rare live appearances – and then suburb after suburb, as I anxiously tried to clear the Bay area before nightfall. Bicycles are not allowed on the freeways in the Bay area, so I had to weave my way through the backstreets and make frequent stops to ask for directions. In the Pittsburg district, a police car pulled up alongside me and the Officer warned me to be careful, as I was entering a very dangerous area with lots of drugs and crime. The patrol car shadowed me for several miles, before the Officer leaned through his window again to shout 'Well done – you made it!' through his loud speaker, before speeding away.

Darkness began to fall, and I was still not clear of the residential districts. There was no sign of a motel or trailer park, so I decided to seek permission to camp on private land. The first house I tried was set back from the road a little and had a big yard, but the dressing gown-clad man who opened the door seemed horrified at my request to camp on his land and warned me that this was a very bad area. He then slammed the door shut in my face, before I could explain that this was precisely why I was trying to avoid having to ride further in the dark, or make camp at the side of the road! There was more joy at the next house, where a young couple answered the door together and pointed me to a small field across the road. The field was owned by a neighbour, they explained, who was away in Australia, and it would be OK to camp there as long as I did not make a fire or leave any mess. There was a small barn in the centre of the field with a water supply and a table and chair, so I was able to make myself quite comfortable, and the perimeter fence afforded just enough security to enable me to drift off to sleep fairly easily.

It was raining heavily in the morning and a howling wind was blowing, so I sheltered in the barn until mid-morning. Eventually, with the weather showing little sign of improving, I accepted my fate and started riding. The fierce, swirling wind made it hard to keep my balance at times, as I finally left the city behind and followed a busy highway due east. It took nearly four hours to cover just twenty-five miles to the city of Stockton, by which time I was feeling quite exhausted. This may have been partly due to the lingering effects of the virus that had laid me low in San Francisco, so I decided not to ride any further that day. There was a trailer park on the outskirts of the city, and the lady in the office there said that if I was crazy enough to consider camping in this weather then she would not charge me!

It was another miserable, rainy morning as I made my way out of Stockton, and then eastwards into the heart of the San Joaquin Valley, which stretches for five hundred miles from north to south. This is one of the richest farming valleys in the world, producing an incredible variety of fruits and vegetables. It is also renowned for its fine, sunny weather, so this was not a typical day! I was feeling stronger now though, and made good progress until a large road sign stopped me dead in my tracks. The sign stated in big letters that the Tioga Pass had been closed for the winter, due to heavy overnight snowfall. It was the news that I had been dreading.

My original plan was to cross the Sierra Nevada in order to visit the Grand Canyon, and then follow a route down through Arizona towards the Mexican border. This was still possible, but I would have to ride several hundred miles south in order to cross the mountain range at a lower pass, and then north again towards Las Vegas and the Canyon. Having resigned myself to the fact that this stage of the journey was going to take several days longer than planned, my thoughts turned to Masahira. I wandered if he had made it across, or whether he had been forced to turn back.

Feeling quite despondent, I turned south at the first opportunity and followed a narrow country lane, which sliced across the pancake-flat farmland of the Central Valley. A decent tailwind helped to propel me along at a good speed and my spirits lifted, as I reminded myself that at least I would not be freezing up in the mountains that night! Instead, I found myself at a comfortable hostel in the lowland town of Merced.

It was the last day of October, and pumpkin faces stared at me from roadside fruit-stands, as I continued south down the valley via a criss-cross pattern of minor roads, which were the only alternative to the busy freeway. The locals certainly seemed to be getting into the Halloween spirit. Stocking up for my evening camp, at a supermarket in Madera, I was served by a ghost! A few miles east of Madera, I set up camp on the shores of Lake Millerton, in the foothills of the Sierra Nevada, as the setting sun turned the whole sky orange.

The next day I made excellent progress, as the bike seemed to sail across the farming plains with just a little encouragement from me. Reaching the town of Visalia, late in the evening, I splashed out on a motel room - allowing myself a rare opportunity to watch television! The news was dominated by the American presidential elections, which were just two days away now.

From Visalia, I turned eastwards again towards the Sierra Nevada. I was hoping to cross the mountains by way of the Lake Isabella Pass, which is considerably lower than Tioga Pass and normally stayed open throughout the winter. It took me all day to reach the foothills so, with the light beginning to fade, I made camp in a derelict roadside building, which had once been a gas station. The stone floor was covered in broken glass bottles and cigarette ends, suggesting that the premises may have been used as a party venue quite recently, but I had the place all to myself that night.

In the morning, the serious climbing began. It was good to run through the gears again, after riding for several days along the flat Central Valley, and it was good to breathe the mountain air at last. After a long, steady climb, I arrived at the village of Glenville for lunch. The locals in the café here warned me of a very steep climb ahead, and they were not kidding! Just a couple of miles further, the gradient increased dramatically and I had to draw on all my reserves of strength for the next few hours. Progress was painstakingly slow and the exertion made me feel quite dizzy. It was some relief when the Pass finally came into view. I had climbed over 2,000 metres from the valley floor, and the rugged, barren peaks of the Sierra Nevada were all around. Lake Isabella glistened below in the late afternoon sunshine, as I rolled down from the Pass to the tiny settlement of Wofford Heights on its northern shores. Checking into a small, lakeside motel, there was another chance to watch some television, and the news came through that a certain Bill Clinton had been elected to the White House. I was pleased for him, but was sure that he had not worked as hard as me that day!

My legs were still aching in the morning, so I decided just to take things easy and spend some time enjoying this beautiful spot in the mountains. After checking out of the motel I rode slowly around the lake and set up camp at Paradise Cove on the other side. The little bay was deserted, so the rest of the day was spent relaxing on my own little private beach and enjoying the solitude. It turned very cold when the sun went down, so I wrapped up warm and spent the evening gazing at stars through the tent window.

Lake Isabella is sandwiched between two mountain ridges, so another big climb lay ahead of me the next day. This time, however, it was a gentle climb, and I made it to Walker's Pass by mid-morning. From here it was a long, winding descent down to Freeman Junction, on the other side of the Sierra Nevada.

Ahead of me were flat desert plains, with the Panamint Mountains forming a thin ridge in the distance. The day was still young and I sped across these arid plains to the town of Inyokern. From here the road followed the boundary of a huge, naval weapons compound, inspiring me to burst into a raucous rendition of Dylan's 'Blowing in the Wind'. It's amazing how you lose your inhibitions when you feel as though you are the only person left on the planet! The empty, barren landscape reminded me of Central Australia, especially as the sun started to go down and the distant hills glowed a deep orange colour. That evening, I asked permission to camp at a trailer park in Trona. The Manager refused my offer of payment and invited me to make full use of the facilities – "Just to keep you off the streets!" he explained.

There were no more settlements marked on my map before the Panamint Mountains. Beyond these lay the notoriously inhospitable terrain of Death Valley, which is one of the hottest and driest places on earth. Summer was behind me now, but the desert sun would still be uncomfortably hot. I set off from Trona carrying six litres of water and a three-day food supply.

A morning ride along the flat shoreline of China Lake - a huge dry salt lake - was a good warm-up for the long climb up through the mountains to Townes Pass, which lies at 5,000 feet. The gradient seemed to increase, as I slowly gained altitude, and the blistering afternoon heat sapped my strength to the point where my legs finally turned to jelly and the peddles would not turn any more. The lowest gear was just not low enough, so I had to admit defeat and push the bike for the last few hundred metres up to the Pass.

Townes Pass marks the western boundary of the narrow strip of desert known as Death Valley, was laid out below. Distant sand dunes were glowing in the late afternoon sun and a strange-looking square of small white blocks was probably a trailer park. It was hard to judge the distance, but hopefully I would be able to get there before nightfall. As I rolled downhill from the pass, the sun started to set and the whole valley was transformed into an artist's palette of deep reds and browns.

November is the peak tourist season in Death Valley, and the trailer park at Stovepipe Wells was full of huge white motor-homes. There was just one other tent pitched on the tiny grassy area reserved for campers. The occupants were a young couple from Pennsylvania, who were cycling in the opposite direction across the States.

My legs were very stiff in the morning, so I settled for a short, gentle ride across the valley floor to the main tourist centre at Furnace Creek. The settlement here is built on a natural oasis, fed by fresh underground springs. It lies at 180 feet below sea level (one of the lowest places on earth) and has a highest recorded temperature of 134 degrees farenheight!

Motor-homes had completely taken over Furnace Creek and there was a country music festival in full swing. I quickly learnt that this was the annual 'Forty-niners' Festival, commemorating events during the Gold Rush of 1849. The story goes that a large group of travellers were trapped in the valley, as they could not find a route through the Panamint Range on the western side. (Having just struggled through these mountains myself, I could understand why!) A party of three young men were sent ahead to try and find a route to safety. They eventually discovered the Townes Pass, but one of them had died on the way. The other two christened the valley 'Death Valley', in memory of their friend, before continuing their journey to the Californian coast. Six weeks later, they returned with a rescue party to bring the others to safety.

The evening was spent relaxing to the sounds of country & western music and chatting with some of the 'old-timers', who seemed to be enjoying their annual pilgrimage.

Leaving the festivities behind, I continued across the valley towards another ridge of mountains, called the Amargosa Range, which forms the eastern boundary of the National Park. Along the way, I made short detours to some of the famous natural features of Death Valley, including Devil's Cornfield and Hell's Gate. The names seemed to reflect how forbidding a place this must have seemed to the early settlers.

The road climbed gently through the mountains of the Amargosa Range to Zabriesky Point, where I stopped to take in a final panoramic view of Death Valley. It was just a short distance further to Walker's Pass, at 3,000 feet, and then a long descent to Death Valley Junction, in the Armogosa Valley. The strange settlement here had all the appearances of a ghost town, although it had an official population of six. Amidst the tiny cluster of deserted buildings was a small Opera House! Apparently the weekend performances here are usually sold out, with Las Vegas tour companies offering city dwellers weekend opera breaks in the desert. I was unable to even buy some lunch here though, let alone catch an opera, as there were no signs of life at all. Perhaps the six inhabitants of Death Valley Junction were all having their afternoon siesta. I climbed back into the saddle and rode a further seven miles to the Nevada State border, where there was an old, Western-style, saloon bar. Walking into the bar was like walking onto the set of a John Wayne film, but the place was entirely genuine and the cowboys inside seemed quite harmless!

The rest of the day was spent riding on a dusty road across vast plains of barren wasteland. The silence was almost deafening at times, as if I was completely alone on the planet. It was back to the land of the living when I finally reached the junction with the relatively busy

Highway 95, which would lead me straight to Las Vegas. There was a truck-stop café and a large rest area at the junction, so I set up camp for the night. The highlight of the evening was an incredible desert sunset.

Las Vegas was still some ninety miles away, but Highway 95 was smooth and flat, and a strong tailwind blew me quickly across the plains. By mid-afternoon, the huge, concrete metropolis of Las Vegas appeared on the horizon. Before long, I was checking into a Backpackers' Hostel on the famous Las Vegas Strip.

Las Vegas is no ordinary city. The downtown area was a mass of glittering motels, restaurants, casinos, instant wedding chapels and sometimes all four rolled into one! Everything seemed to revolve around gambling and entertainment. On my way into the city, though, I had passed a Salvation Army hostel where 'down-and-outs' were queuing down to the end of the street for their daily meal. This immediately brought home to me the huge social cost of the gambling and 'fast living' culture that seems to exist in this city. For every winner in the casinos there has to be several losers.

'The Strip' is a dead straight, five-mile-long road, linking the central downtown area to the major casinos, such as Ceasar's Palace, on the edge of the city. At night, this famous road is brought to life by neon light displays, as each casino tries to out-dazzle the competition and even the supermarkets join in! The winner, in my judgement, had to be the Mirage Casino, with its huge model volcano erupting at fifteen-minute intervals! Inside the casinos, the atmosphere was almost overpowering, with the constant sound of coins falling out of slot machines and endless rows of professional and casual players, gambling the night away. Every few minutes a scream would pierce its way through the general cacophony of noise, as another winner celebrated a sudden windfall. After the peace and tranquillity of the desert, this was all quite a shock to the senses. I had no desire to fritter away my hard-earned Canadian dollars, however, and was happy to spend the next three days enjoying the free entertainment and ridiculously cheap all-you-can eat buffets, which are laid on by all the big casinos to lure people in. For the first time on my travels, I probably put some weight on!

At the hostel, I met Annabel - an English girl, who had travelled from Los Angeles with a Dutchman, called Rene, in an old Landrover. She was now ready to part company with Rene, and was thinking about travelling down to Mexico on her own, so I jokingly suggested that she purchased a bicycle and came with me. To my surprise, she took this suggestion quite seriously, and promised to give it some thought. At breakfast the next morning, she announced that she would definitely be joining me!

I was quite taken aback at this turn of events, but could see that Annabel had made up her mind. The thought of a more permanent travelling partner was a little scary, after riding alone for so long now, but also quite exciting. Travelling alone has many advantages, such as the sense of total freedom that it gives, but perhaps now it was time to enjoy some company. Besides this, it would be a pleasure to introduce someone else to the joys of cycle touring. We agreed that she would continue her journey with Rene as far as Phoenix, and then wait for me at the Youth Hostel there. I expected to reach Phoenix in about ten days' time and, if she had not changed her mind, we would then set about buying a bicycle and other essential equipment.

On my last evening in Las Vegas, Masahira turned up. He had just failed to reach the Tioga Pass before the road was blocked by snow, and had ended up following more or less the same route as me. Somewhere along the way, I must have overtaken him. Understandably, he wanted to spend a few days 'living it up' in Las Vegas, so I set off alone in the morning as planned. He was heading for Phoenix as well, so our paths would no doubt cross again.

After a huge casino breakfast with Masahira, I began a long, gradual climb out of the Las Vegas Valley into the range of hills surrounding Lake Mead. This tranquil, blue lake was created by the incredible Hoover Dam – a giant wall of concrete between the rugged cliff faces of the Black Canyon. The scale of this man-made creation was quite staggering, and I joined the several bus-loads of captivated tourists that were gazing in admiration from the viewing area. Crossing over the Hoover Dam into the State of Arizona, I rode away from the lakeside, and up into the hills again. All the eating in Las Vegas seemed to have given me plenty of energy, and I rode late into the evening before setting up camp in a small picnic area on the banks of the Colorado River.

The next morning, at a roadside café, I shared a table with a painter and his wife from Essex, who were on their way to visit relatives in Arizona. They insisted on paying for my breakfast and brought me up to date with some of the recent news from England. It was good to touch base with home, even in such an indirect way, and this kept me in good spirits for the rest of the day, as I rode on through the hills and across more desert plains to Kingman.

The next day, I followed one of the remaining sections of the historic old highway 'Route 66', which used to run across America from Chicago to Los Angeles. There were several settlements marked on my map along this route, but most of these turned out to be little more than ghost towns. It was a long, hard ride, mostly uphill and against the wind, but I eventually made it to Seligman – a larger settlement where 'Route 66' rejoins the new, modern highway. There was a picnic area behind the general store, and I set up camp for the night here. The steamed up café windows across the road told me that the meal that I had been looking forward to all day would not be long coming now!

Seligman lies at an elevation of 1,700 metres, and it was a very cold night in the tent. Temperatures rose quickly though, as soon as the sun appeared in the morning. I quickly packed up the tent and warmed myself up with a bowl of porridge, before setting off. It was another uphill ride that morning to the town of Williams, where I turned northwards towards the south rim of the Grand Canyon.

The narrow road north led me across a mountain plateau to Valle Junction, which is better known as 'Bedrock City' in 'The Flintstones'! The small community here was certainly cashing in on its Flintstones connections, and there were giant models of the show's characters dotted around the village, as well as several shops selling all sorts of Flintstones memorabilia. There was a large campsite adjoining one of these souvenir shops, but the lady in the shop tried to charge me ten dollars to spend the night there, despite the fact that the water was turned off and the shower block was locked for the winter! There were no other campsites in the town so, determined not to be ripped off by this annoying lady, I peddled onwards towards the Canyon. Late in the evening, as darkness fell, I set up camp by the roadside. Temperatures dropped to minus ten degrees overnight, but I had cycled over ninety miles that day, mostly uphill, so sleep was not a problem.

Though cold and hungry in the morning, I set off from my roadside camp in good spirits, because the Grand Canyon was just twelve miles away. Just before the Canyon, the inevitable McDonald's restaurant was a welcome sight for a change! After a McDonald's breakfast and several coffees, I cycled the last mile to Mather Point on the south rim of the Canyon. The incredible spectacle that lay before me surpassed all my expectations.

At Mather Point, the Grand Canyon is ten miles across and one mile deep. It has been carved out over millions of years by the Colorado River, exposing layers of rock which reveal over two billion years of the earth's history. The rich colours and texture patterns in the rock were constantly altering, as the sun rose higher into the sky that morning, but it was the huge scale of the Canyon that really made a lasting impression.

I cycled a few miles along the lip of the Canyon on South Rim Drive to Grand Canyon Village, where most of the tourist facilities were located. Among the cluster of expensive lodges, trailer parks, shops and restaurants was a small hiker/biker camp. I had not seen one of these since the West Coast, so it was a pleasant surprise. This one even had hot showers, but the charge was still just two dollars a night. Having set up camp here, and stored most of my luggage in the tent, I set off on the bike again to ride further along the Canyon rim. The bike seemed liberated without its usual load, and I sailed along between the numerous lookout points on West Rim Drive, each of which provided a slightly different perspective on the awesome spectacle of the Grand Canyon.

That evening – partly to escape from the cold – I attended a talk and slide show given by one of the National Park Rangers, who had once walked the entire length of the Grand Canyon. The hike had taken him six weeks and much of his route was over very rough terrain, where there are no trails and few people have ever been. He became quite emotional as he described the hardships of this journey - especially the last two days, when he had completely run out of food. There could not be many people alive that knew the Canyon as well as this fellow, who had been a Park Ranger for over thirty years now, and it was a fascinating account.

Inspired by the Ranger's talk, I set off early in the morning to walk down into the Canyon. It turned out to be a memorable hike, and I felt much more a part of the unique landscape by making this journey. The trail plummeted sharply to Indian Gardens – which was formerly the site of an Indian settlement – and from here it was a gentle hike to Plateau Point, on the edge of the sheer-walled inner canyon. The Colorado River was gushing by just a few hundred metres below now, and it was a very steep climb down to the riverside. It felt strange to be standing at the bottom of this great crack in the earth's surface – almost like standing inside the planet. This notion was reinforced by the huge difference in temperatures – from below freezing on the rim to a warm, summer's day at the bottom. Hiking into a Canyon is a bit like climbing a mountain in reverse so, with the hard part still ahead of me, there was no time to linger at the bottom. It was a tough hike back up to the rim, and I only just made it before sunset.

The next morning, after enduring another freezing cold night on the campsite, I loaded up and headed off in an easterly direction along South Rim Drive. Again there were numerous lookout points along the way, the most famous of which was Desert View - which is the highest point on the South Rim, at 7,438 feet. Here I chatted for a while with an elderly American couple, who insisted that I was an Australian and refused to believe that I had cycled down from Canada. (I didn't dare mention that this was just part of a much longer journey!) They seemed convinced that I was trying to make fun of them by giving false answers to their questions, and were shaking with indignation as they climbed back into their car!

Beyond Desert View, the landscape became quite bleak, as the scale of the Canyon reduced rapidly, until it was nothing more than a fairly ordinary steep-walled gorge, barely visible from the road. This was Navajo country, and dotted along the highway were wooden shacks, where the native Indians sold their colourful handicrafts to passing motorists, many of whom would be anxious to purchase a souvenir of their once-in-a-lifetime visit to the Grand Canyon. That evening, I reached a busy little Indian reservation called Cameron, where I was permitted to camp on some stony wasteland behind the restaurant. It wasn't the most comfortable pitch for a tent, but at least I felt safe and the restaurant would provide a warm haven for the evening.

Riding south from Cameron, the barren landscape soon gave way to lush forest and I began to climb again through the mysteriously named 'San Francisco Mountains'. These were actually nothing more than gentle rolling hills and it was a pleasant ride. Arriving that evening in the snow-covered city of Flagstaff, I checked into a Backpackers' Hostel that was more like a beehive, with bunk-beds crammed into every available space.

Among the guests at this hostel was a film stuntman, who went by the nickname of 'Rambling Rob'. Earlier that day, apparently, he had driven a jeep over the edge of the Grand Canyon for the latest Mel Gibson film. He was an eccentric character, with a spare-time hobby of breaking world records. For example, one of the records he claimed to hold was for the world's longest 'non-stop joke telling session'! I would not have believed half of his stories if he had not proudly produced a scrapbook full of newspaper clippings, confirming his many bizarre achievements. In answer to my query as to why he was staying at a Backpackers' Hostel, when he was clearly a rich and famous man, he explained that he was actually staying at the Hilton down the road, and had just popped in for some company!

Being a little behind schedule for my 'rendezvous' with Annabel in Phoenix, I stopped just the one night in Flagstaff. I did, however, make a slight detour on the journey south in order to ride through the Oak Creek Canyon, where nature's forces have cut through layers of rock to create strikingly colourful rock formations. This beautiful canyon is filled with lush coniferous forests, which were displaying their full range of autumn colours that morning. At the southern end of the canyon was the town of Sedona, which was a strange mixture of tourist complexes, cafes and art galleries, clustered around the highway. There were also several places offering clairvoyant services - apparently due to the close proximity of several vortexes, which are spots that are thought to release psychic energy from the earth. It was certainly an unusual place.

Rejoining the main freeway at Montezuma, I rode directly south now through the deep, forested valleys of central Arizona. There was little traffic on the freeway, as it carved its way between huge mountains, and I felt like an ant, slowly making its way across a vast landscape. That evening, I set up camp behind a truck-stop café at Camp Verde, on the edge of the Coconino National Forest. The café had a Mexican feel to it, and the food was delicious. If this was typical Mexican cuisine, then I certainly had something to look forward to across the border.

The morning ride was easier than expected, as I quickly left the mountains behind and a strong tailwind blew me across the plains to Phoenix. Spread over more than five hundred square miles, this huge metropolis covers a bigger area than Los Angeles. It took me over an hour to ride through the sprawling suburbs to the Youth Hostel, which was situated in the heart of the city. Sunning herself in the hostel garden was Annabel, and she gave me a good telling off for being two days late!

Pheonix is a booming city, blessed with over 300 hundred sunny days per year, but to me it seemed a rather dry, dull mass of white concrete blocks, with the Downtown area particularly devoid of interesting features. The Youth Hostel, however, was a wonderful place – largely due to its Manageress, Sue. She was a charismatic character, who made everyone feel welcome and brought people together by encouraging them to participate fully in the day to day running of the hostel. In the evenings, the common room came to life, as guests were encouraged to share whatever creative talents they had, and this helped to create a real feeling of togetherness. Those prepared to provide entertainment were excused cleaning duties, so there was no shortage of willing performers!

Annabel was as keen as ever to come cycling, so we began our search for equipment immediately. After scouring the local newspapers, we purchased an almost new 'Schwinn' hybrid bicycle from a young businessman, who had bought the bike as a new hobby but then decided that a boat would be more fun! He seemed delighted to learn that his discarded toy would be used for such a serious venture, and made us promise to send him a postcard from Mexico City. A strong rack, two large rear panniers and a waterproof jacket were the other main purchases, and in total she had spent around three hundred pounds in gearing herself up for the journey.

The other guests at the hostel took great interest in our proposed bicycle journey through Mexico, especially since Annabel had readily confessed to not riding a bike for several years. One of them – an Irish girl, named Kate - had recently won the Irish lottery, for which the prize was a 'Green Card' (American Working Visa). She had spent a few months working and backpacking around the States, and now wanted to venture further afield. Annabel had struck up an instant friendship with her, and suggested that we invite her along with us.

Slightly worried that the whole thing was getting out of hand, I explained to Kate how tough cycle touring can be, with long distances between settlements and no escape from the unpredictable forces of nature. This only seemed to strengthen her resolve, however, and I could see that she was determined enough to give it a good go. While Annabel was busy going for practice rides around the block, I spent a day with Kate visiting several bike shops, so that she could try out as many different bikes as possible. She eventually settled for a blue 'Giant' mountain bike, and the same luggage and clothing set-up as Annabel.

We were about ready to depart, but Sue persuaded us to stay a couple of days longer in order to share in the Thanksgiving Day celebrations which, she assured us, were not to be missed. It turned out to be a great day, with all the guests contributing to the preparations for a terrific feast. The crowd at the hostel had gelled into one big happy family and it felt like Christmas!

A day late for the Thanksgiving celebrations, Masahira rolled up once more. He needed to stay in Phoenix for several days in order to sort out visas and stock up with equipment, but promised to try and catch us up in Mexico. Our progress would be quite slow at first, with the girls building up their fitness, so this seemed a realistic possibility.

Though seeing little of the city itself, nine days had passed very quickly in Phoenix. The hostel had been a real 'home from home' and it was great to feel a part of the small travellers' community there. Setting off with Annabel and Kate at my side, it felt like the beginning of a whole new journey.

With 'last minute' preparations and final farewells taking the whole morning, it was already a scorching hot November afternoon by the time that we set off from the hostel. We had not got very far when the skies suddenly darkened and the sound of thunder warned of an approaching storm. I did think about taking cover, but the girls were in determined mood, so we rode on through the outer suburbs of Phoenix. Before long, the heavens opened and we were all soaked to the skin. It was a torrential downpour and an early introduction to the harsh realities of cycle travel for my two new road partners. They bravely tried to battle on, but the storm showed no signs of abating and the riding was quite treacherous, as well as extremely uncomfortable! There was nothing for it but to check into a motel on the outskirts of the city. We had not expected to get too far on that first day, but had hoped to at least make it out of Phoenix! We all saw the funny side of the situation though, and I started to realise that this was going to be an enjoyable adventure, no matter how far we managed to ride together.

The next day was more successful, as we managed to make a reasonably early start and covered about twenty-five miles across the plains, to reach the small junction town of Florence by mid-afternoon. The girls were starting to get a little saddle-sore by this point, so we checked into a motel here for the night. Motel rooms in America seem to cost the same, no matter how many people you cram into them, and this one worked out at just seven dollars each.

In the morning, we visited a café in the town for blueberry pancakes and cream, to set us up for the day. As we were about to leave, an old man at the next table collapsed on the floor. Annabel, who was trained in first aid, reacted quickly and administered 'C.P.R.' with the help of a local policeman, who had been sitting at the same table as the old man. The patient's heart eventually started beating again, and he was taken away to hospital in an ambulance. Most of the other diners seemed to be in a state of shock, and paid us little attention as we paid for breakfast and set off on our bicycles. We had barely covered a mile, however, when we were overtaken by the local Police Chief. He jumped out of his car and shook each of us by the hand, explaining that he had received a full account of the incident and thanking Annabel, in particular, for her efforts. As we rode off again, he shouted after us that he was only sorry that he could not fit all our bicycles into his boot and give us a lift to the next town!

We rode slowly south on the Pinal Pioneer Highway, across barren plains that were dotted with Suguaro cactus trees – a species of cactus that grows naturally only in this part of the world. The highway was gradually rising, giving the girls their first taste of climbing, and it turned out to be quite an ordeal. Progress was very slow and we made frequent stops, but they were determined that we would make it to the next settlement at Oracle Junction, forty miles south of Florence.

We stopped for a lengthy lunch break at a rest area that was marked by a monument to the legendary film star Tom Mix, who was killed on this spot when his car rolled over in mystery car crash, involving no other vehicles. The highway was dead straight at this point for as far as the eye could see, so it was hard to imagine how he could have lost control of the car. The uphill riding became even more difficult in the afternoon, as the girls started to tire, and the rest stops became longer and more frequent. As the sun dropped slowly towards the horizon, I secretly accepted that we would probably need to make a roadside camp. However, we kept going and going until the highway finally dipped downwards and Oracle Junction came into view. It was almost dark by now, but we were triumphant!

There was a trailer park at Oracle Junction and the lady in charge gave us permission to set up camp in the corner. However, as we were setting my tent up, she came over and announced that there was a vacant trailer that we were welcome to make use of. The nights were cold at this time of year, and she even went as far as to say that she would not be able to sleep properly if she knew that we were camping! The trailer was warm, with a hot shower and a kitchenette, so we felt well rewarded for our efforts that day.

Feeling refreshed after a comfortable night in the trailer, we set off in high spirits. It was a much easier ride that day, across rolling desert plains to the city of Tucson. After four days in the saddle, both of the girls were starting to walk in a very strange way whenever they climbed off their bicycles, so we decided that it was time for a rest day.

Despite being Arizona's second city, Tucson had a sleepy, 'small town' feel to it. It was once part of Mexico and the Spanish influences were very noticeable. Main Street, in particular, was a reminder of the past, as it once formed part of a famous old road called 'Camino Real' (Royal Highway), that stretched all the way from this northernmost Spanish settlement down to Mexico City. Just off Main Street, we popped into the Mexican Consulate for visas. This proved to be a formality, although the smiling 'Senora' on duty issued them on the express condition that we promised to visit the

Copper Canyon. "The Grand Canyon is nothing in comparison with the Copper Canyon!" she claimed.

Rain was lashing down on the morning of our planned departure, and before long the streets of Tucson had turned to rivers. Eager to get back on the road, Kate and Annabel were quite dismayed at this turn of events, but there was nothing for it but to rest up in the motel for another day.

The weather was far more agreeable the next day, and the floodwaters had all but disappeared, so we were able to ride south towards the Mexican border. The desert terrain was more undulating now and we managed several big climbs. The girls seemed to have built up a good level of fitness in just a few days and coped quite easily with the uphill riding. That evening, we reached the beautifully restored old village of Tubac, which lies at over two thousand feet. The only motel in the village was rather expensive, however, so we decided to ride on a little further and set up camp in the desert.

This was our first camp together, and it soon became apparent that my 2/3-man tent was really only a 2 man at best! I regretted not purchasing a second tent in Phoenix, but it was a cold night and there was nothing for it but to squeeze into the tent together like sardines. It was an uncomfortable night, with each of us trying to avoid the slightest movements, for fear of disturbing the others, but at least we kept warm!

Despite the rather cramped sleeping conditions, the girls seemed to have enjoyed their first camping experience. The mood was good as we packed up camp at first light and warmed up with tea and porridge. We managed to get on the road early, before the desert sun became too oppressive, and by lunchtime we were nearly at the border.

Just outside the border town of Nogales, we stopped at a small roadside café for our last meal in the United States. The Proprietor was a huge man called Charlie, who broke down in laughter when he discovered that we were planning to ride down to Mexico City, and then declared that our meal was on the house. Before long, the locals in the café were gathered around us and warning us of the dangers that awaited us in northern Mexico. The general consensus of opinion was that we would all be shot by bandits within a few hours of crossing the border! Although these comments were not exactly constructive, and clearly based on ignorance, I could see that their concerns for our safety were quite genuine. One of them even gave us his phone number and offered to come and help us if we got into any trouble! We eventually agreed to send postcards to prove our safety, and Charlie promised that he would mount a map on the wall in order to chart our progress!

I was quite used to receiving these kinds of warnings about the perils of attempting to cycle in regions that were notorious for crime. While not ignoring the advice given, I was fully aware that these fears were often based on sensational news reporting, which tends to focus on the unsavoury incidents and give a rather unbalanced impression of the overall situation. There is always an element of risk and vulnerability when travelling, particularly by bicycle, but this was something that I had accepted when I first set off from London. It was some relief, however, to discover that the girls were equally undaunted by these warnings of impending danger. There would be no turning back now.

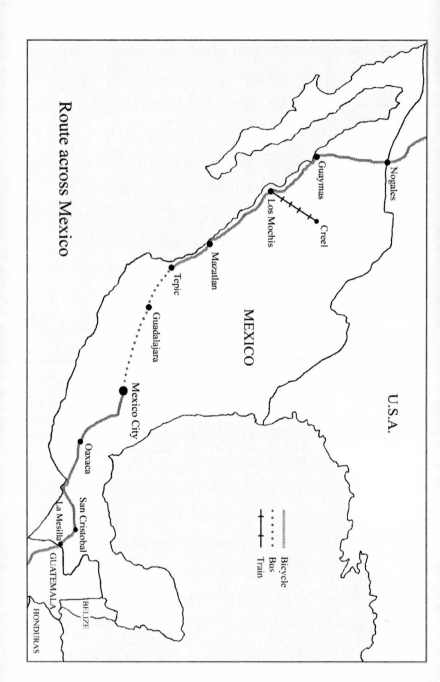

Route across Mexico

U.S.A.

Nogales

Guaymas

Los Mochis

Creel

Mazatlan

Tepic

Guadalajara

MEXICO

Mexico City

Oaxaca

San Cristobal

La Mesilla

GUATEMALA

BELIZE

HONDURAS

Bicycle
Bus
Train

CHAPTER NINE

THREE'S COMPANY

Nogales to the La Mesilla

NOGALES WAS A TYPICALLY CHAOTIC BORDER TOWN, with the border station itself particularly confusing. There were people and vehicles thronging in all directions, and nobody paid us the slightest attention as we battled our way through the crowds. Eventually, we found ourselves on the Mexican side without even having produced our passports! Kate suggested going back for an entry stamp, but one look back at the bedlam behind us was enough to persuade all three of us to just carry on and hope for the best. At least we had our visas.

It was already late in the afternoon by now, so we decided to look for accommodation on the Mexican side of Nogales. The girls were tired now, so I left them at a café and went off to scout for a hotel on my own. It was my first real opportunity to practise the Spanish that I had been studying for several months now, and I was quite pleased with myself on returning with the news that we were booked into a nice little hotel, just a few streets away. Before long, we were settling into a simply furnished three-bed room. It was a relief to be off the noisy streets at last, but the hotel did not turn out to be such a good choice after all. Kate went for a shower and returned a few minutes later looking quite traumatised. She reported that the bathroom floor was covered in human excrement, which she had had to walk through in order to get to the shower! The girls then fell into a state of despondency, as they jumped to the conclusion that every hotel in Mexico was probably going to be like this, while I kicked myself for forgetting to check the bathroom before agreeing to the room.

In the morning, we were all up early, in order to vacate the hotel as soon as possible! We rode through the busy morning traffic and then embarked on a steep climb out of Nogales. There were cheers and whistles coming from all directions, as we slowly laboured up the hill, and the girls stubbornly kept the peddles turning, rather than face the humiliation of having to climb off and push the bikes! We did stop at the top though, and a small girl came running from her house with a plate of melon to reward our efforts!

Once clear of the city, we made good progress across a landscape of scrub desert, with dark pillars of cacti popping out of the desert floor every so often. The narrow, bumpy, highway was not ideal for cycling, but there were no complaints from the girls, who seemed relieved to have left Nogales behind. We covered sixty-five miles that day across hilly terrain, which was incredible really. It was still only a week since we had started our journey together in Phoenix, and I had not expected us to manage this sort of daily distance so quickly. The girls were living proof that you don't need to be super-fit, or to have lots of cycling experience, in order to embark on a long-distance cycle tour. That evening, we arrived at the small town of Imuris, which was a blissfully tranquil place in comparison with Nogales. Having found a modest-looking hotel just off the main street, we gave it a thorough examination before checking in, with particular attention to the bathroom. It was spotlessly clean!

The next day, we rode further across the unchanging desert landscape to another sleepy little town called Magdalene, where we again found excellent, inexpensive accommodation. We were almost across the notorious 'Bandit State' of Sonora now, without having encountered any real hostility, and the girls were at last starting to relax and enjoy Mexico.

From Magdalene, we were faced with a two-day ride to the city of Hermosillo. There were no towns marked on the map before the city, so we loaded up with extra food and water. We had not got very far when we were caught up by a smiling Mexican cyclist, called Francisco, who was riding on an old tandem bicycle. He spoke little English, but we gathered that he was planning to ride all day and all night, in order to reach Hermosillo by the following morning. He was carrying virtually no luggage, but at least had a set of lights for the night riding. Although he had been riding quite fast to catch us up, he did not seem to mind our slow pace and rode along all day with us.

The tiny truck-stop settlement of Corbo Junction marked the halfway point between Magdalene and Hermosillo, so we decided to stop here for the night. There were no hotels at the junction, so we would have to camp. First though, we had a farewell drink with Francisco, before he cheerily waved goodbye and cycled off into the night. A group of curious onlookers gathered around us, as we set up my tent on the stony ground behind the village church. There was a lot of pointing and chattering, as they seemed at a loss to understand how the three of us were going to fit inside such a small tent! Among the crowd was a well-dressed man called Francis, who stepped forward to rescue us from our plight. He spoke a little English, and explained to us that he owned a building nearby where we could spend the night. We duly packed up the tent and followed him to a small, white, stone hut across the road. Rummaging around in his pockets, he produced the key and let us in. The hut was bare, but would at least give us security and privacy! Francis did all he could to settle us in – even erecting some makeshift curtains! He then accompanied us to the truck-stop café for dinner.

In the morning, Francis appeared again for breakfast, which he insisted on paying for. Before we set off, he handed me a short hand-written note. My Spanish was not good enough to translate it on the spot, so I tucked it into my pocket and we thanked him for all his help.

Highway 15 cut across the desert in a long, thin straight line. Riding away from Corbo Junction, I looked over my shoulder several times to see Francis standing there and waving, as we slowly disappeared from his view. It was a moving sight, and his kindness towards us was one of the highlights of our journey across Mexico. We all felt lifted that morning by our experience at Corbo Junction, and remained in good spirits for the rest of the day. The ride ended with a long descent into the sprawling city of Hermosillo.

We rode right into the heart of the city and checked into an old colonial hotel, opposite the lively central market. While we were checking in, the English-speaking receptionist kindly translated Francis's note for us. The gist of it was that he was glad to have been able to help us and sorry that the conditions had been so uncomfortable!

Hermosillo was one of Mexico's fastest growing cities at this time, with its population having increased ten-fold over the previous decade. Tourists were still, apparently, something of a novelty though, and our arrival seemed to create quite a stir. Most of the attention was directed towards the girls, due mainly to their insistence on dressing exactly as they would do on a hot, sunny day in Brighton! They were greeted by a chorus of whistles and catcalls every time that we left the hotel! It was some relief to escape all this attention by hiking to the top of 'Cerro de la Campana' (Hill of the Bell). From the top, we were able to see beyond the city limits to Lake Hermosillo and the rolling desert hills through which we had come.

We had hoped to reach the coastal city of Guaymas in a day, but it was a hilly ride from Hermosillo and progress was slower than expected. As evening began to fall, we were still over thirty miles short of our destination, so we set up camp next to a truck-stop café at Los Arrieros. These places tended to be quite noisy, with some of the truckers keeping their engines running throughout the night, for no apparent reason. However, the sense of security, from knowing that there were lots of people nearby, made this far preferable to a lonely roadside camp. The truckers seemed to be in real party mood this particular evening - intent on shouting and dancing throughout the night! However, the party came to a sudden halt at around midnight, when the heavens opened and a huge downpour sent the merry men scurrying off to their trucks. I had found myself a sheltered spot to sleep beneath the corrugated iron roof of a storage hut, which meant that the girls could have the tent to themselves. There were several rats for company up on the roof, so it was not the most comfortable night, but preferable to playing sardines in the tent again!

Morning came at last. Most of the truckers were still sleeping off their hangovers as we set off at first light. The bumpy highway was deserted at this hour and the silence was broken only by the sound of peddles turning and birds singing, interspersed with the occasional shout of encouragement from farm-workers. The West Coast was firmly in our sights now and by mid-morning we were riding into Guaymas - a busy little port city, squeezed between the ocean and a ring of hills. We rode down to the harbour, from where much of the copper, silver and gold extracted from the State of Sonora is shipped around the world. As we climbed off our bikes, we were besieged by an army of excited children, all anxious to examine the bikes and practise their few words of English on us. We kept them amused for a while, before going in search of accommodation. A very homely, family-run hotel, just a few streets back from the harbour, was to become our sanctuary for the next couple of days.

We were ready for the road again after a good rest in Guaymas. For me it had been active rest, as I had not been able resist the temptation to hike up into the hills around the port, while the girls had preferred to soak up the sun in the hotel garden. The road from Guaymas cut inland, across a strip of coastal farm plains stretching southwards between the mountains of the Sierra Madre and the sea. Annabel and Kate were happily chatting together as they rode along and it seemed that, for the first time since the beginning of our journey together, they were riding in relative comfort now. We managed seventy miles that day, to reach sprawling Ciudad Obregon by early afternoon.

We had the address of a Youth Hostel in this city, where I had promised to leave a message for Masahira, so we stopped to ask for directions. As the young man stared blankly at my scrap of paper, a small crowd gathered around, anxious to help. After some debate we were directed back the way we had come. This seemed a bit strange, as we had not even reached the central area yet, but we eventually found the hostel beside a lake and surrounded by woodland on the edge of the city. It was a large, concrete structure - more like a school building really – and eerily quiet within. As we checked in, I noticed that just one other person had signed in for that night. His name was Masahira!

My Japanese friend had arrived the previous evening, having cycled down from Phoenix in just seven days. This was some going, but he explained that he had been very anxious to catch us up. Unfortunately, he was not in the best of health, having picked up a stomach virus since arriving at the hostel.

We had planned to stay only one night in Ciudad Obregon, but decided on an extra night in order to allow Masahira time to recover from his illness. Though devoid of eye-catching features, the city seemed a particularly friendly place and several people stopped to talk to us as we wandered around the central district. At one market café, run by a mother and her two daughters, we were looked after so well that we returned again in the evening, and then for breakfast the following morning!

Though not fully recovered, Masahira would not have us wait another day and declared himself fit to ride. This led to some debate, but we eventually agreed to ride as far as the town of Navajoa, just thirty-five miles further south. I had already formed a strong bond with Masahira when we rode together in the United States and it was great to be riding with him again. He was a calm, patient guy, who was always able to see the funny side of things and had a quiet determination about him, which was inspirational at times. The girls had met him only briefly, in Phoenix, but took to him readily as well. We must have formed quite a spectacle, as the four of us slowly made our way together through the streets of Ciudad Obregon, and there were plenty of smiles and curious glances from all directions.

Progress was slow that day, with Masahira not having eaten for two days and clearly struggling. It was only a short ride to Navajoa though and, despite taking the journey very slowly, we arrived around lunchtime. We found a hotel close to the centre of this bustling little town, with a room large enough four the four of us – including the bikes! My cooking equipment - consisting of one pot and one small petrol stove - had proved rather inadequate on the rare occasions that I had attempted to cook for myself and the girls. However, with the addition of Mashira's mobile kitchen - including two pots, a frying pan, stove and numerous utensils - we were now well-equipped. We bought some ingredients in the market across the road and managed to produce an excellent meal together.

With the heat becoming more and more intense the further south we rode, it was increasingly important to set off as early as possible. The next morning, we were on the road again soon after daybreak. Mashira was feeling much stronger now, having managed to eat properly the previous evening, but it was about this time that Kate started to complain of pain in her shoulders and neck. Apparently, this had been troubling her for a few days now, but it was much worse that morning and we had to make frequent rest stops. At one of these roadside stops we were surprised by the sudden appearance of a moustached man on horseback, who had the look of a stereotypical Mexican bandit. It soon became clear that he had no ill intentions, however, and he jokingly offered to swap the horse for one of our bicycles. We refused this, of course, but could not resist taking turns to ride on the horse. This was my first experience of bareback riding, and it even made my rock-hard bicycle saddle seem comfortable by comparison!

We crossed the State border into Sinaloa and continued south in fits and starts. Kate's pain was not easing, so we eventually decided to stop for the night at a tiny junction settlement. Setting up camp in something resembling a bandstand, which would at least provide some shelter if it rained, we set about preparing another evening feast. As we were finishing dinner, an old man ambled over and suggested that we follow him to a house nearby. There was a large outbuilding at the back of his property, which he invited us to make our home for the evening. It was yet another act of kindness, which would help to ensure our safe passage through this country.

Back on the highway again early the next morning, we rode into some blustery winds as we headed towards Los Mochis, on the West Coast. Masahira and I took turns at riding in front, so as take the brunt of the wind resistance, as we slowly travelled together across the plains. It was hard going, but we were drawing strength from each other and gradually eating up the distance in front of us to our destination.

Los Mochis is the coastal terminus for the rail route that runs up into the Sierra Madre, via the Copper Canyon. We had promised the lady at the Mexican Consulate in Tucson that we would visit the Copper Canyon, and since learnt that this rail route was the only way of getting there from the West Coast. Masahira wanted to see the Canyon as well, so we hoped to be able to leave our bikes in Los Mochis while we made this trip. Leaving the others at a waterfront café, I went in search of accommodation on foot. It was not long before I tracked down a suitable hotel, with a nice rooftop garden and a storeroom where we would be able to leave the bikes.

With the bicycles safely stored, we headed for the train station at 5am on Christmas Eve morning. We had decided to spend Christmas at the mountain plateau town of Creel, which lies on the Los Mochis to Chihuahua line, just beyond the Copper Canyon. The man in the ticket office could hardly believe that four 'rich foreigners' had elected to travel second class, and he dispensed the tickets rather grudgingly.

The train was not due to leave for nearly an hour, so we went for breakfast at the station café. While we were used to attracting plenty of attention, it seemed to us that this morning we were being stared at even more than usual. The reason for this became clear, however, when somebody passed us a copy of the local newspaper. There was a picture of Masahira, Annabel and Kate – posing in front of the four bicycles – on the front cover! Apparently this picture had been taken while I had been off scouting for accommodation the previous evening. Not realising that the photo was destined for newspaper publication, my companions had not even bothered to mention it to me.

Our minor celebrity status was quickly forgotten, however, when the whistle blew to announce the train's arrival. Pandemonium broke out and we were quickly submerged in a great tide of passengers, suitcases, blankets and shopping bags, as we tried to board the train and secure seats for the ten-hour journey ahead of us. It was quite a scramble, but we managed to claim three seats. This meant that each of us would be able to sit down for at least three-quarters of the ride! The whistle blew again and the train slowly trundled out of the station. Once clear of the city, we crossed farming plains, which glowed a pale yellow colour in the first rays of sunlight, and then began to climb through the fog-shrouded foothills of the Sierra Madre.

After three hours, we crossed the Rio Fuerte Bridge and entered the first of some eighty-eight tunnels. Completed in 1961, the train line from Los Mochis to Chihuahua took almost ninety years to build. As we climbed higher and higher into the mountains, it was easy to appreciate the work that must have gone into creating this engineering masterpiece. Besides the numerous tunnels – some several miles long – the train passed through deep, forested valleys and along ledges that had been cut into near-vertical rock faces.

The train journey became a whirlwind of breathtaking views and seven hours had slipped by almost unnoticed when we stopped at El Devisadero. This tiny settlement sits right on the rim of the Copper Canyon, at an altitude of 2,500 metres. We climbed out of the train and peered over the edge into a sea of forest and cloud, disappearing far below into the endless depths of the Canyon. The scale of the Copper Canyon was almost too much to comprehend and we all stood in silence, lost in our own thoughts.

For the rest of the journey, the train travelled through thick pine forest - skirting the edge of the Canyon, without ever getting close enough to see down into it again. That brief stop at El Devisadero was to be our only glimpse of the Canyon, but that moment alone had made the journey worthwhile.

Getting off the train at Creel, we made straight for a guest house on the town square called Margarita's, which was famous on the backpackers' grapevine at this time for its excellent hospitality. We were not to be disappointed, although the tiny place was a little over-full! The policy was clearly not to turn anyone away and there seemed to be backpackers lurking in every corner! Annabel and Kate were lucky to get a double room to themselves, while Masahira and I had to make do with a mattress each on the lounge floor. The evening meal had to be served in several sittings in the cramped dining room, but the atmosphere was very relaxed and friendly

– so much so, that some of the guests had been 'resting' at Margarita's for several months now!

There were a number of Indian communities in this region, where Tarahumarra Indians continued to lead simple and self-sufficient lives – living in adobe huts and subsisting mainly on corn and beans, which they grew themselves. While maintaining their own traditions and rituals, many of them seem to have embraced Catholicism, which was now Mexico's main religion. On Christmas Day, Tarahumarra Indians filled the Cathedral in the town square for morning mass. After the service, the square came to life as they filed out of the Cathedral and began to sing and dance. The celebrations lasted all day, with most of Creel's population either joining in or just watching from the sides. It was as if the community was one big family, and the backpackers were distance relatives that had come to stay for Christmas. Margarita had enlisted the help of several of her neighbours in order to create an extra special Christmas dinner for all her guests, so the day was rounded off with a huge feast. This was my third Christmas on the road, and probably the most enjoyable.

We spent a couple more days in Creel, soaking up the atmosphere at Margarita's and exploring some of the surrounding villages and caves, before returning to Los Mochis on the night train. The girls did not want to start cycling straight after the train journey, so we decided to spend another night in Los Mochis.

Masahira, however, was anxious to get back on the road straight away. He had been finding our pace a little slow for his liking anyway, so he set off alone on the road south to Mazatlan. I was sorry to see him go, but we had always had an understanding that we would not hold each other up if one wanted to ride and the other wanted to rest.

Despite a good night's sleep at the hotel, we were still feeling a little sluggish after the Christmas festivities in Creel and the long train journey. After a late breakfast, we rode slowly out of Los Mochis and followed the highway through fields of corn and cotton to the small town of Guasave, thirty miles south. Kate had already started to feel the pain in her neck and shoulders again, so we stopped here for the night. This was becoming quite a concern now and I wondered how much further she would be able to cycle.

The next day we rode much further, mainly because we were helped by a strong tailwind, which propelled us across rich agricultural plains to the big, industrial city of Culiacan. Founded in 1531, this is one of the oldest cities in Mexico and the capital of Sinaloa. As usual, we headed towards the central market area, where the cheap hotels are often located. Culiacan was notorious at this time for its crime and drug problems, but the biggest danger to us seemed to be the aggressive driving! This is probably why the girls rode so close behind me that, when I stopped at a junction, Kate flew straight into the back of me! Neither of us were injured in the collision, but her front wheel had sliced right into my rear pannier! After that little mishap it was quite a relief to find the sanctuary of a hotel room, where I was able to repair the pannier with strong tape that Masahira had left with me for just such an emergency.

We set off again early in the morning, while the streets were still relatively calm. Not far south of Culiacan, Annabel came to a sudden halt at the sight of a couple of light crop-spraying aeroplanes, which were parked up outside some roadside farm buildings. She had felt a sudden, uncontrollable, urge to go up in one of these planes, so we decided to enquire as to whether this would be possible. The farm manager pointed out, apologetically, that the planes were all single-seaters, but he invited us to join his family for breakfast instead. A folding table was set up in one of the barns, and his wife and two children carried in trays of fresh fruit, bread and boiled eggs. The family seemed delighted to have interrupted their working day to entertain us, and they loaded us up with parting gifts of fruit and honey.

A little further down the road, we reached the start of a brand new toll highway to Mazatlan, eighty miles further south. The new highway looked much safer for cycling, with a perfectly smooth surface and wide shoulders. Unfortunately though, the over-officious toll booth operator refused to let us pass on any account. He just kept waving his arms and shouting 'no bicycles, no bicycles'! Eventually, an English-speaker arrived on the scene and explained to us that cycling was against the rules of the company that owned and managed the new highway. He suggested that we backtrack five miles and follow a much longer route to Mazatlan, through the hills.

The girls were tired by now and in no mood for backtracking, so we decided to hitchhike instead. Until now, all offers of lifts from passing truck drivers had been steadfastly refused, but I realised that now we needed a helping hand. In any case, it was New Year's Eve and it would be great to celebrate New Year in the resort town of Mazatlan. No sooner had we made the decision than a two-truck convoy pulled over to offer us a ride. Annabel and Kate quickly disappeared into the cab of the first truck, while I sat with the bikes in the back of the second. A couple of hours later, we were duly deposited on the sea front in Mazatlan.

The Pacific Coast of Mexico had seemed refreshingly underdeveloped up until now, but Mazatlan had all the hallmarks of a premier beach resort and package holiday destination. The centrepiece was a long, golden, crescent-shaped beach, separating the 'Golden Zone' at the northern end from 'Old Mazatlan' at the southern end. The 'Golden Zone' was an area of expensive resort hotels, time-share condominiums, tacky bars and discotheques, where holiday-makers can easily throw away more money in a week than the average Mexican earns in a year. Those wishing for a 'flavour of Mexico' would be able to wander down the beach to Old Mazatlan for a few hours, before returning to their holiday paradise for another evening of partying.

There were a few very basic hotels situated within Old Mazatlan itself, so we were able to find cheap lodgings there. This enabled us to escape the artificial world of the 'Golden Zone' and to avoid blowing our budgets in one night! Once settled in, we celebrated the New Year with a meal at one of the excellent seafood restaurants, for which Mazatlan is famous.

The girls showed no sign of appearing for breakfast the next morning, so I set off to explore the narrow, cobbled streets of Old Mazatlan by myself. Just a few yards from the hotel entrance, however, I bumped into Masahira! It was great to see him, but neither of us were particularly surprised, as we were getting used to these chance encounters. It was almost as if it was destiny that our paths should keep crossing. He had been in Mazatlan for a couple of days now, having taken the road through the hills in order to avoid the toll highway, and was staying at a hotel just around the corner.

We spent another three days in Mazatlan, with Annabel and Kate spending most of their time sunning themselves on the beach, while Masahira and I explored every inch of the town on foot. Once or twice, we even wandered up to the 'Golden Zone' for an over-priced drink with the package-tourists, before returning again to the real world.

With Masahira rejoining our ranks, we set off from Mazatlan. Ahead of us was a tough ride, as Highway 15 wound its way inland, up into lush hill country. The traffic was quite heavy on this narrow old highway and we had to stay tight to the edge of the road, as trucks came hurtling around the sharp bends. As the day wore on, we passed through several hill settlements, with shady plazas and old colonial buildings, where the pace of life seemed much slower than down on the plains. One of these was Acaponeta, just inside the State of Nayarit. We stopped for the night here at a cosy little guest house, with a balcony facing across the plaza to an ancient Cathedral. The plaza came alive in the evening, as the locals turned out in their 'Sunday best' to enjoy live music and various delicious snacks from food stalls that seemed to spring up from nowhere.

We had not got very far from Acoponeta when Annabel began to feel sick. We stopped to rest at a roadside café, where it soon became clear that she was in a bad way. On top of this, Kate was suffering from the shoulder pains again, which had dogged her for a couple of weeks now and seemed to get worse every time that she climbed on the bike. It was obvious that neither of them were going to be able to ride any further that day, so one of the locals in the café flagged down a bus that was heading to Tepic - the capital city of Nayarit. Masahira kindly offered to come with us on the bus, but I would not let him. His cycle journey had been unbroken, since it began at the northern tip of Alaska, and I knew that he would regret it if he took the bus with us now when he did not really need to.

The bus was almost empty and the driver helpfully loaded our bikes into the centre aisle. As we pulled away, and I watched Masahira slowly fading away into the distance, a strange feeling came over me that this was to be our final parting. This indeed turned out to be the case, for reasons that did not become apparent until I received a letter from him a year later. He wrote that he had been robbed at gunpoint on the road to Mexico City, just a few days after our parting. The bicycle, together with most of his possessions, was taken from him and he was left with little more than the clothes that he was standing in. Fortunately, most of his money was in travellers' cheques, so he was able to get these refunded in Mexico City, before returning to Phoenix by train in order to buy camping equipment and a replacement bicycle. He then returned to Mexico City by train and continued his journey from the exact spot where the robbery had taken place. This was so typical of Masahira. He had great strength of character and incredible determination, which I had come to admire so much in the time that we travelled together.

It was only an hour's journey to Tepic, but on the way Kate came to the decision that her cycle touring days were over. It was obvious that the shoulder problem was not just going to go away and there seemed no point in taking the risk of aggravating the injury. She decided that she would travel by bus to Mexico City and then try to sell the bike there, or exchange it for a backpack. Annabel and I agreed that we would travel with her on the bus to Mexico City and help her to get fixed up for backpacking, before continuing our cycle journey together from there.

Having taken these decisions, there seemed no real point in staying in Tepic. On hearing that we wanted to travel straight on to Guadelajarra, the bus driver arranged for one of his friends at the bus station to transport us across the city to the national coach terminal. As we sped across the city in a small white van, the young man enthusiastically pointed out various places of interest, including the Government Palace and the sixteenth century Temple of the Cruz de Zacate – a former Franciscan convent, which now housed the State Ministry of Tourism. We arrived at the terminal just in time to catch an inter-city coach that was about to depart for Guadalajara. The Tepic connection had been incredibly smooth! Three hours later, we were checking into a small hotel in the heart of Guadalajara's 'Historical Centre'.

Many famous symbols of Mexico originate in Guadalajara, including tequila and the sombrero! Mexico's second city was pleasantly cool, as it lies at an altitude of over 1500 metres, on the edge of Mexico's Central Plateau – an immense chunk of land, which covers two thirds of the country.

Annabel decided to spend a day in bed, recovering from her bout of sickness, so Kate and I set off to explore the 'Historical Centre'. This area around the hotel contained several beautiful plazas, decorated with statues and surrounded by churches, museums and palaces - many of which dated back to the sixteenth century. The twin-towered Cathedral forms the centrepiece, but perhaps the most impressive building was the 'Teatro Degollada'. An array of intricate sculptures adorned the front of this theatre, while the ceiling inside was covered in a huge mural depicting a scene from Dante's 'Divine Comedy'. We enjoyed strolling around these grand old buildings, most of which were policed by small groups of enthusiastic students, who were anxious to practice their English on us!

The bed rest seemed to do Annabel a world of good, and she was up and about again the next day.

We repeated our 'Historical Centre' tour for her benefit, before travelling by night bus across the Central Plateau to Mexico City, 150 miles east. Arriving at dawn on a Sunday morning, we rode through the deserted city centre streets to a hotel that had been recommended to us by a German traveller called Marcus, who had waved us off from the hostel in Phoenix a couple of months before. To our amazement, the first person we encountered, as we lifted the bikes through the entrance porch, was Marcus himself! He seemed delighted -if slightly surprised - to see that we had made it down to Mexico City and were still together!

Covering nearly 800 square miles, the huge, sprawling metropolis of Mexico City was the largest in the world at this time, and its population was estimated at over twenty million. Despite lying at an altitude of some 2,300 metres, the city was notorious for its incredibly high levels of pollution. Breathing the air for one day here was, apparently, equivalent to smoking two packets of cigarettes! Not having smoked a cigarette in my life, it was perhaps not surprising that the pollution seemed to affect me straight away. I spent most of that first day in bed with a thumping headache and, when I did finally venture out of the hotel, my eyes were constantly watering.

The next day was marked by the arrival at the hotel of Konrad, Maurice and Paul - three young Australian backpackers that we had met previously in Creel. Annabel and Kate had established rather close relationships with Konrad and Maurice respectively, so this may not have been as much of a coincidence as it appeared! Leaving them to renew their ties, I set off to discover Mexico City.

Having heard all the negative things about Mexico City – pollution, high crime rates and dreadful slums - it was good to discover that the city also has much to be proud of. The 'Historical Centre' was even larger than that of Guadalajara and centred around the 'Plaza de la Constitution' - which was first paved in the 1520s and remains one of the world's largest city plazas. At the northern end stood the enormous Metropolitan Cathedral, which was covered in scaffolding. Apparently, the building was suffering from subsidence, partly due to a major earthquake in 1985. Not far from the Plaza, I bumped into Paul, who was also doing his best to avoid the romantic couples! Paul and I had not really 'connected' in Creel, but now found that we had a lot in common, particularly an interest in literature. We spent the rest of the day browsing through bookshops and drinking coffee in the numerous continental-style cafes that were dotted around the 'Old Town'.

Not far from Mexico City stand the ruins of an ancient Aztec settlement called Teohuatican, which dates back to 200 BC and grew to be one of the world's largest cities by 600 AD. It declined rapidly after that, and was eventually abandoned, but has remained an important pilgrimage site for the Aztecs. Accompanied by the Australians, we reached the ruins by local bus and proceeded to climb the 'The Pyramid of the Sun', which was the focal point of the settlement. It was surprising to learn that 'The Pyramid of the Sun' is the world's largest pyramid, containing over three millions tonnes of stone! The 248 steps looked quite manageable, but we were at an altitude of over 4000 metres now and the lack of oxygen turned this into quite a challenge! We all made it though, and from the top it was easy to appreciate why Teohuatican was once regarded as the New World's greatest city.

A week had slipped by very easily in Mexico City and it was now time for our Australian friends to return home by plane. With the emotional farewells completed, Annabel announced that she was ready to ride south. Kate stuck to her decision to end her cycle journey here, but had not been able to bring herself to sell the bicycle. Instead she boxed it up and sent it home to Ireland by surface mail. She had cycled over a thousand miles from Phoenix and seemed to have enjoyed the experienced. Perhaps more importantly though, she had gained the confidence to travel on through Southern Mexico and Central America alone, if necessary. It was hard to leave her behind, but she seemed positive about things and had already found some new friends with whom to share the next part of her journey.

Following signs to Puebla, we found ourselves riding out of Mexico City on an eight-lane highway with no hard shoulder. The traffic was moving at a furious pace, the noise was deafening and our lungs were choking in the polluted air. It took a whole morning to clear the suburbs, and we were both pleasantly surprised to find ourselves still alive at the end of it! The real hard work, however, was yet to come.

The most direct route to Puebla was by way of another new toll highway, and this time there were no objections to the bikes. We were waved through the toll barrier and onto the shiny new highway, which, thankfully, had a wide hard shoulder for us to ride on. Ahead of us was a long, gradual climb to a pass at 3,500 metres, before dropping down into the Puebla Valley. Physical exercise of any kind becomes quite difficult at this kind of altitude, due to lack of oxygen, so it was not long before we were struggling. Progress became slower and slower, until Annabel eventually resigned herself to having to walk. We were offered several lifts, as she slowly pushed her loaded bike up the hill, but these were stubbornly refused.

As the afternoon drew to a close, it became clear that we were not going to reach the pass before dark, so we decided to seek permission to camp behind a roadside café. The café was run by a cheerful, plump woman called Rosa, with the help of her eight-year-old son, Alexandra. The small boy led us to the grassy spot in the fields behind the café and waited patiently while we set up the tent. He then produced a football and we had a kick-a-round before dinner.

There was a power cut in the café that evening, so we had a candlelit supper. Several trucks pulled up for the night and the atmosphere was quite lively. Rosa carried out steaming plates of chicken and rice, while Alexandra cleared the tables and served the drinks. Once everyone had had their fill, the tables were cleared and the card games began. We refused all invitations to join in but watched for a while, before returning to our camp.

We awoke to find Alexandra waiting outside the tent for another game of football! I duly obliged him, while Annabel started to pack things together for the journey ahead. The truckers had already left and Rosa was still sleeping, but Alexandra insisted on waking his mother so that we could have a hot breakfast before we set off. This boy was mature beyond his years!

Refreshed after a good night's sleep, Annabel was able to ride again and we easily made it up to the pass. Far away to the south, as we descended into the rich, fertile Puebla Valley, we caught our first glimpses of two of Mexico's biggest volcanoes – Popocatepetl ('Smoking Mountain') and Iztaccihuatl ('White Woman'), both of which rise above 5,000 metres. The descent brought us right down into the ancient city of Puebla itself, where we checked into a simple guest house in the downtown area.

As well as being a city of some historical significance, having been the scene of many great episodes in Mexico's history, we found Puebla to be a lively, modern city. We spent a day exploring the downtown area, which was an interesting mixture of old colonial buildings, continental-style cafes and fashionable shops that were selling all the top brands. Wandering further afield, we found ourselves in pretty residential districts where each house was painted in bright, contrasting colours.

From Puebla, we rode south on Highway 190 – an old road, which skirted the southern foothills of Mount Popocatepetl. It was a clear day and this huge, conical volcano dominated the landscape all day long. With the gradients generally in our favour that morning, we made good progress to reach the old colonial town of Atlixco, which lies in the heart of an avocado-producing region. The next thirty miles were nearly all uphill and again the climbing became quite an ordeal for Annabel. A few miles short of Acatlan, she finally had to resort to walking, and this time we accepted a short truck ride into the town.

Another long, tough climb awaited us the next morning. Annabel was in determined mood, however, and patiently slogged away. The terrain of southern Mexico was proving to be far more mountainous than we had expected though and I was starting to realise that it was simply too much for her. This was unfortunate, because she had built up a good level of fitness by this time and would easily have coped with cycle touring in most parts of the world. We covered thirty miles – sometimes riding, sometimes walking – before again hitching a ride, and this was to develop into a pattern over the next few weeks, as we travelled south through the mountains. On this occasion, salvation came in the form of a small lorry carrying sugar to the city of Oaxaca, ninety miles further south. The bikes were carefully loaded on top of the sugar and we squeezed into the cab alongside the driver and his mate.

Set on a mountain plateau in the heart of southern Mexico, Oaxaca was an attractive old colonial city with a relaxed, easy-going atmosphere. We were dropped off in the central market district, which was full of lively street cafes and stalls selling colourful, locally-produced handicrafts. That evening, having settled into one of the numerous small hotels dotted around this area, we walked a few blocks to Cathedral Plaza, where musicians and street dancers were entertaining the evening diners and strollers. Here we encountered another cycle tourist, pushing his heavily loaded bike towards us, through the middle of the crowded plaza.

Our new friend's name was Bill – a young Californian - and he had just arrived in the city, having cycled down from his home city of San Francisco. He had followed the West Coast all the way down to Acapulco, before turning inland through the mountains to Oaxaca. Like us, he had been surprised at just how tough these mountains were for cycling and, though clearly an experienced cyclist, had pushed himself almost to the point of exhaustion while riding up from the coast. We directed him to our hotel, arranging to meet up with him later in the evening for a meal.

We stayed three days in Oaxaca, relaxing and exploring the cultural treasures of this fascinating city. Perhaps the most interesting of these were the nearby Zapotec Indian ruins at Monte Alban ('White Mountain'). Dating back to 700 BC, these well-preserved ruins have a spectacular setting, on a flattened hilltop overlooking the three valleys of Oaxaca. The site grew to become a city of more than 50,000 people by 300AD, with the residential districts built on terraces around the hillside. The effort that must have gone into levelling the hilltop and carrying stone up from the valleys was hard to comprehend. The eventual decline of Monte Alban was probably due to the lack of a natural water source, and by 700 A.D. it had become more of a religious site. We visited a number of elaborate tombs, built by the Miztec Indians, who had started to dominate the Zapotecs by this time.

Although Bill was travelling in our direction, we decided not to ride together, as our combination of cycling, walking and hitchhiking would not have suited him. He was clearly on a mission to cycle all the way down to South America and it would have been a shame for him to break his ride on our account. We did not encounter him again, but I did receive a postcard from him several months later, on my return to England. The card came from Peru and described his chance meeting on the road with a certain Japanese cyclist named Masahira! Apparently, Masahira was singing a Bob Dylan song that I had taught him, when Bill caught up with him, and he became quite emotional at hearing news of us. The two of them were to cycle together for several weeks in South America.

We rode for twenty miles or so across flat terrain, before starting the inevitable climb out of the wide basin in which Oaxaca lies. We broke the climb with a stop at the village of Tula, in order to visit the famous 'Tula Tree' – a cypress tree which was claimed to have the biggest girth of any tree in the world. Thought to be over two thousand years old, the Tula Tree stood in the village churchyard, completely dwarfing a tiny church. We wondered whether the church had been built deliberately small in order to emphasise the size of the tree!

We stopped again at the next village of Tlacolula, where the weekly market was in full swing. It was a colourful spectacle, with most of the traders in traditional dress. One that we spoke to had walked for miles from his mountain farm, with a packhorse that was loaded with vegetables. The next settlement marked on our map was over forty miles away, so we stocked up with food and water here before continuing our slow journey through the mountains.

It turned into another torturous ride. We had to walk some stretches, but we kept going and managed to reach the tiny settlement of El Tepenene, just as the sun was falling behind the mountains. We set up camp close to one of the small white stone houses that were clustered around the highway. As we were preparing dinner, an old man emerged from the house carrying a kerosene lamp. Seeing that we had all the food and drink that we needed, he insisted on lending us the lamp for the evening. The mountain sky was especially clear that night and it was a lovely camp at the end of a long, hard day.

The next day was somewhat easier, as we came down from the mountains, and it ended with a long, gradual descent to the town of Tehuantepec, just a few miles in from the Pacific Coast. Some farm workers gave us permission to camp on their small farm on the outskirts of the town, despite the owner being away at the time. With their day's work finished, many of the workers gathered round to watch, as we set up the tent and then prepared our evening meal over my tiny petrol stove. A couple of them carried over a small wooden table, a couple of stools and a lamp so that we could dine in style, and then they all respectfully dispersed as we began to eat.

Later in the evening, the owner himself turned up. He greeted us cheerfully and insisted that we should come and stay at his house, as he was fearful that the farm dog would bother us. We dutifully packed the tent up and followed him to a large, walled property on the edge of the farm. As we had already eaten, we were served a light supper, and the evening was spent chatting with the owner and his wife on a terrace by the swimming pool. They spoke little English, but seemed quite impressed at our dismal attempts at conversing in Spanish. As if we were not struggling enough with the Spanish, they even taught us a few words of Zapotec – the language of the local Indian community. As the evening drew to a close, our hosts retired inside, leaving us to sleep on our mats by the pool. This was a little surprising, as we had been expecting to be invited in, but it was a warm night and we slept comfortably. We did not see the owner or his wife in the morning, but the maid carried out a breakfast of omelettes and toast, and invited us to make use of the outdoor showers before setting off. It had been a strange night, and perhaps our hosts were a little wary of us, but we were grateful for their hospitality and sent them a card a few days later to let them know.

The highway south followed flat coastal plains, which should have been a huge relief as we had been climbing or descending almost constantly since leaving Mexico City. There was to be no respite, however, as we now had to battle against fierce crosswinds which made riding almost impossible. After two hours we had managed less than ten miles, which is about walking pace! To our rescue that morning came the 'Angele Verdes' ('Green Angels'). Provided as a free rescue service by the Mexican Government, the Green Angels were a fleet of bright green trucks, patrolling the main Mexican highways in search of motorists that were in trouble. The driver of this particular Green Angel had seen that we were struggling to keep our balance against the stormy winds, and stopped to offer us a lift. He was so insistent on helping us that we both agreed at once, without even bothering to consult each other. We were dropped off at a junction about twenty miles further on, which marked the edge of his patch. There was a large truck-stop café at the junction, so we would be able to shelter here and there would be no trouble hitching another ride if we needed it.

After drinking coffee for a couple of hours at the café, there was still no sign of a break in the storm, so we did decide to hitch. As usual, Annabel's long, flowing hair appeared to do the trick, and we had barely made it to the side of the road before we were offered a lift by two young guys in a pick-up truck. They were carrying a load of tropical fruit and seemed intent on eating as much of it as possible on the way, so we munched our way to the next truck-stop at Tapanatepec, a further eighty miles south. Our plan was to head inland from here, so we were dropped off with a supply of fruit to last us for the next few days!

It was dark by now, so we started looking for a place to camp in amongst the trucks that had pulled in for the night. As we were starting to fix up the tent, however, one of the truckers approached us and insisted that we should sleep in the back of his truck, as it would be safer and warmer. His offer seemed genuine enough, so we followed him to his truck and loaded everything in. He then accompanied us to the café, where he introduced us to some of his friends. His English was very good, on account of his having lived in the United States for a few years, and we had an entertaining evening in the company of these good-natured Mexican truckers.

When morning came, we were slightly alarmed to discover that the driver had locked us inside the truck, presumably for our safety. However, I was able to climb through the tarpaulin, which formed our roof, much to the amusement of the other truckers, as our friend hurried over to unlock the back door. He then took us for breakfast and fixed us up with a ride inland to the city of Tuxtla Gutierrez, in the mountainous State of Chiapus.

Having been warned that the road up to Tuxtla was incredibly steep, we were certainly glad of the assistance!

Chiapus is Mexico's southernmost State, and perhaps the most beautiful. Perched precariously on some concrete slabs, in the back of a builder's pick-up truck, we were carried up into the lush, forested mountains on a narrow, winding highway. The driver seemed intent on breaking all mountain speed records, and on some of the hairpin bends we had to cling onto the sides of the truck in order to avoid flying off into space. To make matters worse, Annabel was desperate for the toilet and the driver did not seem to understand my signals for him to pull over. He seemed to be interpreting them as friendly greetings and just kept giving us the 'thumbs up' in return! When we eventually reached Tuxtla, he stopped outside a car showroom. Annabel jumped out of the truck and ran inside, demanding immediate access to a toilet, while I thanked the driver and assured him that we had thoroughly enjoyed the ride.

Tuxtla was a surprisingly modern city, having benefited in recent years from the discovery of oil in the north of Chiapus. The central plaza was surrounded by high-rise office blocks and plush hotels, but we did not have to wander far to discover the more old-fashioned market area, where we were able to find cheap lodgings for the night.

Back on the bikes again, we were not far out of Tuxtla when the highway passed right over the mouth of the Sumidero Canyon. The near-vertical canyon walls disappeared far away below us to the Grijalua River, slowly flowing by a thousand metres below. It was a spectacular sight, which was all the more enjoyable as we had not been expecting it at all. We lingered at the Canyon for quite a while, before riding on to the old colonial town of Chiapa De Corzo – a quaint little settlement which has been lived in almost continuously since around 1500 BC.

From Chiapa De Corzo, we were faced with a long, steep climb up to San Cristobal de las Casas. We rode until Annabel was ready to drop, with the road rising endlessly around bend after bend. When it became obvious that we could not go any further, we pulled into a lay-by and waited for a lift. However, with the bends so close together, it was not a good hitching spot. We had to wait for over two hours until a truck finally swerved in to pick us up and carry us the remaining distance to San Cristobal.

Situated high in a pine-clad valley, San Cristobal de las Casas is a colourful, colonial city, with brightly painted, red-roofed houses lining narrow cobbled streets. The city owes its strange name to the sixteenth century cleric, Fray Bartolome de las Casas, who was its first Bishop and spent much of his life fighting a political campaign to protect the indigenous people of the Americas.

We checked into one of several hostels that were dotted around the town and spent the next four days simply relaxing, and getting to know other travellers from all corners of the globe. Among them was a 'National Geographic' photographer called Steve, from Canada, who was busy trying to capture the native Indian culture for the magazine. We accompanied him one day to the village of Chamula, which nestles high up in the hills above San Cristobal. There was a small handicrafts market in the village square, where a small group of Indian women, dressed in intricately embroidered traditional costumes, were eagerly awaiting the daily arrival of tourists from the city below. Across the square was an imposing white church, where some rather strange religious practices were said to take place, including the sacrifice of 'coca-cola' bottles to pagan Gods. As with many of the Indian communities in Latin America, the Chamulans seem to have somehow merged the Catholic teachings of the Spanish missionaries with there own time-honoured pagan practices. Steve explained to us that there was a huge variety of customs and beliefs among the native Indians. The Chamulans, for instance, believed that Christ rose from the cross to become the sun.

The night before our departure from San Cristobal, we joined a large group of intrepid travellers that were gathered in a tavern for a talk on Guatemala, given by an English aid worker, who had been living there for the past twenty years. It turned out to be a depressing evening, however, as he advised us not to cross the border into Guatemala under any circumstances! Although there was no war at present, he explained to us that the country was under military rule and that crime had spiralled out of control – mainly because the military were not really interested in the job of policing. We took the advice seriously, as the speaker clearly had first-hand knowledge of the situation, but were both determined not to turn back. We resolved, however, to be particularly careful to stop cycling well before dark and to camp close to civilisation whenever possible – preferably on private land.

In the morning, we duly headed off towards the border. We were both feeling refreshed, after our stay in San Cristobal, and rode fifty miles through lush forested hills to the bustling market town of Comitan. After rapidly consuming a plate of tasty enchiladas at a café on the town plaza, we rode on until the evening and set up camp in a village churchyard, just fifteen miles from the border. The village consisted of no more than a small cluster of houses, and did not even appear to have a name, but did boast a small, sandy basketball court! Having set up the tent, I joined some of the local children for a game of basketball, which did not finish until the last rays of the sun were blocked out by the surrounding mountains.

It was a steep climb from our village camp to the border town of Ciudad Cuauhtemoc, where we were informed that we should have had our passports stamped at an immigration hut four miles back down the hill! Having employed a small boy as a security guard for the bikes, we jumped on the back of a crowded passenger truck, which was heading back down the hill. We had used up all our Mexican currency, so I produced a crisp one dollar note with which to pay for the ride. The note was carefully passed through the hands of virtually every passenger, before finally reaching the conductor. Back in Ciudad Cuautemoc, the border formalities were now completed smoothly, and we rode across into the Guatemalan town of La Mesilla.

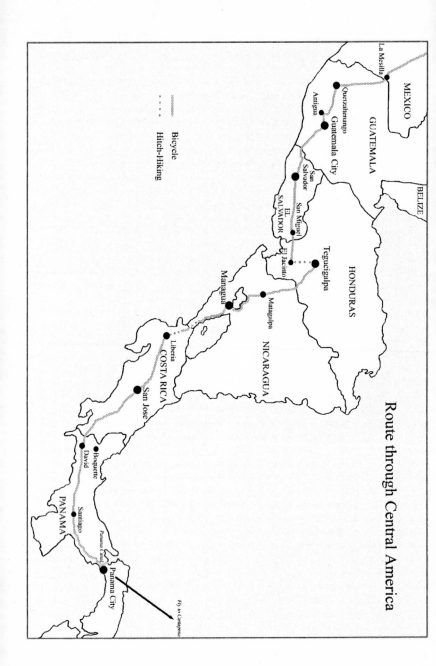

Route through Central America

434

CHAPTER TEN

RIDING THROUGH CLOUDS

La Mesilla to Panama City

BORDER TOWNS CAN BE CHAOTIC - EVEN ugly - places and rarely warrant more time than is absolutely necessary to complete border formalities, but La Mesilla was different. Nestling at the foot of a towering volcano, it certainly had a spectacular setting, but it was the people that made the real impression. The Guatemalans seemed far more reserved and respectful than their Mexican neighbours across the border, although just as friendly in their own way. Children waved at us and their parents would acknowledge us with a smile, but nobody fired questions at us from across the street, or whistled at Annabel, as we had grown used to in Mexico.

Our initial impressions of the Guatemalan people were reinforced as we rode further into the country. Stopping at a marketplace in the first village that we came to, a few locals gathered around as we purchased some groceries, but they kept a respectful distance and asked nothing of us – except for one of the stall-holders, who suggested that we take his photograph! Another striking feature of this mountain village was the traditional dress worn by most of the women and children. Gone were the American-style tee shirts and jeans – so popular in Mexico – and in their place were bright, multi-coloured robes and headscarves.

The Western Highlands of Guatemala is a lush region of forested volcanoes, steep-sided canyons and rushing streams. Though slightly wary at first, after hearing so many stories of highway robberies and general lawlessness, we were soon able to relax and appreciate the beauty of our surroundings. We chose our first campsite carefully, however – seeking permission to set up the tent within full view of a petrol station and a couple of farmhouses, so that we would be able to summon help if necessary. The night passed without incident, however, and we rode on the next day to the large town of Quetzaltenango, which lies at an altitude of 2,000 metres, in the shadow of the huge Santa Maria volcano.

Having heard that there were a few language schools in the town offering short, low-cost Spanish courses, we made enquiries straight away. At the first school we visited, we found ourselves enrolling on an intensive course, which would start the following morning. For the all-inclusive price of seventy-five dollars, we would receive twenty hours of individual tuition, spread over five days, and full board at the home of a local family. It seemed an incredible deal and too good an opportunity to miss. Having completed the enrolment forms, we were taken to meet our host family, who lived just around the corner from the school. Their home was built around an open, stone courtyard with cool, spacious rooms. We were warmly welcomed by the whole family and invited to move in straight away.

The week passed very quickly. Each morning was filled with lessons and the afternoons were set aside for school trips to local places of interest. In the evenings we would practice our Spanish over dinner with the family, before meeting up again with some of the other students at one of the intimate little drinking holes in town.

The day before our departure from Quetzaltenango, I set off with a couple of the other students from the school to climb Santa Maria. It was a steep climb, with the trail rarely deviating from its direct course up the side of the volcano, but four hours later we were standing on the summit, at an altitude of over 4,000 metres. It felt like being on the 'top of the world', with the mountain tops of the Western Highlands laid out below us to the north, and the southern plains of Guatemala stretching all the way to the Pacific Ocean in the opposite direction. Much closer to us, the highly active Santa Ana volcano was completely obscured by clouds, but frequent rumblings, as well as the occasional puffs of smoke that forced their way up through the clouds, reminded us of its presence.

Armed with a slightly improved command of the Spanish language, we cycled eastwards into Central Guatemala. The highway followed a narrow ridge that cut its way through the mountains, before dropping down to the town of Solala - a bustling market town that sits on a wide ledge overlooking the famous blue waters of Lake Atitlan, 500 metres below. Ringed by three towering volcanoes, this large crater lake must me one of the most beautiful spots in Latin America. We spent a while taking in the incredible views, before embarking on a descent to the lakeshore.

The zigzag road that led down to Lake Atitlan was so steep that my hands were sore from squeezing the brakes by the time that we arrived at the lakeside village of Panajachel. This idyllically situated village has long been a favourite travellers' haunt and was full of hostels and guest houses. The one that we selected consisted of several cabins dotted around a grassy courtyard. As we were wheeling the bikes into our cabin, a man with long blond hair, who we immediately recognised, emerged from the cabin next door. His name was Steve and we had met him at Margarita's Guest House in Creel, where we had spent the previous Christmas. Steve was a rather laid-back American traveller, who tended to stay in one place for several weeks before moving on to the next. He seemed delighted to see us and took us for a meal at one of the American-style pizza restaurants in the village.

We stayed a couple of days at the rather artificial backpackers' paradise of Panajachel. During the daytime, we took boat trips across the lake and then tackled some of the numerous hiking trails, which invariably led uphill to spectacular viewpoints. In the evenings we relaxed with other travellers at the video bars and restaurants around the village.

It would have been easy to laze around for much longer in these comfortable surroundings, but we resisted the temptation. After a final breakfast with Steve, we set off on the zigzag road back up towards Solala. Coming down this near-vertical road had been hard enough, but riding back up again was a virtual impossibility and we admitted defeat after just a few hundred yards. It was not long before a small truck came into view, inching its way up the hill from Panajachel, and a few minutes later we were lifting the bikes into the back of it. Squeezed between the driver and his mate, we continued up the hill at little more than walking pace. It took over an hour to cover no more than ten miles to the junction with the Pan Am Highway, just the other side of Solala, where we were dropped off.

We gazed across the stunning Lake Atitlan for one last time, before climbing onto the bikes again and riding eastwards through the mountains. It was a tough ride, with the lowest gears frequently coming into play, but we kept going until early evening to reach the village of Patzicia. There were no lodgings here, so we sought permission to camp on the lawn in front of a Mormon Church. A knock on the door of a small house next door to the church was answered by a young American missionary, who greeted us enthusiastically and readily agreed to our request. As we were setting up the tent, his wife came over and invited us to supper. Over supper, they described some of the difficulties that they had experienced while adapting to life in this remote mountain village, where they had been stationed for three months now. In particular, they had found it hard to get used to the slow pace of life and lack of punctuality!

The village was still sleeping as we packed up the tent at first light. The missionaries were already up and about though, and called us in for breakfast. After that, we left them to their evangelical work and rode on through the mountains to Chimaltenango. This town had certainly woken up and a bustling market was in full swing. The Pan Am Highway continues eastwards from Chimaltenango towards Guatemala City, but we rode out of town in a southerly direction on a bumpy, gravel track, which wound its way down the mountainside to the ancient colonial city of Antigua.

Annabel and I had often wondered how Kate – our former cycling companion – was faring, so it was a lovely surprise to bump into her as we explored the tranquil, cobbled streets of Antigua. After we parted company in Mexico City, she had travelled straight down to Guatemala and enrolled on a Spanish Language Course in Antigua, similar to the one that we had just completed in Quetzaltenango. The only difference was that her course lasted a lot longer and she was now into her fifth week. It was great to catch up with her again and we stayed longer than planned in Antigua as a result.

Kate urged us to join one of the daily tours to the highly active Volcan Pacaya. The local tourist authorities were advising against this trip, due to reports of several recent tourist muggings on the volcano, but local tour companies had stepped up their security in response and you could now make a trek up the volcano under the protection of armed guards. Kate had been on one of these tours, and she assured us that it was an experience not to be missed.

The trip began early one evening, as our group of a dozen or so intrepid adventurers gathered at the appointed meeting place. Together with our guide, and no less than five armed guards, we were driven about half way up the volcano, before continuing on foot. As we hiked towards the summit, it began to turn dark and the night sky was turned completely red by several explosions of lava and burning rocks. We were being treated to an incredible display of natural fireworks, which became increasingly spectacular as we neared the crater. By 10pm, we had reached a sheltered lookout point that was no more than two hundred yards from the crater's edge. The flying rocks were landing just a few feet in front of us now, so it was definitely not safe to venture any further! We huddled together at the lookout point for about half an hour, witnessing this awesome spectacle. The volcano erupted every few minutes and a river of lava was flowing down its far slopes from the other side of the crater.

By the time that we had been safely transported back to Antigua, I had long forgotten my initial apprehension about the tour. In fact, I would gladly have sacrificed my camera and a few dollars to the muggers in exchange for such a breathtaking experience!

Ironically, after surviving Pacaya, I had my handlebar bag – together with all its contents – stolen the following day, when I took my eyes off it for a few seconds in the local post office! This was the only blemish on a memorable stay in Antigua.

Guatemala City was only thirty miles away, in the next valley. There was a long, steep climb up to the ridge that separates the two valleys, however, so it was not going to be an easy ride at all. We set off early in the morning, so that we could tackle the climb before it got too hot, and by mid morning we were at the pass, staring down on the biggest city in Central America. The sprawling suburbs beneath us seemed to occupy an enormous area but we made quick progress through them, as we freewheeled down into the city, and before long we were right in the centre. The dusty downtown streets were choked with noise and exhaust fumes, so it was some relief to find sanctuary at a small hotel in a quiet side street.

Guatemala City has been subjected to several earthquakes over the years, including one as recently as 1976, which caused extensive damage to the Historical Centre. Much of the city's colonial past has been obliterated by these natural disasters, but the grandeur of this era seemed to be represented by the majestic, eighteenth century Metropolitan Cathedral, standing steadfastly on one side of the vast Plaza Mayor de la Constitution. We spent just a day in the city, losing ourselves for a few hours in the tangled maze of streets and alleyways around Plaza Mayor and then visiting the huge central market, before escaping to the cinema.

On a muggy Sunday morning, with heavy clouds protecting us from the scorching sun, we rode out through seemingly endless, overcrowded suburbs and followed the Pan Am Highway up through the ring of mountains that surround Guatemala City. Then, with one last look back on the vast, ever-expanding, concrete metropolis behind us, we descended into the lush, tropical southern lowlands. It was like entering a different world and we glided swiftly over green, gently rolling hills to the town of Jalpatagua, just twelve miles from the El Salvador border. Here we checked into a small, family hotel, run by a local businessman called Ceasar, who spoke some English and was eager to assist. Once we were settled in, Ceasar showed up again and invited us out to the local ice cream parlour. He certainly knew how to look after his guests!

We set off from the hotel in Jalpatagua straight after breakfast, by which time the heat and humidity levels were already uncomfortably high. We were soon into our cycling rhythm, however, and an hour later we had reached the border town of Las Chinamas. We did not even need to obtain visas – the requirement having been recently lifted for British passport holders – and were swiftly ushered across into El Salvador. We were both quite sorry to be leaving Guatemala, which, though crippled by economic, political and social problems, must be one of the most beautiful and friendly countries in the world.

Ahead of us now was the tiny, war-torn nation of El Salvador – a country rarely visited by Westerners, except for news reporters, relief workers and missionaries. The civil war that had raged for several years in El Salvador was now officially in a state of cease-fire, conveniently for us. However, we had been warned that crime rates were extremely high, in a country where so many that were used to fighting, either for Government or guerrilla forces, were now unemployed. The nation was in the grip of a desperate economic crisis, and hardened fighters with time on their hands will sometimes resort to desperate measures when there are hungry mouths to feed.

In soaring, midday heat, we were faced with a long climb from the border, but there was plenty of encouragement, as small children ran from roadside shacks with gifts of fruit and lollipops to keep us going! Spurred on by these touching gestures, we slowly peddled away for several hours to reach the town of Ahuachapan, where we were able to find a hotel for the night. As we explored this small town, later that evening, several locals approached us and warned us to be wary of thieves and to avoid certain streets. It seemed that the ordinary townsfolk were anxious that we should think well of their country and not have our visit spoilt by the criminal element.

The next day, we rode north to Santa Ana, which is the country's second city. The policemen here wore army fatigues and directed traffic with automatic rifles slung over their shoulders. Though the war was officially over for the time being, it seemed as though it could start up again at a moment's notice. It was still early in the day, so we continued east towards the Cerro Verde National Park. We were back on the Pan Am Highway now and rode quickly along the busy dual carriageway to reach the Cerro Verde junction at El Congo. Here we turned off onto a very steep, winding mountain road, rising 2,000 metres to the summit of Cerro Verde – one of three huge volcanoes in the region.

It was a long, steep climb, but by various means – including pushing, towing, three short truck lifts and even a spot of cycling – we somehow made it up to the dormant crater of Cerro Verde. The clouds had long since enveloped us, but we managed to find our way to a small camping area on the summit, next to a rather grand-looking tourist hotel.

On a clear, crisp morning, the panoramic views of western El Salvador reminded us why we had struggled up to this lofty camping spot. A thousand metres below us was the large, blue Lake Coatepeque, shimmering in the early morning sunlight, while much closer was the summit of the perfectly conical Volcan Izalco. This famous volcano is dormant now, but used to be extremely active - breathing fire and smoke for so long that it became known as the 'Lighthouse of the Pacific'. Hotel Montana, next to our campsite, was built to provide tourists with a comfortable base from which to gaze down into the seething crater of Izalco. However, the fires went out almost as soon as the hotel was completed, and it now stood virtually empty.

To the east lay the third great volcano, called Santa Ana, which is the biggest of the three. There was a trail leading from our campsite on Cerro Verde to the summit of Santa Ana, so we set out to follow it. Somewhere along the way, however, we managed to lose the trail and ended up scrambling over loose rocks to the crater. The small crater was filled by a green sulphur lake, from which smoke was gently rising. The views from the rim were even more extensive than from Cerro Verde and, far away in the distance, a huge grey mass of concrete could only be the capital city of San Salvador.

After another night camped atop of Cerro Verde, we dropped back down to the Pan Am Highway and continued our journey east, through a broad, fertile valley. We made good progress, with cloud cover affording us some relief from the intensity of the sun, and by lunchtime we were soaking in the volcanic hot springs at Los Chorros, just twelve miles from San Salvador.

There was a steep little climb from Los Chorros and, when Annabel decided to walk the last few hundred yards, an old man rushed up and insisted on pushing her bicycle to the top for us. He then stood at the top, smiling and waving at us, as we cycled down into San Salvador.

On the outskirts of San Salvador we rode past a huge shanty town of wooden shacks with tin roofs. We later learned that the majority of this city's inhabitants lived in overcrowded shanty towns such as these, or in slums scattered along the edge of the river. The downtown area had a much more prosperous feel to it, with broad boulevards and gleaming white office blocks, but even this seemed superficial because the pavements were covered in potholes and there were plenty of other signs of neglect and decay. With unemployment in the country running at over 60% at this time, it was no surprise to find the downtown streets lined with people trying to make a living by selling whatever they could.

We checked into a large, rather drab hotel, with stone floors and threadbare sheets, not far from the central market. It was getting late now, so we just dumped our things and went straight out for dinner at one of the numerous food stalls that lined the streets around the hotel. There was a cheerful atmosphere among the locals gathered at the stall and I began to get a sense of the strong community spirit that seemed to exist in this city. The mood was lightened even further when I stepped forward to make my order and promptly fell into a huge pothole!

San Salvador is not really a city for sightseeing, so we decided to use our time here to investigate the possibility of doing some voluntary work in the country. We were both in need of a rest from the cycling and keen to learn more about a country whose people seemed to have retained their dignity and sense of humour, despite having experienced so much hardship during the years of civil war. We started by visiting the offices of an organisation called ITAMA (Instituto de Tierra. Agua y Medio Ambiante), which is concerned with improving technology in the rural communities of El Salvador. Here, we were received by Carmen Medina - a Salvadoran lady who spoke excellent English, having studied for several years in the United States. Carmen told us a little about the work of ITAMA and invited us to visit one of their projects.

The next morning, we piled into the back of a pickup truck with a group of Salvadoran health workers, a Scottish relief worker and the French Director of a European relief agency. We were heading for a rural settlement called Gualcho, around eighty miles north-east of San Salvador. We followed the Pan Am Highway east towards San Miguel and then turned north onto a dirt track, which seemed unlikely to lead anywhere until, after bumping along for a couple of hours, we suddenly came upon a large cluster of tin shacks. This was Gualcho.

The 1,200 people living here were all former refugees who had fled to Honduras and Costa Rica during the civil war. When the cease-fire was finally called, they had returned to El Salvador, only to discover that their own village had been destroyed in the fighting. The Government's solution to this problem had been to allocate them this remote site, far away from any existing amenities or infrastructure, on which to build a new village. Unfortunately, the building work had recently come to a halt, due to lack of funds, and most of the families were still living in makeshift homes and surviving with just the barest living essentials. Our small party did at least bring them some hope that work would be getting under way again soon, not least thanks to the presence among us of the French Director, who would have the authority to release significant funds. The community leaders received us like royalty and guided us to the communal dining room. This was situated within an old brick farmhouse, which seemed to be the focal point of the community.

Nearly all the villagers who we met that day bore scars from the fighting, such as missing limbs or knife wounds. Despite the traumas that they had lived through, however, they could not have been more cheerful and welcoming. Their common plight seemed to have bound them together and the community spirit was very evident. Although there would be no building work taking place in the immediate future, as we had hoped for, we resolved to return with our bikes and help out in any way that we could, before continuing our journey east.

Back in San Salvador, we spent a few more days exploring the city, while waiting for the next ITAMA truck to set off for Gualcho. To pass the time, I caught a bus to Colonia Escalon – an affluent area, full of embassies and large mansions – in order to read some English newspapers at the British Club. This was a fairly exclusive ex-patriots 'hang out', and a well-dressed 'retired General-type' solemnly informed me that I would have to pay the annual membership fee of £150 if I wished to enter. However, on hearing that I was just passing through the city on a bicycle and only wanted to know what was going on in the world, he finally relented. The rest of the afternoon was spent browsing through a selection of English dailies that had just arrived from London.

Carmen was able to arrange for our transportation back to Gualcho and we departed a few days later, in the company of another group of local health workers. It was quite cramped in the back of the truck, with our bikes and luggage taking up much of the space, but nobody complained.

Arriving in Gualcho when the midday sun was at its most intense, we were welcomed back to the community and shown to a shady spot where we would be able to set up our tent. However, as we were struggling to set the tent up on the thorny, sun-baked land, two small boys came running with an invitation for us to share a small workshop building with three Salvadorans from another village. They had just arrived themselves and were planning to spend a few weeks here teaching new farming methods to the Gualcho settlers. The three teachers seemed delighted to share their cramped lodgings with us and offered us fresh mangoes that they had brought with them from their village.

For the next couple of nights we slept on the stone floor of the workshop and took our daily meals in the communal dining room. The food was filling and wholesome, although a little lacking in variety, with beans and rice forming the basis of every meal. In the mornings we worked alongside the local farmers in the surrounding fields, as this seemed to be the only work available at that time. The heat was quite unbearable for us though, and by noon each day we were both suffering from headaches and dizziness.

We only stayed a few days in Gualcho, but the whole community seemed to appreciate our visit, which was clearly a source of light entertainment to most of them! We would have loved to stay longer, but were finding it hard to cope with working in the fields in such blistering heat, and it did not seem right to share their limited resources if we could not make a more meaningful contribution. The building work was not due to re-start for several weeks, so we reluctantly decided that it was time to move on.

The road leading out of Gualcho had turned into a mud bath, due to a surprise overnight downpour, so cycling out of the village would not be possible. However, the shared community truck had to make a journey to San Salvador for supplies, so we were transported through the mud bath and back to the junction with the Pan Am Highway. From here we watched the truck disappear into the distance, before climbing back onto the bicycles and heading off in the opposite direction.

The highway sliced its way across a landscape of rolling plains, dominated by the massive San Miguel Volcano, which loomed over us for the rest of the day. That night we reached the town of San Miguel itself, which is the biggest town in eastern El Salvador. We rode around the town centre - full of old colonial buildings in varying states of disrepair - before checking into an old hotel that could almost have been described as derelict. In the hotel bar, I got talking to a young man called Ramon, who had spent several years exiled in America while the fighting was going on. Unfortunately, his American visa papers had been stolen in Virginia, so he had left his young family there while he came back to El Salvador to apply for a replacement visa. However, the process of obtaining a new visa was painfully slow and he had been waiting in San Miguel for over a year now. With no work available, he spent much of his time drinking and smoking in this dingy bar. It was a story of frustration, which was typical of many that I had heard in this country.

Setting off early to avoid the heat, we rode east across barren rolling plains to the Honduran border. We seemed to be the only travellers, among numerous border officials and soldiers milling around the frontier post, but nobody paid us too much attention and the border formalities were completed swiftly. The day was still young but we were both feeling quite weak, having had stomach upsets in San Miguel, so we decided to stay the night in the Honduran border town of El Amatillo. That evening, we reflected on our journey through El Salvador. Despite the turmoil, with so many people trying to rebuild their lives in a country ravaged by war, it was a welcoming place and people seemed to really appreciate the effort that we had made to visit their country. It was as if our visit had been, for some, an encouraging sign that El Salvador was at last beginning to get back to something resembling normality.

From the border, the highway followed a direct course eastward, across lowland plains to the junction town of El Jacinto, where we stopped at a café. The Hondurans have a reputation for being the most 'laid back' people in Central America, and the young girl who took over an hour to produce our breakfast, despite the absence of any other customers, did nothing to damage this reputation!

We had planned to ride up to Tegucigalpa, the capital city, which lay fifty miles to the north, at an altitude of over 1,000 metres. However, it was a particularly hot day, even by Central American standards, and we decided against attempting the long climb on the bikes. Instead, we found a suitable hitching spot just outside El Jacinto. Within ten minutes, we were loading the bikes into the back of an old pick-up truck. Slowly, we were carried up into the sparsely populated, mountainous interior of Honduras. We sat with the bikes in the back of the truck, from where we could see for miles across a lush landscape of forested hillsides, with a few scattered adobe huts being the only signs of civilisation.

Eventually, the red-tiled roofs of Tegucigalpa came into view. From a distance, it seemed like a fairytale, mountain-top city, but, as we made our way through its narrow streets towards the centre, decaying buildings and huge piles of rubbish rather spoiled the effect. We crossed over the muddy waters of Rio Choluteca, which divides the city in two, to reach Parque Central - the central plaza and main hub of the city.

Not far from Parque Central, we checked into a simple hotel, consisting of a ring of small wooden compartments built around a stone courtyard. Annabel had decided to go scuba diving off the north coast for a few days, while I explored the area around Tegucigalpa, so this would be our base and luggage store until we met up again in a week's time. We both felt that a few days apart would be good for us, as we had rarely been out of each other's sight for nearly five months now!

Following Annabel's departure the following morning, I caught a bus up to Parque A La Paz – a small patch of green lying on top of a wooded hill, with a large monument to peace as its centrepiece. When arriving in a new city, I always liked to get my bearings by finding a high vantage point. From this hilltop, the whole of

Tegucigalpa was laid out beneath me, sprawling in rather haphazard fashion over the barren hillsides.

The relationship between Honduras and the United States has always been an uneasy one, with America having established banana plantations in the north of the country at the beginning of the nineteenth century, displacing many of the poor inhabitants of that region to the underdeveloped central areas. Backed by the U.S. Government, the banana companies took virtual control of the country for many years. The main priority was to ensure the swift transportation of bananas to the United States, with little thought given to the needs of the Honduran people and the development of the interior.

That night, a 'friendly' soccer match between Honduras and U.S.A. was due to take place at the National Stadium, near the centre of the city. With such a strong historical connection between the two countries, this promised to be an intriguing clash, so I went along to watch. The U.S.A. were ahead one-nil at half time, but the Hondurans came back strongly, scoring four times without reply in the second half. Some of the supporters took to celebrating this 'turn of events' by throwing half-full cans of beer at me from the back of the stand, one of which cut me on the side of the head. They had obviously taken me to be the token American in the crowd, and decided to target me. In order to avoid further injury – not least to the people around me – I decided to leave early. As I made my way to the exit, a woman ran after me to say how ashamed she was at the behaviour of a few of her drunken countrymen.

During my stay in Tegucigalpa, I made several journeys by bus to different parts of the interior, including one to the historic city of Comayagua. This small city was the Honduran capital for three centuries, until the Government moved to Tegucigalpa in 1880. While Tegucigalpa has developed quickly into a big city, Comayagua has stayed small and retained much of its old colonial charm. It felt almost like exploring a forgotten city, as I wandered around the near-deserted plazas and ancient churches. Sitting on a bench near the seventeenth-century Cathedral, I got chatting to a young lad called Alexander, who invited me to visit his family for dinner. Not having any other plans for the rest of the day, I followed him down one of the streets leading off the plaza. The paved street soon turned into a muddy track, which led us through a maze of simple little brick houses, each with its own small plot of land, and tiny courtyards where the children played. Along the way, Alexander proudly introduced me to several of his friends and neighbours, before we finally arrived at his home. Here, we received a big welcome from his mother, two elder sisters and younger brother, almost as if my visit had been long awaited. Like Alexander, the two girls had learned some English in school, so we were able to converse quite easily. Alexander's younger brother, Oscar, was severely effected by cerebral palsy.

The burden of caring for Oscar seemed to rest fully on the family, without any of the support and advice that would be taken for granted in the U.K. The family seemed to have very little understanding of his condition and lived in the forlorn hope that, by some miracle, Oscar would one day be able to go to America for an operation that would cure his cerebral palsy.

Later in the evening, Alexander's father arrived home from work and we all sat down to dinner. It was nice to be made so welcome by this family, having been wandering about on my own for the last few days, and the evening passed very quickly. As it started to get late, a bed was made up for me in the corner of the living room. My day trip to Comayagua had turned into an overnight visit!

Back in Tegucigalpa, Annabel duly returned from the Bay Islands, complete with her international scuba diving licence. Our original plan had been to ride back down to El Jacinto and then follow the lowland highway east to Nicaragua. However, I had learned in conversation with locals that the southern border crossing had been long closed - due to the collapse of a bridge, several years previously! It seemed that our best route was to follow a narrow highway, running due east through the mountains to a smaller border station further north.

The highway rose steeply out of the city, so it was hard work right from the start, especially for Annabel, who had been 'living it up' with partying backpackers for the past week! However, she was in a determined mood and managed to reach the pass under her own steam, despite having to push her bike on the steeper sections of the climb. After the pass, we were able to gather some momentum as we rode through the forested mountains to the town of Danli, not far from the Nicaraguan border. We checked into a small hotel right on the central plaza of this tranquil little town, and then tried in vain to find a restaurant that would be expensive enough to use up the last of our Honduran currency!

In the morning, we were faced with another long, winding climb up to the border station. Again this turned into quite an ordeal for Annabel, but we eventually reached the border around lunchtime. The crossing procedures seemed particularly complicated, so we enlisted the help of a small boy to guide us around the numerous offices where forms had to be filled out, and various questions asked, before our passports could be stamped.

Before continuing into Nicaragua, Annabel confessed that she had lost her appetite for cycle touring. The mountains had taken a heavy toll, draining her reserves of energy and enthusiasm to the point that she was no longer enjoying the journey. I was sorry to hear this, but the announcement was fairly inevitable. Since Mexico City, we had been constantly battling our way across mountainous terrain, in a climate that was certainly not conducive to physical exertion! Annabel was a strong cyclist now, but these mountains just seemed to go on forever and she had had enough. I could see that she had firmly made up her mind, so did not try too hard to persuade her otherwise. We decided that we would travel together through Nicaragua and into Costa Rica – a more prosperous country, where she would hopefully be able to get a good price for the bike.

From the border station, we cycled twenty miles through rugged mountain country to Ocotol, and then on to the larger town of Estelli, a little further south. Estelli was once renowned as a stronghold for the 'Sandanista Rebels', who had recently been defeated in their struggle against the American-backed Government forces, but remained a potent force in the country. Westerners in Central America are generally assumed to be American, as we had long since discovered, so we were not too sure what sort of reception we would receive in Estelli. However, the town seemed a typically sleepy mountain settlement and the locals barely gave us a second glance as we rode slowly through the dusty streets towards the central plaza. On reaching the plaza, an old man looked up from the flowerbed that he was attending and helpfully pointed us to a small hotel nearby.

In the morning, Annabel decided to travel by bus from Estelli, so we arranged to meet up again in Matagalpa that evening. It felt strange to be riding alone again, although it was nice to be able to go at my own pace. Ironically, it turned out to be quite an easy ride that morning, across a flat, grassy mountain plateau to the town of Sebaco. From here the climbing began again though, as the road turned northward, and it took most of the afternoon to cover the remaining eighteen miles to Matagalpa.

Matagalpa was another Sandanista stronghold and is famous as the birthplace of Carlos Fonseca – 'The Father of the Sandanista Revolution'. Like Estelli, however, the town had a rather sleepy, 'laid-back', feel to it, and the only signs of revolution were the occasional slogans daubed on wall around the town plaza. The shady plaza was pleasantly cool, so I sat on a bench there until it was time to meet Annabel's afternoon bus. In the short time that I was sitting there, several passers-by stopped for a chat. They all seemed to be fascinated by the loaded bike and one elderly couple even thanked me for visiting their country!

Annabel's bus duly arrived and we checked into an empty hostel for a couple of nights. It was a rather spartan place, with stone floors and whitewashed walls, but we soon made ourselves at home. Shopping for food that evening, we were surprised at how high the prices were. Nicaragua was the poorest country in Central America at this time, with extremely high rates of unemployment, and we wondered how people could survive if they had to pay these prices for food. No doubt self-sufficiency was the key.

After a rest day in Matagalpa, I rode alone again down into the southern lowlands, where the heat and humidity was much more intense. Helped by a strong tailwind and downward gradients, I managed to cover eighty-five miles to reach the shores of Lake Managua. The road then followed the lakeshore into the capital city of Managua itself.

The whole central area of Managua was devastated by a huge earthquake in 1972 and, with more earthquakes expected, had never been rebuilt. Cycling through the downtown district, I could hardly believe that this was the centre of Nicaragua's capital city. The urban wasteland was dotted with derelict buildings, including the ruins of the old Cathedral. The walls of the Cathedral were overgrown with weeds, both inside and out, and the roof was completely missing! It was a haunting spectacle, and perhaps a symbol of this impoverished nation. It was here that I met up again with Annabel, as planned, and we made our way to a guest house that had been recommended to us.

The following morning, we began our city tour with a visit to an extraordinary museum. Contained within were the footprints of men, woman, children and animals, who had been running towards Lake Massaya, not far from Managua, in a desperate bid to escape an eruption of the Masaya Volcano. The prints were thought to be over ten thousand years old and had been buried under layers of lava and ash, which preserved them until their discovery in 1874. Outside the museum, I chatted for a while with a young Nicaraguan man, called Carlos. Despite having obtained an engineering degree at University, and speaking excellent English, Carlos was unable to find work in the city. His only means of support was his father, a shoemaker, who supported a family of twelve with his meagre earnings. Unemployment in Managua was running at around 70% at this time, and Carlos's story was fairly typical. In this city, even bright, young educated people like Carlos were sucked into a desperate struggle for survival, against an economic climate of sky-high unemployment and inflation.

Annabel continued her journey by bus, while I enjoyed a gentle ride across flat farming plains to the lakeside town of Masaya, where we met up again. It was Saturday afternoon, but the main street seemed eerily quiet, with just the sound of an occasional horse and cart trundling past to break the silence. We checked into a small hotel on the main street, where the Proprietor explained to us that most people would be at the weekend markets, on the other side of town. Once settled in, we paid a visit to the markets ourselves, and then wandered down to the shores of Lake Massaya. Across the water stood the bulky form of the famous Volcan Masaya, which claimed so many lives when it last erupted, a hundred years previously.

Rising early the next morning, we hitched a lift around the lake to the foot of Volcan Massaya, and then hiked up to the crater. Legend has it that, at times of volcanic activity, the native Indians used to throw women down into the boiling lava within the crater, in order to appease the Goddess of Fire and prevent a major eruption. There was a large wooden cross on the edge of the crater, which was apparently planted by the colonising Spaniards, in order to dissuade the Indians from such 'heathen' religious practices. Fortunately, the volcano was lying quite dormant now, so there was no need to throw Annabel in.

Another short ride east brought me to the old colonial city of Grenada, on the shores of Lake Nicaragua, which is the largest lake in Central America. In line with our usual routine now, Annabel had taken the bus and our rendezvous took place in the town's central plaza. The Semana Santa (Easter Holiday) celebrations were in full swing now and the leafy plaza was alive with final preparations for a carnival procession that was about to begin. We spent a few hours watching the celebrations and soaking up the atmosphere, before wandering off in search of a hotel.

Grenada was an elegant city, with plenty of trees providing shade and horse-drawn taxi-carts adding a touch of character to the old cobbled streets. Best of all, a cool breeze blowing in from Lake Nicaragua helped to make this an excellent place to unwind for a day.

Our next stop was the small town of Rivas, just thirty miles or so along the lakeshore. Annabel decided to hitchhike with a French backpacker called Guylaine, who we had met in Grenada, while I rode alone across fertile lakeside farming plains. By the time that I reached Rivas, Annabel and Guylaine were waiting for me at a café by the side of the road into town. Our plan was to take a boat trip from here to Isla Ometepe, in the centre of Lake Nicaragua, so we stored the bikes at a hotel and caught a bus down to the ferry port at San Jorge. We arrived just in time, as the packed ferry was about to set off for the island.

Isla Ometepe is the largest of over three hundred islands on Lake Nicaragua, and consists of two huge volcanoes joined together by lava flows. We berthed at the port of Moyogalpa, which is a tiny village lying in the shadow of the perfectly conical 'Volcan Concepcion'. There were several guest houses dotted around the harbour, so we checked into one of these for the night. We stayed on Isla Ometepe for two nights, but did not venture too far from Moyogalpa, as the island's bus service had been suspended for the Easter Holiday and, of course, we did not have the bikes. Instead, we spent the time relaxing and getting to know some of the locals. They were cheerful people, who seemed to live a fairly carefree, self-sufficient kind of lifestyle, cut off from the mainland stresses of a country in economic turmoil.

There were too many people for the morning ferry back to Rivas, but the resourceful locals did not take long to find another boat to carry the excess passengers. Back in Rivas, we collected the bikes from the hotel and parted company with Guylaine, as she was heading back to Grenada. The Costa Rican border was just twenty miles east on the Pan Am Highway. Annabel did not feel like cycling this stretch, however, so we hitched a truck ride there so that we could negotiate the border controls together.

Costa Rica means 'Rich Coast' in Spanish. The name seemed quite appropriate as we rode away from the border because the landscape suddenly turned lush and green, in contrast to the rather barren terrain of southern Nicaragua. There were other signs of greater prosperity as well. For example, the improvised shacks of wood, tin and cardboard that we had been used to seeing in Nicaragua were now replaced by more solid-looking structures of brick and concrete.

The first settlement that we reached was La Cruz, where we stopped by a roadside 'Civil Guard' checkpoint and waited for a ride to the larger town of Liberia. The Civil Guard was a kind of military police force with full responsibility for the defence of the country, due to the absence of a regular army. The three young recruits at the checkpoint looked barely old enough to be out of short trousers, but they were fully kitted out in jungle fatigues and armed with machine guns. Despite their rather intimidating appearance, however, they could not have been more friendly and served us with ice-cold Coca-Cola while we were waiting for our ride. It was not long before an old pick-up truck slowly trundled to a halt in front of us.

Lifting the bikes into the back of his truck, our driver explained to us that we would be making a little detour to a coastal village, before continuing on to Liberia. The ride turned out to be quite an adventure, with the detour taking us along a dirt road through lush, tropical rainforest, where wild monkeys were swinging from the trees. We ended up at a beautiful sandy cove on the Pacific Coast, where there were two secluded holiday villas at which we stopped to deliver supplies. Annabel and I sat on the deserted beach to watch the sun go down, while the driver and his companion were concluding their business, and then jumped back into the truck for the ride back up to the highway. A few hours later, we were deposited at the entrance to a small hotel in the centre of Liberia. Having started out from

Isla Ometepe that morning, it had had been a long day's journey by boat, bicycle and truck.

Liberia seemed a lively, prosperous town. The well-stocked shops were still trading, late into the evening, and continental-style cafes lined the streets. There were no obvious signs of hardship at all and it seemed as though we were suddenly a world away from Nicaragua.

The next morning, we hitched a short ride along the highway to Canas, from where we planned to travel up into the mountains of central Costa Rica. Our driver was on his way to San Jose and spoke excellent English. On hearing that Annabel was hoping to sell her bicycle, he immediately offered $250 for it, which was the exact amount that she had paid for it in Phoenix. His readiness to part with this kind of money for a bicycle was another sign of this country's relative prosperity. We agreed that we would contact him when we arrived in San Jose.

With the sale of Annabel's bike now agreed, we decided to have one last ride together. From Canas, we set off on a narrow highway, leading northwards, and rode slowly up into the hills. The landscape was greener than ever now and all kinds of colourful creatures, such as butterflies and frogs, shared the road with us. We rode all afternoon through this tropical wonderland to reach the still blue waters of Lake Arenal, nestling in the shadow of the huge, conical 'Volcan Arenal', which is Costa Rica's most active volcano. Completing the picture was the small lakeside village of Arenal and it was here that we sought lodgings for the night. Accommodation standards seemed to be much higher in Costa Rica than we had been used to for some time, and that evening we found ourselves in a very comfortable private apartment, with a veranda looking over the lake.

The road leading eastwards around the lake was unpaved and extremely rough, but we were able to hitch a ride to the start of a sealed rode on the other side. I could not resist the temptation to ride again from here, so Annabel stayed in the truck, which was heading for the mountain settlement of Fortuna, and we agreed to meet there in the evening. Suddenly alone with nature again, I climbed back on the bike and followed the sealed road, which led away from the lake and skirted Volcan Arenal. The volcano loomed overhead like a slumbering giant, with deep rumbling noises emanating from its depths every few minutes. It was another wonderful ride, with the road cutting through thick tropical rainforest as it climbed higher into the mountains, and I did not really want it to end. Eventually though, Fortuna came into view and Annabel materialised at the roadside. With its close proximity to Volcan Arenal, this town was full of hostels and guest houses, so it did not take us long to find lodgings.

Annabel decided that she would stay in Fortuna for a couple of days, exploring the area around the Arenal Volcano and relaxing with some of the backpackers that we had met there, before continuing to San Jose by bus.

In the meantime, I would ride on alone through the mountains to San Jose.

Ahead of me was one of the toughest rides of my entire trip. The day began with a fairly comfortable twenty mile stretch across rolling hill country, but then the road began to turn upwards. For the next thirty miles, it wound its way steeply up into the mountains. The clouds rolled in by mid-morning, providing welcome relief from the scorching sun, but also obscuring the panoramic mountain views. Occasionally, I was able to rest my legs by hanging onto the back of a slow-moving truck for a tow, but this respite was usually short-lived as the sharp bends made it too dangerous to hang on for long. As the road climbed higher and higher, my energy was draining fast and I began to feel as though I was never going to reach the pass. When a truck finally pulled over to offer me a lift to San Jose, the temptation was great. However, after all the hitching with Annabel recently, I was determined to battle this one out.

As evening fell, and the sun dropped behind the mountains, the road finally levelled out and I rolled into the town of San Ramon, which lies at the junction with the Pan Am Highway. By now, my legs had virtually turned to jelly and I just about had enough energy left to find a hotel and stagger into town for some dinner!

By contrast, the next day's ride was little more than a 'loosening-up' exercise, as I rolled thirty miles or so along the flat Pan Am Highway into San Jose. Here I met up with Annabel again at a Backpackers' Hostel in the downtown area of the city.

San Jose was a smart, modern city with an air of prosperity. The downtown streets were dotted with plush shopping malls, containing department stores and most of the popular American food chains. At night time, the street lights and neon signs glowed brightly to create a glitzy atmosphere. Even the coffee tasted a little richer than usual, perhaps because Costa Rica - unlike her Central American neighbours – does not have to export all her best quality coffee beans.

We managed to contact the man who had given us a lift to Canas, a few days previously, and Annabel's bicycle was sold. This confirmed that, after travelling together for the past five months, our journey together was at an end. It was a sad moment, but Annabel had long since decided that there were better ways than cycling to travel through the mountainous Central American countries, so it was probably for the best. We hoped to meet up again soon, as we were both heading towards Panama City, but for now we would be travelling independently. For me this held no fears, as I was quite used to it, but for Annabel it would be a new challenge. However, she had gained an incredible amount of confidence from our cycling expedition and did not seem at all fazed by the prospect.

We spent our last couple of days together wandering around the shopping plazas and cafes of San Jose, as well as making short excursions into the mountains that surround the city. These included visits to the mountain village of San Pedro de Poas, with its beautiful plaza full of all kinds of tropical flora, and the historical old town of Heredia.

The Pan Am Highway rose steadily though the Central Valley, as I rode east from San Jose to the town of Cartago, which lies at 1500 metres above sea level. Despite being a sizeable town, I was only able to find two budget hotels and they both had a sorry, neglected look about them. At one of these I was offered a room for 1,000 colones (around five pounds), but managed to negotiate a fifty per cent reduction on account of the fact that my room had no curtains and the bed had a big dip in the middle! My main reason for stopping in Cartago was to visit the 'Iglesia de los Angeles', which was renowned as one of the most beautiful churches in Costa Rica. Having settled into my humble lodgings, I strolled across town to the church, which had a tranquil setting on the edge of a leafy plaza. The church itself was quite magnificent, with its six elaborate angel statues adorning the roof.

After breakfast, in the early morning street market across the road from the hotel, it was back to the Pan Am Highway. Ahead of me lay a very long, steep climb up to a pass called 'Valle des Angeles' – the highest point on this famous highway, at 3,600 metres. In fact, this was the highest altitude that I have ever attempted to reach on a bicycle! It was a cloudy morning with light drizzling rain, which kept things refreshingly cool as I slowly forced the pedals round for what seemed like an eternity. As the highway soared high above the valley floor, the mist closed in as well and visibility was reduced to no more than a few feet. I rode on and on until, around mid-afternoon, the gradient suddenly levelled out and a barely visible signpost, marked 'Valle des Angeles', announced my arrival at the pass. The views from here are probably quite stupendous on a clear day, but all I could see was mist, as if standing in the middle of a cloud.

Despite the anti-climax of not being able to see anything, I stood in triumph at 'Valle des Angeles' for a few moments, before gingerly embarking on the descent. The road down was even steeper than the road up and it was necessary to brake heavily for much of the way, as I plunged down into the valley below. As the mist cleared a little, the lush, forested valley finally revealed itself fully. The road continued to plummet and had dropped down to an altitude of just 1,000 metres when

I reached the town of San Isidro, after a twenty-three mile descent. It was evening now and already dark, as I checked into a small hotel on the main street.

My main enemy the next day was the heat, as I rolled eastwards across the southern lowlands. The terrain was gently undulating but the sun was relentless, making the hills seem twice as high as they really were. An opportunity for a rest came when another cyclist appeared on the horizon, riding towards me. His name was Lucas, from Belgium. Lucas had began his bike ride on Tierra Del Fuego, at the southern tip of South America, and was riding to Mexico City. He warned me to be extra careful in Panama, where he had been robbed three times – twice at knifepoint and once at gunpoint! Two of these incidents had occurred while riding out of Panama City, and he advised me to stick to the main highway into this city, rather than taking a shorter route through some of the more dangerous inner suburbs. It was a valuable piece of advice, which I would try not to forget! Despite his misfortunes, Lucas appeared to be in good spirits and remained positive about his journey. Among the items that he had lost, however, was his camera, and he had not yet been able to purchase a replacement. In order to mark his ride across the southern lowlands of Costa Rica, I took a couple of photos of him, against the backdrop of a pineapple field, and promised to send them to him in Belgium. After chatting with Lucas for an hour or so, I rode onwards – though in somewhat less of a hurry to reach the Panamanian border!

The highway entered a steep-walled river gorge, which provided welcome relief from the intense heat, enabling me to ride along more comfortably in the latter stages of the day. At the junction settlement of Palmer Norte, I checked into an old Chinese hotel for the night. The proprietor was a cheerful little man, who welcomed me in and helped to carry the loaded bike up the stairs to my room. When I enquired about local restaurants, he asked me what I fancied and then hurriedly disappeared to the kitchen to prepare a large plate of 'chow mein'.

The next morning I was up at first light in order to ride as far as possible before the sun reached its full intensity. Unfortunately, though, my plan was strangled at birth when I discovered that the gates leading out of the hotel courtyard were locked. The hotel clearly did not cater for early starters and I had to wait for over an hour until the smiling old Chinese man finally appeared. He was in such a cheerful mood again that I could not bring myself to complain about my detention!

Banana plantations flanked the highway, as I finally rode eastwards from Palmer Norte, on what proved to be another scorching hot day. Before long I began to feel quite sick, as the sun beat down on me from a cloudless sky. My head started to thump as well and it was not long before I had to admit defeat. Having reached the small town of Neilly, just ten miles from the Panamanian border, I checked into another Chinese hotel and spent the rest of the day in bed.

Feeling much better in the morning, after a good long sleep, I rode to the border. It turned out to be my easiest border crossing in Central America, and within fifteen minutes I was across into Panama. The Panamanian border officials sprinkled the Spanish that they spoke with American words (for example, 'El Flashlight?', when enquiring as to whether or not I was carrying lights), and the Panamanian dollars, which I received in exchange for my remaining Costa Rican colones, were almost exactly the same as American dollars. This was the first indication of the massive influence that the United States has had on this tiny country that links North and South America.

The terrain was barren and lifeless, in comparison with the lush Costa Rican landscape behind me. I was glad of the easy ride though, as the smooth Pan Am Highway cut across gently rolling plains to the town of David, which is the main settlement in Western Panama. Arriving early in the afternoon, I made my way to the central plaza, where a group of young lads were idling the day away. My arrival seemed to stir them into action and they gathered around to examine the bike. On hearing that I was in need of lodgings, one of them promptly jumped onto his own bicycle and escorted me to a modest little hotel called the Pension Costa Rica, just a couple of blocks away.

Having decided on a rest day in my namesake town, the only task that I set myself was to replace one of my tee shirts, which had almost disintegrated. Conveniently, the main shopping street was lined with clothes shops, all stocked to bursting point with American-style jeans and tee shirts. Outside each store, shop assistants were loudly banging together pairs of flip-flops, in order to attract customers. With all the stores adopting this tactic, it was hard to see where any advantage was to be gained. As I ventured into the first store, one of the assistants laid down his flip flops and doggedly followed me around the store, smiling and pointing out various colourful garments. When I finally selected a plain tee shirt that he had not even suggested, he seemed quite disappointed and conducted the sale rather grumpily. It was a bizarre shopping experience to say the least!

Feeling a little more adventurous, after another good night's sleep at the Pension Costa Rica, I took a local bus to the mountain village of Boquette, twenty five miles north of David. The bus slowly trundled its way up through the hills to Boquette, which sits in a lush, green valley that is renowned for its colourful flowers, as well as being the main coffee-growing region in Panama. Rising high above the valley stood Volcan Baru, which is Panama's highest mountain. Boquette itself was a pretty little village, as its name might suggest, and a tranquil place after the hustle and bustle and 'flip-flop banging' of David! The day was spent hiking in the hills around the village, before returning to David on the evening bus.

In contrast with the lush Boquette region, the landscape east of David was bleak and empty, save for the volcanoes of northern Panama, which were dimly visible in the distance. Each settlement marked on my map turned out to be little more than a cluster of houses on either side of the highway, but I had hopes of finding accommodation at the town of Tole, where most of the buses seemed to be heading. Set in the hills a couple of miles to the north of the highway, Tole turned out to be nothing more than a small village, however, and there were certainly no hotels. I was just about to head off again, and look for somewhere to camp, when somebody mentioned that there was an old lady in the village who sometimes rented out a room to the occasional travellers that ended up here. Before long, I had tracked the old lady down. She greeted me warmly and showed me to a bare, stone-floored room that was furnished with just a lumpy mattress and a bucket of water with which to wash. This was quite satisfactory and far preferable to the option of camping by the roadside, in a country where highway robberies were said to be commonplace. There were no restaurants in the village, so I walked down to a truck-stop café on the highway for a fish supper. By the time that I had walked back up the hill to the village, I was ready for the lumpy mattress!

The next settlement marked on the map was the town of Santiago, lying about sixty miles further east and almost in the exact centre of the country. After a long, energy-sapping climb from Tole, it was rolling hills all the way again. There was hardly any traffic on the highway and few features on the landscape to catch my attention, so I sang to myself to pass the time, while peddling away under the baking sun. Arriving in Santiago, I checked into a large, empty hotel that was run by a rather excitable Chinese man, who babbled away in what sounded like a mixture of Spanish and Chinese. I could not understand a word of it, so he eventually gave up and just pointed me to my room. I had planned a rest day in Santiago, but an evening stroll was enough to persuade me otherwise. There was little to interest me here, so I decided to ride on in the morning after all.

East of Santiago, it was more of the same barren landscape. I began to reach the conclusion that, while Panama may be one of the richer Central American countries, it had missed out badly when it came to scenery allocation! Running into a strong headwind, I stopped for an early lunch at a roadside café just outside the settlement of Aguadulce. While preparing my meal, the cook kept popping his head out of the kitchen to ask me questions about my journey – questions that I had been asked so many times that the answers came out automatically, even in Spanish! It was nice to have some conversation though, having been starved of this for several days now. The headwind failed to let up all afternoon, turning what promised to be a relatively easy ride across flat terrain into a hard slog. Eventually though, I made it to the small town of Penonome.

The next day was cloudy, which came as a tremendous relief after several days of riding under a relentlessly hot sun. There was also a strong wind blowing in my direction of travel, so I hurried breakfast down and jumped on the bike as quickly as possible. The bike flew along the Pan Am Highway that morning, and by lunchtime I had reached the seaside resort of San Carlos, which had been my target for the evening! The wind had dropped a little but a thick blanket of cloud was still protecting me from the sun so, after resting on the beach for a while, I decided to keep going.

As the highway turned inland again, the terrain became hilly and progress was a little slower. Eventually, on reaching the Capira in the early evening, I decided to call it a day. On asking after accommodation, a roadside fruit-seller, named Isidro, apologetically informed me that the nearest hotel was ten miles further on, in the larger town of Chorrera. However, he then brightly suggested the alternative of staying the night at his home in the nearby village of Santa Rosa.

Together we walked a couple of miles, following a dirt track across ploughed fields to reach the tiny village, where his family and various other relatives lived in four or five huts that were clustered together on the family farm. Everyone gathered to welcome me, and before long I was sitting down with Isidro's parents and three sisters for an evening meal of noodles and roast chicken. After dinner, I was shown to my quarters, which seemed to be a storage hut, where a bed with mosquito net had been set up for me. The rest of the evening was spent at another hut, belonging to Isidro's Aunt Gladice, who seemed very excited at my unexpected arrival and bombarded me with questions. Panamanians tend to speak a particularly high-speed version of Spanish and I had to concentrate hard, in order to pick up the gist of the conversation. After a couple of hours of this my head was spinning, so I politely excused myself and retired to my quarters.

Breakfast was a plateful of delicious fried dough cakes, and a few more were put into a bag for me to take with me. After a photo session and endless goodbyes, Isidro escorted me back down the track to the highway, where I helped him to set up his fruit-stand before climbing onto the bike again. My overnight stay in Santa Rosa had been an uplifting experience, and was certainly the highlight of my journey through Panama.

Having rode much further than expected the previous day, it was just thirty-five miles further to Panama City. It was hot and muggy, with the sun just making occasional appearances in the grey sky, as I rode to Chorrera, from where a brand new section of the Pan Am Highway stretched all the way to Panama City. There was a nice wide shoulder on the new highway, allowing me to ride at a comfortable distance from the high-speed trucks and buses that thundered past, towards the big city.

Soon after lunch, I reached the famous 'Bridge Of The Americas' – a majestic suspension bridge, spanning the entrance to the Panama Canal. Down below, a queue of vessels of all shapes and sizes, ranging from small yachts to ocean liners, lay at anchor as they waited to begin their passage from the Pacific to the Atlantic. On the other side of the bridge lay the huge metropolis of Panama City, marking the end of my journey through Central America.

Riding into the city, I somehow took a wrong turning and ended up riding through one of the notorious slum districts that Lucas (the unfortunate cyclist who had been mugged three times in Panama) had warned me to avoid. The narrow streets were overhung with wooden balconies, connected by numerous washing lines, and there were piles of garbage everywhere. Remembering what had happened to Lucas, I rode as quickly as possible and tried to stick to the busier streets. Without mishap, I reached the safer district of San Felipe, which is the oldest part of Panama City and full of ancient colonial buildings – some of which were clearly in urgent need of renovation. It was a district full of colour and character, right in the heart of the city, so I decided to look for lodgings here. It did not take long to find a modest, but stylish, old hotel, built around a shady courtyard, just behind the Cathedral.

My first port of call was the General Post Office, where I received mail from home and a message from Annabel. Apparently, she had been in the city for a couple of days now and was staying at a pension just around the corner, so I went to call on her straight away.

We spent the next few days exploring this diverse city together, from the crumbling streets and old colonial buildings of San Felipe to the modern, central business district of Via Espana, full of huge banks, hotels and smart shopping and entertainment complexes that any city would be proud of. There seemed to be an air of hostility in some areas of the city, as cold stares were directed towards us. The sense of unease was heightened by the fact that both of us had already met other Westerners at our hotels that had been mugged on the streets in the past few days. However, we had learned to walk city streets in this part of the world with just a few dollars in our pockets, and not even a simple watch to tempt a potential mugger, so I was not unduly concerned.

Venturing slightly further afield, I caught a local bus out to the Miraflores Locks – one of three sets of locks on the Panama Canal. Incredibly, the locks were about one mile long, with two channels that were wide enough to accommodate 94% of the world's shipping, at this time. I watched from the viewing galley, as a huge cargo ship passed through one of the channels. Meanwhile, a taped running commentary explained the operation of the locks and proudly presented a brief history of the Panama Canal. The project was actually started by a French company, but had to be abandoned after numerous problems with landslides, flooding and tropical diseases, costing the lives of many of the construction workers. The Americans took over the project in 1889 and work was finally completed in 1914. Since then, over 700,000 ships had passed through the canal - and another fifty were scheduled for today. One interesting statistic was the average toll fee of $35,000, which seemed rather expensive, although this would be considerably cheaper that the alternative of a three-week voyage around Cape Horn! The toll fee varies according to the size of the vessel, of course, and the lowest fee ever charged was just 36 cents – to the athlete, Richard Haliburton, who swam through the Canal in 1928!

The Pan Am Highway comes to an end just south of Panama City, giving way to the mountains and jungles of the Darrien Gap, which were penetrable only by a combination of river-boat and foot. The highway begins again on the other side of the Darrien Gap, in Columbia, and continues down through South America. It had been my original intention to travel through the Darrien Gap, by whatever means possible, and then continue by bicycle down through South America to Tierra del Fuego. However, my journey through Mexico and Central America had taken much longer than expected, and my finances had diminished to the extent that there was not enough left to enable me to travel very far in South America. I decided, therefore, to save the journey to Cape Horn for another time. Instead, I would fly to Cartagena, on the north coast of Columbia, and then ride along the Caribbean coast to Caracas, in Venezuela. This would take around six weeks and use up the remaining money. My flight back to England, from Caracas, would have to be on plastic.

Annabel had decided to fly to Cartagena with me, so we met up at the international airport in Tocumen, about twenty miles east of Panama City. There was a slight hitch when one of the airport officials insisted that my bicycle had to be packed in a box. This was the seventh flight of my journey, and it was the first time that this requirement had been enforced. However, the baggage handlers were eager to help and my only expense was a roll of tape!

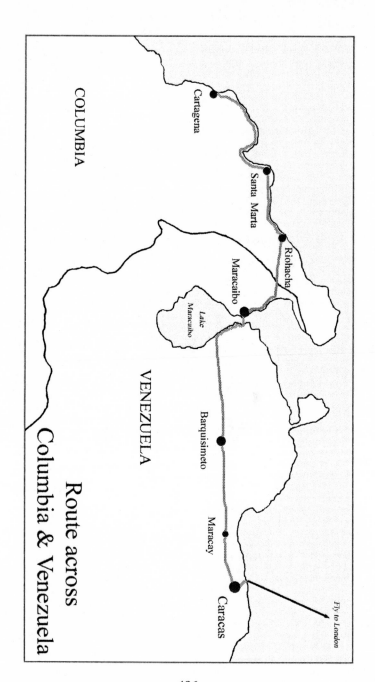

Route across
Columbia & Venezuela

Chapter Eleven

Highway Robbery

Cartagena to Caracas

Founded by the Spaniards back in 1533, Cartagena was one of the first settlements in Columbia. Within a short time it had blossomed into a major port and became known as the 'Gateway to South America'. The walled city continued to flourish throughout the colonial period, and was regarded as the most important city of the Spanish Empire. Today it has less global significance, but remains an impressive living museum of Spanish architecture and one of the most popular destinations for the relatively small number of tourists that ever make it to Columbia.

For us, Cartagena provided a positive introduction to a country that was notorious at the time for drug smuggling and kidnappings. There was a good range of accommodation options, with the backpacker end of the market well catered for, and we were soon settled into a friendly little hostel, just outside the walls of the Old Town. A walk across the street and through the entrance to the Old Town was like stepping back in time, as you entered a bustling maze of narrow streets, dotted with ancient palaces, churches and quaint little plazas, where people continued to live and work.

Annabel had decided that she would not be travelling any further south than Columbia. Instead, she would take the bus down to Bogota and then fly north to Canada, where she hoped to find work for the summer. Our last day together was spent on a Caribbean cruise around a small archipelago of coral islands, lying a few miles off the coast. The sea was almost as blue as the sky and we encountered all kinds of wildlife, including a sea otter that came and sat on my lap, as we were relaxing on one of the golden beaches.

The next day, I celebrated my twenty-seventh birthday with a big breakfast at one of the Old Town cafes, before seeing Annabel onto the bus. It was time for me to be moving on as well, so I loaded the bike up and rode out of Cartagena in an easterly direction.

The end of my journey was not far away now and my mind was buzzing, as I contemplated this prospect. There was disappointment at not being able to travel as far into South America as intended, mixed with excitement and some trepidation at the thought of returning home and trying to settle into a more conventional style of life once more. With these thoughts running through my head, I peddled like mad along a flat highway, which followed the direction of the Caribbean shoreline. Conditions were perfect for riding that day, with virtually no wind and a blanket of cloud blocking out the tropical sun, and the bicycle seemed to be eating up the highway in front of me. Small villages were dotted along the way and locals shouted out friendly greetings as I rode by. My responses were fairly mechanical however, as my mind was too preoccupied to allow me to take full notice of all that was around me.

By evening time, I had covered over ninety miles to reach the outskirts of Barranquilla – Columbia's fourth largest city and major seaport. Despite its big city status, however, many of the downtown streets were unsealed and recent rains had turned them into a mud-bath. Eventually, as I headed towards the heart of the city, it became impossible to ride, so I had to climb down and push. On finally reaching a suitable hotel, I then had to find the energy to carry the loaded bike up four flights of stairs to my room!

Barranquilla seemed a particularly noisy and chaotic city. The narrow downtown streets and alleyways were lined with traders, turning the whole place into a giant street market, as I wandered around that evening. The atmosphere was quite different to Cartagena, where people were accustomed to the daily influx of tourists and I was able to walk around fairly anonymously. Here, people stopped me in the street to ask where I was 'coming from' and what I thought of their city. The attention was all very good-natured and made me feel welcome. It was these more 'ordinary' places - where I obviously stuck out like a sore thumb – that would stay in mind the longest.

Splashing through the muddy streets once more, I made my way out of the city and back onto the coastal highway, towards Santa Marta. The highway crossed flat, brown coastal plains, with the snow-capped mountains of the Sierra Nevada de Santa Marta lying ahead of me in the distance. This is the highest coastal mountain range in the world, containing Columbia's two highest peaks of Simon Bolivar (at 5,775 metres) and Cristobal Colon (at 5,770 metres).

There was no cloud cover that day and the intensity of the Caribbean sun made riding a much more difficult proposition. I tried not to ride too hard and took a long break during the hottest part of the day at Cainanga, which was the only settlement of any size en-route to Santa Marta. As I was resting beneath a palm tree, a small crowd seemed to materialise from nowhere. They gathered around to examine the bike and ask me questions about my trip in broken English. They seemed excited at my sudden appearance in their community, and kept me chatting for a couple of hours.

Late in the afternoon, I arrived in the breezy, seaside resort of Santa Marta, which is the oldest surviving town in Columbia. Close to the waterfront, I checked into a crowded, travellers' hostel called 'The Miramar', where a dormitory bed for the night cost less that one pound.

In the morning, I caught a local bus to the fishing village of Taganga, set in a deep bay a few miles north of town. There was an idyllic tropical beach here, and the day was spent swimming and relaxing on the sands. There was hardly anyone else around, apart from an Irishman called Mark, who was living in Santa Marta with his Colombian wife. We shared a taxi back to Santa Marta that evening, because the buses had stopped running due to heavy rain, although Taganga was still soaked in sunshine. This sudden cancellation of services was explained when we arrived back in Santa Marta to find the whole town flooded. Some of the streets were more than a foot beneath water. Mark told me that that this was quite common here, and that once he had seen a bus floating down the street!

The floodwaters had cleared by the next morning, so I rode twenty miles eastwards to the Tayrona National Park, which is a lush, coastal paradise of jungle-covered mountains and white sandy beaches. There were no roads in the park, and the jungle trails were not really suitable for cycling, so I checked into a guest house right by the entrance to the Park.

At first light, I hiked to the tiny beach settlement of Arrecifes. The beach here was one of the most perfect that I had ever seen. It was almost deserted, apart from a small group of backpackers that I recognised from the hostel in Santa Marta. They had spent the night here in rented hammocks and were planning to laze around in these idyllic surroundings for a few more days. I spent the afternoon relaxing with them, before making my way back through the jungle to the guest house. It rained a little on the way back, which seemed to bring the rainforest to life and helped to round off a wonderful day.

Leaving the mountains of Tayrona behind, I rode further east on the coastal highway towards Riohacha. There was little traffic in this remote north-eastern part of Columbia and it was an enjoyable ride, across lush, green, coastal plains. Lunch was a plate of fried fish and yucca (a root vegetable that tastes a bit like sweet potato), at one of the roadside cafes that seemed to pop up every few miles. Unfortunately, the meal did not agree with me at all, and the stomach cramps started almost as soon I was back on the bike. The rest of the day was punctuated by frequent roadside toilet stops, but I somehow made it to Riohacha.

Riohacha was a quiet, seaside town, with plenty of reasonably priced accommodation, and I ended up in a very comfortable hotel by the waterfront. Feeling much better, after a good night's sleep, I headed for the Venezuelan Consulate to apply for a visa. The officials here informed me, however, that I would have to obtain a ticket out of the country before they could issue the visa. There seemed no way around this obstacle, so I went to a nearby travel agent and purchased a flight from Caracas to London. The best deal that I could get was a ticket costing nearly one thousand dollars, with a five-hour stop in Miami. The sixteenth of June, 1993, was the date set for my return. Armed with my ticket, I returned to the Consulate to find the officials still very reluctant to give me the visa. Eventually, after waiting for several hours, I was grudgingly issued with a three-day transit visa costing thirty dollars! The visa would have to be extended in the Venezuelan city of Maracaibo, across the border.

The next day was incredibly eventful. It began with an early morning ride to the large, industrial town of Maicao, fifty miles further east along the coastal highway. The coastal plains were featureless, so I just focused on the road ahead and peddled hard until Maicao came into view. After some lunch at a truck-stop café on the ring road, I rode on to the border town of Paraguachoi, just seven miles further along. Unusually for a border town, there were no hotels in Paraguachoi. There was no obvious place to camp either, so I decided to cross the border and look for somewhere to spend the night on the other side. With my three-day transit visa in hand, the border officials nodded me through into Venezuela with the minimum of fuss.

Beyond the frontier post, the highway was hemmed in by thick forest on either side. I was no more than a couple of miles into the country when three wild-looking bandits sprang from the trees and lined themselves up across the road to block my way. They were armed with semi-automatic machine guns and one of them kept thrusting his weapon threateningly towards my forehead, shouting "La plata, la plata, rapido!" I can still picture his face now, with sweat pouring down it and a look of desperation in his eyes. Overcome by a rather British sense of indignation at this turn of events, I just responded with a negative shrug of the shoulders and a stubborn "No entiendo". This was technically correct, as I had not heard the expression 'La plata' before, although it was quite obvious that they wanted cash. My lack of co-operation only served to infuriate the bandit, and he kept shouting the same instruction louder and louder.

There was a timely diversion at this point. A big truck pulled up and the driver started to climb down from his cab. One of the guns was immediately pointed in his direction, however, prompting him to quickly jumped back into the cab and drive off! This little distraction served a purpose, however, as it brought me back to my senses and I started to think rationally. Self-preservation was the priority, so I dug deep into one of the front panniers to produce my wallet. It contained about sixty pounds worth of Venezuelan currency, which I had just obtained by exchanging the last of my American dollars at the border. One of the bandits snatched the notes straight away, without bothering to take the wallet itself, or the credit card that was still inside. Still waving their guns in the air, they vanished back into the forest as quickly as they had appeared.

There seemed little point in going back to the border, as the credit card would be no use there, so I rode onwards, in a bit of a daze, to the town of Guajira. There was another border checkpoint here, manned by a couple of young police officers, so I tried to explain to them what had just happened. They got the message, eventually, but did not seem at all interested or appear to understand why I was bothering to tell them about it at all.

Feeling quite demoralised at this apathetic response from the police, I rode on slowly to the larger town of Paraguaipoa. It was evening now and I had just ten American dollars (kept separately for emergencies), with which to pay for accommodation and food. To make matters worse, the banks were shut for the next three days, due to a public holiday. This was before the global spread of A.T.M.s, so my credit card would probably be no use until then. Strangely though, my cash-flow problem did not bother me too much, as I had travelled long enough now to feel confident about coping with a little crisis such as this. My main feelings were that of anger at what had happened and relief that I had escaped unharmed from a life-threatening situation. There was just one hotel in Paraguaipoa, so I shelled out half of my emergency cash to pay for a room there.

Later that evening, I was sitting at a street café, dining as cheaply as possible on 'arepas' (a kind of maize pancake), when a crowd of people suddenly gathered around me. One of them starting patting me on the back and asking me if I was O.K. Looking up, I immediately recognised the driver of the truck that had stopped on the highway, and realised that he had told everyone about the unsavoury incident that had taken place there. It had been a long, traumatic day, but this was a nice way to end it. Since entering the country that morning, I had been robbed and not received a kind word from anyone. Now, suddenly, the true face of Venezuela was showing itself to me. A huge slab of roast chicken was piled onto my plate and, when the meal was over, I was shepherded to a local bar, where everybody wanted to buy me a drink. My last five dollars remained in my pocket, and I woke up in my bed the next morning without even being able to remember how I had got back to the hotel!

Out on the lonely road once more, I skirted the shores of the enormous Lake Maracaibo towards the city of Maracaibo itself. After the events of the previous day, I was feeling a little apprehensive and half expecting bandits to jump out of the bushes at any moment. Even the machete-wielding farmers in the fields looked menacing, until their faces broke into smiles as they waved at me.

Oil was first discovered in Venezuela back in 1917, turning a poor debtor country into the richest nation in Latin America. The economy had suffered in recent years, however, with declining world oil prices plunging the country back into heavy foreign debt. Huge refineries dotted the landscape as I approached Maracaibo, which is Venezuela's second largest city and the centre of its oil industry.

Torrents of traffic sucked me in towards the cluster of towering skyscrapers concentrated in the central part of the metropolis. I headed for the oldest part of the city, where the cheapest hotels are often located, and began my search for accommodation. Unfortunately, I was disadvantaged by the fact that I only had two dollars left to my name! Most of the hotels appeared to be full anyway, with oil workers taking up virtually all of the rooms on a semi-permanent basis, due to a lack of alternative accommodation. Eventually, I found a hotel with one vacancy and quickly carried the bike up three flights of stairs to claim the room, before explaining to the receptionist about my cash-flow difficulties. The hotel did not accept credit card payments, and the girl did not seem too impressed when I explained to her that I would not be able to pay in cash until the banks opened again in a couple of days' time. However, she agreed to call the manager, so that I could explain the situation to him. An hour or so later, an old Italian man appeared and listened to my story, in faltering Spanish, of the highway robbery, which had led to my cash shortage. After considering the matter for a few minutes, he seemed to sense that the story was genuine. He told me to make myself at home in the hotel, and even went so far as to lend me ten dollars from his own pocket for food.

With my immediate crisis resolved, all I had to do now was wait until Tuesday. The old colonial district, in which the hotel was situated, was a quaint area, but the city did not have too much else to offer in the way of sightseeing and the time passed incredibly slowly.

Tuesday came, at last, and I was able to use the credit card to obtain enough Venezuelan currency ('Bolivars') to last me the rest of my trip. My next job was to try and get an extension to my three-day transit visa, which was about to expire. The rest of the day was spent drowning in a sea of bureaucracy, as I was shunted from one office to another, as bad-tempered government officials tried to shift the problem onto one of their colleagues. My simple request for a two-week extension, so that I could stay in the country until the day of my booked flight from Caracas, seemed to create endless confusion. Eventually, I was directed to the immigration office at the airport, ten miles out of the city.

An hour later, after an expensive cab ride, I was faced with another immigration officer, who immediately tried to deflect the problem by telling me to report to the main immigration office at Caracas airport the next day. This, I explained, would be very difficult, as I was travelling by bicycle and did not think that I could ride 450 miles in one day! Fortunately, he seemed to find this quite amusing and, after making a phone call to his superiors, finally stamped my passport and issued me with a letter that I could present to the office in Caracas within two weeks. At last, the paperwork was sorted and I was free to continue my journey.

On a wet and windy morning, I headed east out of Maracaibo on a direct route towards Caracas. The first obstacle in my way was the huge Lake Maracaibo, which was spanned by a five-mile long bridge. On reaching the tollbooth, however, a rotund toll collector barred my way, insisting that it was far too dangerous to cycle across the bridge in such atrocious weather conditions. Instead, he flagged down a truck and asked the driver to take me across.

On the other side of the lake, I took shelter at a service station café, in the hope that the rain – now torrential - would ease off a little. Several hours later, with the downpour finally petering out, I climbed back into the saddle and rode off to a round of cheering from the waiters, who were probably wandering whether I was ever going to leave!

Anxious to make up for the long delay, I rode hard along the highway, which followed the eastern shores of the lake. Several of the lakeside villages were awash with floodwaters, following the heavy rains, but the highway was built on higher ground and still usable. One of the villages was a hive of activity, as its inhabitants prepared to evacuate their flooded homes and bed down for the night in the local church hall. Just before sunset, I reached the town of Bachaquero, which had escaped the flooding, and checked into a motel for the night.

The floodwaters had moved right down into Bachaquero by morning, which meant that my planned route eastwards to Corora was completely cut off. The only possible way out of the town was in a southerly direction, and even that road was under half a foot of water. It would certainly not be possible to cycle, so I hitched a lift on the back of a truck, asking the driver to set me down as soon as we had cleared the floodwaters. We had travelled about five miles when he dropped me off, having drawn me a rough map of the circuitous route that I would have to follow in order to get back onto the highway to Corora.

The skies were clear that morning and the sun beat down relentlessly as I peddled away from the flooded region. On reaching the highway, I started to feel quite dizzy from the heat and thought about stopping for the night. However, there were no service areas where it might be possible to pitch the tent and, with the highway robbery still fresh in my mind, I was reluctant to consider camping in a lonely spot by the roadside. Instead, I set my sights on the town of Corora and rode on determinedly.

Ten miles short of Corora, the skies blackened once more to indicate that another storm was imminent. Fortunately, a pick-up truck pulled over and transported me the rest of the way into town. There was no room for me in the cab, so I sat with the bike and a cargo of cheese urns in the back. We had barely started moving when the storm began. It was another ferocious one and I felt its full force, with giant hailstones raining down on me as we trundled slowly along. By the time that we reached Corora, my head was quite sore from the bombardment!

The unpredictable weather continued the next day, with strong headwinds and the scorching sun creating the problems. At least the highway was a good one though, with four lanes and a wide shoulder. It sliced its way across undulating terrain towards the mountainous central part of the country. There was plenty of opportunity for breaks, with transport cafes every ten or fifteen miles serving a tempting array of delicious snacks. These places were always very friendly and it was sometimes hard to get away! Most people wanted to ask me the same old questions as usual, such as 'Where do you come from?', 'How do you pay for your trip?'

and 'Why don't you travel by bus?' but I always tried to answer cheerfully, as though it was the first time that anyone had thought to ask.

Having completely lost track of the distance covered that day, I was filled with joy when Barquisimeto suddenly appeared on the horizon. With a population of over one million, this was a big, modern city. Riding towards the downtown area, I passed by the Cathedral, which was shaped like a giant urn! Not far from the 'Urn', I checked into a cosy little guest house for a couple of nights. Barquisimeto is known as 'La Ciudad de los Crepusculos', or the 'City of Sunsets', and a particularly beautiful one lit up the night sky that evening.

Riding out of Barquisimeto, I was chased down by a Venezuelan racing cyclist, named Carlos, who was out on a training ride. Carlos was an architect and spoke excellent English, having studied his trade at Nottingham University for several years. Chatting with him, as we rode along the hard shoulder together, I learnt something of the economic and political turmoil that the country was going through at that time. The crash in world oil prices was causing considerable hardship, while the President, Perez, had recently been arrested on corruption charges.

Carlos lived in Barquisimeto and, when we reached the village of Chivacoa, he announced that it was time for him to turn back. The highway forked in two at Chivacoa, so I had to decide whether to take the coastal route to Caracas, or the more direct route through the mountains. Carlos advised the coastal route, as we discussed the two options over coffee, but I was feeling energetic that day and could not resist the pull of the mountains.

The climbing began almost immediately, and it was an uphill slog for the rest of the day. Towards evening, an extremely unpleasant incident occurred. A group of young lads were standing at a bus shelter with a large black Labrador. As I slowly peddled by, the dog started barking loudly, and then suddenly darted across the road towards me. Unfortunately, it had not seen the truck that was coming up the hill behind me. The truck was travelling fast and only one conclusion was possible. The dog flew up into the air, as it rebounded off the bumper, before landing in a heap right in front of me. This brought me to a sudden halt and I stood there in a daze, as the truck hurtled on and the onlookers came rushing across the road to assess the damage. It was immediately apparent that the dog was dead, so they mournfully dragged the corpse to the side of the road. No blame was attached to me, but I was left badly shaken.

A little further up the hill, I checked into a hotel in the mountain settlement of Nirgua. As well as being in a state of shock, I seemed to have picked up another stomach bug. Half the night was spent running up and down the corridor between my room and the communal toilet!

Despite feeling no better in the morning, and having no appetite for breakfast, I decided to ride another thirty miles through the mountains to the larger town of Bejuma. This was mainly because I could not face the monotony of lying in my miserable little hotel room all day, feeling sorry for myself. It was a painfully slow journey, as I fought against the aching limbs and nauseous feeling in my stomach, but at least the lush mountain landscape lifted my spirits on a lovely, sunny day. Arriving in Bejuma, I was immediately besieged by curious locals, including three policemen, who were anxious to make friends and establish the details of my journey. It was hard to cope with this, when all I wanted to do was to lie down, but they seemed to realise that I was in need of rest and soon directed me to a hotel. It was wonderful to be able to collapse into a comfortable bed, in a room that even had the luxury of a radio. The short ride had taken a lot out of me, but the rest of the day would pass quickly now, so it had been worth the effort.

Feeling slightly better the next day, after a long sleep and a light breakfast, I decided on another short ride to the ancient city of Valencia. It was an arduous ride and, with my energy levels still low, on some of the steeper climbs I had to climb down and push. However, every mile was bringing me closer to Caracas and an overwhelming desire to reach my journey's end was spurring me on now.

Arriving in Valencia shortly after noon, I rode straight to the 'Historic Centre'. The area was full of beautiful old Spanish buildings and monuments, giving an indication of the important part that Valencia has played in Venezuela's history. In fact, the country gained its independence following the Battle of Carabobo, which took place here in 1821. As in Maracaibo, finding accommodation was not easy, with many of the cheaper hotels full of people that had arrived from other parts of the country in search of work. Eventually, I did manage to find a room, but had to pay twice the normal price in order to persuade the proprietor to let me sleep there for just one night.

Following the signs to Maracay, I found myself riding out of Valencia on a choked six-lane highway with no hard shoulder. It was a nerve-jangling ride, especially when trying to bridge the frequent slip roads. With the deafening traffic noise ringing in my ears all morning, I made it half way to Maracay before being pulled over at an army checkpoint. Here a young soldier kindly explained that there was a much safer, quieter road to Maracay, and he even drew up a rough map to show me how I could reach it.

Once off the busy highway, the ride to Maracay became a pleasurable experience. The traffic noise was replaced by the sound of friendly Spanish greetings, as I rode through tiny villages, with Lake Valencia to the south and the rugged mountains of the Henry Pittier National Park to the north.

Maracay was an attractive city, with tree-lined avenues and leafy plazas. My humble lodgings were located right in the shadow of the huge, whitewashed Cathedral, which stood serenely on the central plaza. With the city lying at five hundred metres above sea level, the evening was pleasantly cool for strolling. This was probably my favourite place in Venezuela so far.

Following the advice of one of the reception staff at my hotel, I jumped on a bus the next morning to the coastal village of Puerto Columbia, thirty miles north of Maracay. It was an exhilarating journey, with the bus climbing over the narrow range of mountains that form the Henry Pittier National Park. The driver negotiated a series of hairpin bends at alarming speed, narrowly avoiding a head-on collision at one point, as we climbed right to the top of range. Here, we paused briefly to take in a fantastic panoramic view across densely forested mountains, with Maracay nestling in the valley to the south and the deep blue Caribbean Sea to the north. The descent was even more hair-raising than the climb, and I was relieved to get off the bus in one piece when we reached Puerto Columbia.

With its idyllic natural setting, Puerto Columbia seemed a relatively unspoilt little fishing village, with just a handful of cafes and gift shops to cater for the steady trickle of foreign visitors and Venezuelan holiday-makers that make their way here. From the village, I followed a steep trail over the hills to a beautiful palm-fringed sandy beach, called Playa Choroni. It was a secluded spot in a tropical paradise and I spent the rest of the day here, resting and swimming, before catching the last bus back to Maracay.

Doing my best to avoid the busy Caracas highway, I rode east from Maracay on a circuitous route across gently rolling hill country to the town of Camas. On asking for directions here, an old man laughingly informed me that Caracas was too far away to cycle and then pointed vaguely in the wrong direction. I rode out of town for several miles before realising that I was heading back to Maracay! Back in Camas, I found a more reliable source of information and continued eastwards.

With the day was slipping away fast, I embarked on a steep, fifteen-mile climb to the city of Los Teques, where I planned to spend the night before the final push to Caracas. Several passing trucks slowed down to offer me lifts, but I waved them on. My long journey around the world was almost at an end now and I wanted to savour these last few moments on the road. With just a couple of miles further to climb, my legs suddenly turned to jelly. I had hit 'the wall', as marathon runners say, and there was no strength left in them to turn the peddles. Just at that moment, however, a slow-moving cattle truck came past, and I was able to let my arms do the rest of the work by hanging on to the back for a tow.

Though situated dramatically on top of the mountain range, Los Teques was an ugly city of huge concrete blocks, which almost seemed like a scar on the beautiful landscape. My search for accommodation was a long, frustrating one. As with Maracaibo and Valencia, all the cheap hotels were full of itinerant workers, but persistence finally paid off. My room was not much more than a broom cupboard, but they had somehow managed to squeeze a bed into it!

After battling my way through the early morning city traffic, I hurtled downhill from Los Teques for a few miles, before rounding a bend to see the whole of Caracas laid out before me in the broad valley below. It was downhill all the way now and before long I was battling with heavy traffic once more, as I made my way into the heart of the city. Surprisingly, budget accommodation seemed to be quite plentiful here, and I was soon checked into a small hotel just across the road from the central bus station. The reception staff, who did not seem to have much work to do, spent the rest of the afternoon taking turns to ride up and down the street on my bicycle. Normally I was reluctant to let people mess around with my most treasured possession, but the bike had done its job now and it didn't seem to matter any more.

Since World War Two, Caracas had grown faster than any other South American city, except for Sao Paulo, and its population was now in excess of four million. With the surrounding mountains restricting outward expansion, it seemed to have grown mainly upwards. Much of the city centre was a mass of vast, characterless, high-rise office blocks and shopping precincts.

Not far from my hotel doorstep, the oldest part of the city seemed to have been left relatively unspoilt by the rapid urban growth. There were some beautiful old colonial buildings here, such as the Cathedral and Government House, centred around Plaza Bolivar. Simon Bolivar was a figure that I was becoming quite familiar with, as virtually every Venezuelan town seemed to have a plaza named in his honour – usually complete with statue. Known as 'El Libertador', he was responsible for ending colonial rule through a series of battles from Venezuela all the way down to the borders of Argentina, so his hero status was probably well-deserved.

With elections pending, and the political situation quite unstable in Venezuela at that time, there seemed to be very few Westerners in the country, and I only met one during the four days that I spent exploring

Caracas. He was an American student called Keith, who I came across as he was eating a hamburger in a shop doorway. He was studying Spanish at a language school for foreigners, but was currently the only student in his class. As we chatted, it transpired that we had both attended the same Spanish school in Guatemala, where we even had the same teacher!

Simon Bolivar International Airport was situated twenty-six miles outside the city, at the small Caribbean port of La Gaira. In between lies a huge, green wall of forested mountains, called Parque Avila, which would present me with one final challenge.

With my flight to Miami booked for early in the morning, I decided to ride to the airport the day before and spend the night in the departure lounge. It was just after midday when I loaded the bike up for the last time.

Conditions were good for riding, with an overcast sky blocking out the hot, tropical sun, as I rode quickly through the affluent northern suburbs of Caracas. The neatly landscaped gardens and flowering trees made quite a contrast from the high-rise concrete jungle down below. There was a motorway running from Caracas to La Gaira, but I had decided to travel by an old highway across the mountains. This road did not seem to be sign-posted at all, and I had to ask directions several times before finally managing to locate it. Once on the right road, I settled into a good climbing rhythm and was soon gliding high above the city.

Reaching a narrow pass, high in the mountains, the Caribbean Sea came into view once more and I could see the old highway winding down in front of me towards the airport. It would probably be possible to freewheel all the way and there was a twinge of sadness as it struck me hard that this really was the end of my journey. However, there was still time for one final adventure!

I was in full flight when an army checkpoint came into view and three or four soldiers started waving their arms to flag me down. Braking hard, I managed to pull up just a few metres past them, and then turned round to see what they wanted. One of the officers ordered me to wait in the lay-by, explaining in broken English that it was not safe for me to be using this highway, as it was a drug-smuggling route. With my destination just a few miles further down the road, it seemed a little late to be telling me this now but, with a shrug of the shoulders, I obediently sat down in the lay-by and waited to see what would happen next. It seemed almost certain that a bribe would be asked for at some point, but it would have to be a small one, as I was down to my last few dollars.

A few minutes later, a truck came trundling down the hill and the soldiers immediately spread themselves across the road to bring it to a halt. The driver and his three companions were ordered out and then roughly forced to stand against the side of their truck with their hands above their heads. As two of the soldiers guarded the captives at gunpoint, the others began to ransack the truck, presumably searching for drugs. Midway through the search, one of the guards turned to me and declared that it was now safe for me to go. Though rather curious to witness the conclusion to these dramatic events, I quickly climbed back on the bike and rode away before they had time to change their minds.

Arriving at the airport without further incident, I checked everything in and watched my faithful green bicycle disappear down the luggage conveyor. Making myself comfortable in the departure lounge, my thoughts turned to England. How would people react to me after such a long time away, and how easy would it be to find work and settle down again? How much would I miss the travelling lifestyle and how long would I be able to resist the lure of the road? The future was a little uncertain but for now, at least, it was good to be going home.

POSTSCRIPT

It is now over twelve years since the journey ended. As time goes on, the memories start to fade, but looking through my old diaries and writing this book has brought them all flooding back again. Although there were some hard times on the road, the journey was a wonderful experience, which has shaped the rest of my life. In those three years I was truly alive and gained a real appreciation of the diverse world in which we live, as well as discovering inner resources that I had never been aware of.

After the initial euphoria of returning home and reuniting with family and friends, the process of adjusting back to life in England began. This proved to be far more difficult that I had expected. My outlook on life had changed and much of what I saw around me seemed irrelevant and even distasteful. In particular, the relentless, blinkered pursuit of material riches that seems to motivate people so much in our society.

Other travellers had warned me that surprisingly few people back home would really want to hear about my experiences, and this proved to be the case. Polite enquiries about my 'extended holiday' were nothing more than that, and there seemed to be little genuine interest in the world beyond these shores. Potential employers certainly took a negative view of the long gap in my employment history, if the number of rejection letters that I received is anything to go by. It took me nearly three months to find work, by which time I had gone from feeling like I had conquered the world to wondering whether there was still a place for me in society. In time, however, I came to realise that the real value of making a journey such as this cannot be measured in terms of the effect that it has on other people, or on society in general. It is very much a personal thing and the rewards are to be found within. Perhaps this is why it has taken so long to produce this book!

The old bicycle still sits in the garage and gets a run out every so often. My working life has prevented me from making any more long cycle tours, although the 'travel bug' never leaves you and I take the opportunity to get away as often as possible – always somewhere new, by preference. A couple of years ago, I even managed to get down to Tierra del Fuego at last! Nothing can compare, however, to the feeling of setting off on a long journey, without knowing where you will end up or when you will return. To anyone that has ever considered it, I would say one thing: Give it a go!

APPENDIX ONE

Main Items of Equipment Carried on Departure

Clothing:

1 set of waterproofs (breathable fabric, Agu Sport)
1 light windproof cycling jacket
1 sweatshirt
1 cycling shirt and 2 tee-shirts
1 pair racing shorts and 1 pair touring shorts
1 pair dark, lightweight trousers
   (Mountain Equipment)
1 pair thin tracksuit bottoms (Ron Hills)
1 pair cycling/hiking shoes (Merrell) and 1 pair of
   flip flops
1 pair cycling goggles and a cap

Camping Gear:

1 lightweight tent (Robert Saunders: 'Jetpacker')
1 three/four season sleeping bag (Mountain
   Euipment: 'Green Dragon')
1 Sleeping Mat

1 Petrol Stove (MSR: 'Wisperlite')

1 deep billy can

1 Swiss Army Knife

Plastic food containers, candles, washing powder, plastic crockery

Toolkit:

Headset and bottom bracket spanners

Crank removing tool

Large adjustable spanner

'Park Tool' (small screwdrivers and alum keys)

Pair of pliers

Chain whip and freewheel removing tool

Chain link extractor

Cable cutters

Spoke key

Two puncture kits

Electrical tape and 1 small tub of grease

Spares:

20 spokes

2 spare inner tubes

Spare chain links

Brake and gear cables

4 brake blocks

APPENDIX TWO

Facts about the Journey

Vital Statistics:

Distance covered by bicycle (logged daily):	19,764 miles
Daily average (cycling days only)	55 miles
Highest altitude reached by bicycle:	3,700 metres (Valle des Angeles, Costa Rica)
Number of countries visited:	27
Number of flights:	8
Approximate gross cost of journey (incl. flights):	£6,500
Amount earned en route (minus living expenses)	£3,000
Approximate net cost of journey:	£3,500
The bicycle:	Ridgeback 603' mountain bike

Main bicycle equipment used:

4 Sets of tyres (various makes, 'Specialised Touring' were best)

3 Rear freewheel blocks (Shimano XT)

3 Chains (Shimano XT)

2 Sets of gear changers (Shimano XT)

3 Sets of handlebar grips ('Grab Ons')

2 Headsets (Shimano XT)

1 Set of hand-built wheels (Mavic rims)

1 Saddle (Turbo)

Front and rear rack (Blackburn)

Printed in the United Kingdom
by Lightning Source UK Ltd.
112918UKS00001BA/1-27